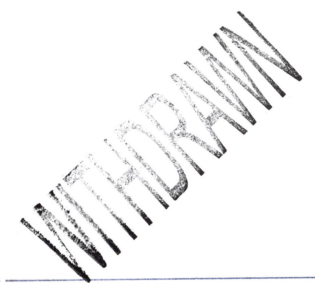

Advances in Criminology

Series Editor: David Nelken

Titles in the Series

Deleuze and Environmental Damage: Violence of the Text
Mark Halsey

Globalization and Regulatory Character: Regulatory Reform after the Kader Toy Factory Fire
Fiona Haines

Family Violence and Police Response: Learning From Research, Policy and Practice in European Countries
Edited by Wilma Smeenk and Marijke Malsch

Crime and Culture: An Historical Perspective
Edited by Amy Gilman Srebnick and René Lévy

Power, Discourse and Resistance: A Genealogy of the Strangeways Prison Riot
Eamonn Carrabine

Hard Lessons: Reflections on Governance and Crime Control in Late Modernity
Edited by Richard Hil and Gordon Tait

In Search of Transnational Policing: Towards a Sociology of Global Policing
J.W.E. Sheptycki

Informal Criminal Justice
Edited by Dermot Feenan

Becoming Delinquent: British and European Youth, 1650–1950
Edited by Pamela Cox and Heather Shore

Migration, Culture Conflict and Crime
Edited by Joshua D. Freilich, Graeme Newman, S. Giora Shoham and Moshe Addad

Critique and Radical Discourses on Crime
George Pavlich

RE-THINKING THE POLITICAL ECONOMY
OF PUNISHMENT

Re-Thinking the Political Economy of Punishment
Perspectives on Post-Fordism and Penal Politics

ALESSANDRO DE GIORGI
University of Bologna, Italy

ASHGATE

Published by
Ashgate Publishing Limited
Wey Court East
Union Road
Farnham
Surrey, GU9 7PT
England

Ashgate Publishing Company
Suite 420
101 Cherry Street
Burlington
VT 05401-4405
USA

Ashgate website: http://www.ashgate.com

British Library Cataloguing in Publication Data
De Giorgi, Alessandro
  Re-thinking the political economy of punishment :
  perspectives on post-Fordism and penal politics. -
  (Advances in criminology)
  1.Punishment - Philosophy 2.Sociological jurisprudence
  3.Emigration and immigration law
  I.Title
  364.6'01

Library of Congress Cataloging-in-Publication Data
De Giorgi, Alessandro.
 Re-thinking the political economy of punishment : perspectives on post-Fordism and penal politics / by Alessandro De Giorgi.
      p. cm. -- (Advances in criminology)
  Includes bibliographical references and index.
  ISBN 0-7546-2610-5
 1. Punishment. 2. Imprisonment--Social aspects. 3. Imprisonment--Economic aspects.
4. Prisons--Social aspects. 5. Social control. I. Title. II. Series.

  HV7419.D44 2005
  364.6--dc22

                                                                            2005028248

Transfered to Digital Printing in 2012

ISBN 978-0-7546-2610-7

MIX
Paper from
responsible sources
FSC® C018575
www.fsc.org

Printed and bound in Great Britain by the
MPG Books Group Ltd, UK

Contents

Acknowledgements

I would like to thank Stefania De Petris, Chris Hale and Ian Loader for their useful comments and helpful support. Many thanks also to Dario Melossi and Richard Sparks for their patience and encouragement. I owe a special debt of gratitude to David Nelken, who recommended my work for publication.

To Stefania

Introduction

Paris, 1657

We expressly prohibit and forbid all persons of either sex, of any locality and of any age, of whatever breeding and birth, and in whatever condition they may be, able-bodied or invalid, sick or convalescent, curable or incurable, to beg in the city and suburbs of Paris, neither in the churches, nor at the doors of such, nor at the doors of houses nor in the streets, nor anywhere else in public, nor in secret, by day or night … under pain of being whipped for the first offence, and for the second condemned to the galleys if men and boys, banished if women and girls.[1]

New York, 1997

… Subway stations became shantytowns for the homeless and aggressive begging increased, exacerbating a climate of fear, compounded by a significant and notorious decline in the quality of life as a whole … Then as you entered Manhattan, you met the unofficial greeter of the city of New York, the squeegee pest. Welcome to New York City. This guy had a dirty rag or squeegee and would wash your window with some dirty liquid and ask for or demand money. Proceeding down Fifth Avenue, the mile of designer stores and famous buildings, unlicensed street peddlers and beggars were everywhere … This was a city that had stopped caring about itself. There was a sense of a permissive society allowing certain things that would not have been permitted many years ago. The City had lost control.[2]

At first sight, it would seem that very little has changed in the three centuries separating the Paris of the *Hôpital Général* from the New York of *Zero Tolerance*. In fact, the legislators of the seventeenth-century edict and the former chief of New York Police Department, William Bratton, seem to share a common philosophy. That is, a logic of contempt for the extreme poverty that shows itself overtly, thus contaminating the urban environment; a logic combining moral motives to eugenic allusions; a logic of hostility against whatever can disturb the quiet and orderly flux of metropolitan productive life, injecting into it the infections of non-work, economic parasitism, and urban nomadism. Above all, an identical object of discourse emerges here: the implicit equation between social marginality and criminality, between poor classes and dangerous classes.

However, a deeper analysis would show that this analogy is only apparent. The cited edict belongs to the historical period that witnessed the transition from a regime of power which Michel Foucault defined 'sovereign', toward a 'disciplinary' paradigm

---

[1]   French edict establishing the creation of the *Hôpital Général*, quoted in Michel Foucault, *Madness and Civilization. A History of Insanity in the Age of Reason* (London, 1967), pp. 48–49.

[2]   William Bratton, 'Crime is Down in New York City: Blame the Police', in Norman Dennis (ed.), *Zero Tolerance. Policing a Free Society* (London, 1997), pp. 33–34.

of control. Confronted by the spectacle of vagrancy, material poverty and moral dissolution of the European poor, between the seventeenth and the eighteenth centuries the strategies of power started to change, shifting gradually from a negative function of destruction and physical elimination of deviance, toward a positive function of discipline and normalisation of the 'other'.

It is here that the age of the 'Great Confinement' started. No longer would the poor, vagrants, prostitutes, alcoholics and criminals of any sort be tortured, quartered, executed and symbolically eliminated through a spectacular destruction of their bodies. Much more discretely, silently and efficiently, they would be confined. Reclusion emerged as an alternative to the destruction of the body because it became clear that these 'outsiders' constituted a mass whom the emerging technologies of discipline could forge, normalise, transform into productive individuals: into a labour-force. From the 'right of death' to the 'power over life'; from the brutal neutralisation of 'infamous individuals' to the productive regulation of the populations inhabiting the urban territories: what the edict foresaw, and at the same time invoked vigorously, was the birth of *bio-politics*.[3]

By intersecting the discipline of the body and the regulation of human groups, bio-politics organised an efficient power over life; it assembled a complex of technologies of government which replaced the dissipation of bodies, energies, resources and power with a rational management of productive forces. Following Foucault, again:

> The adjustment of the accumulation of men to that of capital, the joining of the growth of human groups to the expansion of productive forces and the differential allocation of profit, were made possible, in part, by the exercise of bio-power in its many forms and modes of application. The investment of the body, its valorisation, and the distributive management of its forces were at the time indispensable.[4]

This is the emergence of that model of disciplinary control which would affect the age of expansion of the 'industrial society', reaching its apogee in the period of Fordist capitalism. In fact, it is particularly in the first half of the twentieth century that the project of a perfect articulation between the discipline of the body and the regulation of whole populations came to completion, embodied as it was in the economic regime of the factory, in the social model of the *welfare state* and in the penal paradigm of the 'correctional' prison.

Zero Tolerance and its practice of discourse, on the other hand, emerge in a radically different context, and illustrate the crisis and gradual abandonment of the disciplinary project of capitalist modernity. No longer will technologies of discipline offer themselves as efficient instruments for the control and the government of the dissipation and waste of labour-force: perhaps precisely because dissipation and waste no longer exist. The poor, the unemployed, the immigrants: these are the new dangerous classes, the 'wretched of the metropolis' against whom new technologies of control are deployed in contemporary Western societies.[5]

---

3   'One might say that the ancient right to take life or let live was replaced by a power to foster life or disallow it to the point of death', Michel Foucault, *The Will to Knowledge. The History of Sexuality, vol. 1* (New York, 1990), p. 138.

4   Ibid., p. 141.

5   I am paraphrasing here Frantz Fanon, *The Wretched of the Earth* (New York, 1963).

However, the strategies of power set in motion here seem quite different from the disciplinary ones. The first object of these strategies is to identify the new *dangerous classes* and to separate them from the *labourious classes*. This task is becoming increasingly problematic. In the post-industrial metropolis, the growing precarisation of work, the flexibilisation of employment and the constant overlapping between the 'legal' economy and the many hidden, informal and illegal economies is producing a gradual fusion of work and non-work, mixing the labouring and the dangerous classes together and making any rigid distinction between the two almost impossible. A paradigmatic example is offered by the migrant labour force. At the same time 'dangerous' and 'necessary', non-Western immigrants stand at the core of this process, and their condition (both as privileged targets for new social control strategies and as objects of a renewed economic over-exploitation) symbolises its intrinsic paradoxes.

The second object seems to be the neutralisation of these new dangerous classes through the development of risk based technologies, articulated mainly in the forms of surveillance, urban seclusion and mass confinement.

If we look at the technologies of control emerging at the dawn of the third millennium, we could argue that a second 'Great Confinement' is in fact taking place. Urban confinement, through the new ghettos (or hyper-ghettos, following Loic Wacquant's definition). Penal confinement through the explosion of mass imprisonment. Global confinement, through the many 'immigration detention centres' which mark the borders of the Empire.[6] However, far from representing a plain reproduction of the Foucauldian 'Great Confinement', this contemporary version does not seem to cultivate any disciplinary utopia. Instead, confinement appears today as an attempt to define a new space of containment and to draw material and immaterial borders around those 'surplus' populations 'inassimilable' by the contemporary system of production and its post-welfarist model of social regulation.

Perhaps we could say that we witness here a dramatic dissociation between bio-political rationality and disciplinary strategies. As a paradox, bio-political imperatives are fulfilled through a refusal of disciplinary technologies. In other words, we can still see a bio-political power regulating the productivity of populations and controlling the fluxes of labour force in the global economy. However, what seems to be disappearing is the 'anatomo-politics of the human body' described by Foucault, the productive 'fostering of life' which complemented, at the level of individuals, the regulation of whole populations in the disciplinary era. This can be described also as the disappearance of those technologies of subjectivation whose aim was to transform the subjects through individualised control.

The aim of contemporary power technologies (in the broadest sense) seems no longer to be 'to foster life *or* disallow it' but 'to foster life *by* disallowing it'. It is precisely the 'disallowance' of life imposed today to an increasing fraction of the global labour force, that is becoming the main requisite for the 'fostering' of life in post-Fordist economy.

A new right of death emerges here. I refer to the 'death' imposed to some 'undeserving' categories of people by the strategies of control which sustain the capitalist organisation of society: this death bears upon the affective, social and

---

6   On the concept of Empire see Michael Hardt and Antonio Negri, *Empire* (Cambridge MA, 2000).

economic existence of individuals and appears as a brutal limitation of individual expectations, as an expropriation of possibilities, as a systematic violation of the freedom of movement. I conceive of 'death' as a biographic experience of the contemporary labour force, rather than as a biological event. This death is exemplified by the biographies of the hundreds of migrants who constantly die at the borders of the 'Fortress Europe' while attempting to exercise a 'right to escape';[7] it is exemplified by the biographies of the millions of prisoners confined in the 'American gulag', or of those social groups – ethnic minorities, the unemployed, immigrants, refugees, and many other 'collateral effects' of neo-liberal economy – whose life-horizon is defined by the borders of a local or global ghetto.

In his works, Michel Foucault traced a genealogy of disciplinary power firmly inscribed in the formation of the capitalist system of production and in the consolidation of a Fordist industrial society. Disciplinary power cannot be separated (both theoretically and historically) from the process of constitution of the industrial economy. Conversely, the development of industrial capitalism is structurally linked to the strategies for the production of subjectivity and labour-force embodied in the disciplinary techniques. However, what we are facing now seems to be precisely the overcoming of the system of capitalist production to which these disciplinary technologies have been connected for a long time.[8]

We perceive clear signs of this process. There are several descriptions, analyses, definitions and critiques of the transition from Fordism to post-Fordism, and a growing economic and sociological literature is concentrating on the consequences of this transition.[9] 'Post-Fordism' is a definition that is becoming increasingly popular in the sociological, political and economic discourse as well as in the common language, and points to a paradigmatic change that is reconfiguring our experience of social life. At the same time, we witness the emergence of analyses pointing to the transformations which take place in the field of social control and penality. Terms like 'society of control'[10] and 'surveillance society',[11] just to give two examples among the many possible, indicate the epilogue and the overcoming of the disciplinary regime: a process of transition whose dynamic is rooted in the crisis of the Fordist system of production.

However, if the work of Michel Foucault inscribed the genealogy of disciplinary control directly in the materiality of capitalist relations of production – that is, in those processes which led to the constitution of an industrial proletariat and to the formation of a Fordist labour force – contemporary analyses of social control seem reluctant to take this fundamental step. Although we are in the condition to say that disciplinary control appears more and more inadequate to the new forms of production and to the new labour force, we are still unable to connect this inadequacy to the processes of transformation affecting the economy.

---

[7]   The concept of migration as the exercise of the 'right to escape' is borrowed from Sandro Mezzadra, *Diritto di fuga. Migrazioni, globalizzazione, cittadinanza* (Verona, 2001).

[8]   See Luciano Ferrari Bravo, 'Sovranità', in Adelino Zanini and Ubaldo Fadini (eds), *Lessico Postfordista. Dizionario di idee della mutazione* (Milan, 2001), pp. 278–284.

[9]   The transition from Fordism to post-Fordism will be analysed in Chapter 2.

[10] Gilles Deleuze, 'Postscript on the Societies of Control', *October*, 59 (1992): 3–7.

[11] David Lyon, *Surveillance Society. Monitoring Everyday Life* (Buckingham, 2001).

Thus I come to the object of this work: an attempt to find some new hypotheses which could help to fill this apparent gap. The aim is to describe some significant transformations taking place in the field of social control, starting from the emergence of a new system of production, and to investigate in which ways these new control strategies can be connected to the emergence of a post-Fordist economy. However, this means that the analysis of contemporary social control has to be complemented with a description of some significant features of the contemporary labour force. It is here, when we turn to the analysis of the post-Fordist labour force, that the concept of *multitude* becomes central.[12]

The term 'multitude' is useful because it describes the rhizomatic, nomadic and composite character of the post-Fordist labour force: a labour force for which a series of distinctions and descriptions referring to the traditional 'Fordist working class' seem to lose much of their meaning. Thus, multitude refers to the extreme flexibilisation of the labour force, to the blurring of times of work and non-work experienced by large sectors of the labour force, to the fragmentation and diffusion of the production process in the society and beyond the walls of the industrial factory, to the crisis of the idea of a 'working life' and to the 'corrosion of character' which follows it.[13] But multitude refers also to the increasing mobility of the labour force, to the diffusion of multi-skilled productive roles, to the end of the 'assembly-line' with its repetitive tasks and the emergence of creativity, inventiveness, communication as the main productive tools of the post-Fordist labour-force, to the crisis of the Taylorist 'time-motion-oriented' management and the diffusion of innovative, just in time, lean production systems.

However, I should make clear that the concept of multitude does not refer to any definite subjectivity, nor to the emergence of a paradigmatic identity of the labour force, as was the case with the industrial workforce: the multitude is not simply what comes after the industrial working class in a post-industrial economy. Instead, the term defines a *process* of subjectivation, a 'becoming multiple' (in Deleuze and Guattari's terms) of the new forms of work, to which post-disciplinary strategies of social control are directed. Hence, multitude refers primarily to the impossibility of any *reductio ad unum* of the diverse productive subjectivities, comparable to that which allowed sociologists and economists to conceive the industrial working class as the hegemonic subject of the Fordist age.

Thus, starting from the concept of multitude, we will see that what at first sight appears as the inadequacy of the disciplinary techniques to exercise control over the contemporary productive system, can also be described (taking the point of view of the post-Fordist labour force) as a surplus expressed by the object of control (the new social labour force) toward the disciplinary dispositives: a new dimension of work irreducible to the processes of normalisation and subjectivation imposed by disciplinary technologies of power.

But before approaching these conclusions, it is necessary to situate these transformations within a broader theoretical framework. The political economy of

---

[12] This concept has been adopted by Hardt and Negri in *Empire*, to describe the contemporary labour force.

[13] See Richard Sennett, *The Corrosion of Character. The Personal Consequences of Work in the New Capitalism* (New York and London, 1998).

punishment seems to offer such a framework. This is a critical orientation – inspired by Marxian and Foucauldian analyses – which emerged within the sociology of punishment in the 1970s, with the aim of investigating the relationships between the economy and penal control.[14] As we shall see, this critical tradition has concentrated mainly on the relationship between the prison and the factory and between unemployment and imprisonment, describing in particular the connections between the labour market and penal policies in a Fordist scenario. In this respect, some of its assumptions seem to be outdated, given the recent transformations of the economy and social control. However, the critical tools forged by the political economy of punishment – both through the historical reconstruction of the birth of the prison and through the analysis of the contemporary relationships connecting the economy and punishment – are an important starting point, from which we can move in order to identify some new directions for a critique of post-Fordist social control.

In Chapter 1 I illustrate the main positions which emerged within the political economy of punishment, and describe their theoretical assumptions, both in a historical and contemporary perspective. This will allow me to identify some limits of this perspective, due mainly to the transformations taking place in the field of the economy. In Chapter 2 I turn to these transformations, attempting to identify their tendencies and to describe their effects on the labour force. At that point I can start my analysis of the new strategies of social control. In Chapter 3 I offer some preliminary incursions in this field, arguing that the new strategies articulate themselves around three main technologies: generalised surveillance, selectivity of access and mass confinement. In Chapter 4 I examine mass incarceration as a post-disciplinary strategy of control, and describe how a new conception of 'categorial risk' is giving birth to actuarial technologies. I will argue that the 'new penology' should be understood as a technology for the punitive management of the 'surplus populations' produced by the post-Fordist economy. Finally, in Chapter 5 I take Western immigration policies as a clear example of the emergence of a post-disciplinary and risk-based philosophy of social control. The condition of immigrants in Western societies is in fact paradigmatic for the arguments presented here: at the same time a vital part of the post-Fordist labour force and a typical example of 'dangerous class', their condition intersects the new economy with the new strategies of social control.

---

[14] The classic text is Georg Rusche and Otto Kirchheimer, *Punishment and Social Structure* (New York, 1968).

Chapter 1

The Political Economy of Penality and the Sociology of Punishment – Past and Present

Introduction

Toward the end of the 1960s, the criminological field saw the emergence of some critical perspectives which in fact revolutionised the theoretical coordinates of this discipline. At its origins, 'criminology' was the study of the problem of crime, more than the study of the problem of punishment. That is to say, criminology considered punishments, criminal policies and strategies of social control only under the point of view of their impact on crime. For a long time criminology has been a *savoir* whose object was the production of effective strategies for the government of deviance and criminality. Thus, it is easy to understand why the study of social and individual causes of crime played such an important role within the priorities of criminological research.

A result of what Michel Foucault defined as the 'inquisitorial society', criminology emerged as a knowledge inseparable from the technologies of power built around the field of deviance. Its history is part of the process of 'governamentalisation' of the State which took place between the eighteenth and nineteenth centuries. In that period, the science of government (and police science) became more specialised, giving birth to different forms of knowledge about the population: social statistics, urban studies, social psychiatry and criminology itself.[1] The 'inquisitorial' attitude of criminology produced a set of new discourses around the *homo criminalis*, the recidivist, the criminogenic environment and the dangerous class.[2]

Before the 1960s, criminological research did not question the rigid epistemological structure of its own origins: the influence of positivism was perhaps still so strong to make it virtually impossible for different perspectives to emerge. Nor had criminology ever dealt with an analysis of social reactions to deviance, separating these (at least methodologically) from their object (i.e. deviants). It was only with the development of the labelling approach that social reactions to crime emerged within criminology as a separate field of inquiry. In the political context of the 1960s, with their radical critique of repressive power in its diverse expressions (the family, the church and

---

[1] Michel Foucault, 'Governmentality', in Graham Burchell, Colin Gordon and Peter Miller (eds), *The Foucault Effect. Studies in Governmentality* (Hemel Hempstead, 1991), p. 104.

[2] On the relationship between criminology, disciplinary society and governmentality, see Pasquale Pasquino, 'Criminology: the Birth of a Special Saviour', *Ideology and Consciousness*, 7 (1980): 17–33.

total institutions), some space was opened for a sociological perspective in criminology. The growing awareness of the failure of the prison stimulated critical criminologists to question the role of this institution and to try to uncover the reasons for its persistence in the present.

Labelling theorists had already started a revision of criminological knowledge, but confined their research within the boundaries of a micro-sociological perspective. They were 'empowering' the deviant against the structures of power, but without developing a deeper analysis of the social power to label. On the one hand, the deviant world described by labelling theorists seemed incapable of any resistance except at an individual level. On the other hand, power was never analysed beyond those face-to-face interactions taking place in the microcosm of total institutions. These aspects of American liberal sociology were in fact the targets of Alvin Gouldner's famous critiques:

> The attitude of these zookeepers of deviance is to create a comfortable and human Indian Reservation, a protected social space, within which these colourful specimens may be exhibited, unmolested and unchanged. The very empirical sensitivity to fine detail, characterising this school, is both born of and limited by the connoisseur's fascination with the rare object: its empirical richness is inspired by a collector's aesthetic.[3]

These critiques pointed to the importance of a materialistic analysis of social control. According to Gouldner, the main difference between *liberal* and *radical* sociology lies in the willingness to focus critical attention on the labellers (power institutions) as well as on the labelled (their victims):

> ... I think that radical sociologists differ from liberals in that, while they take the standpoint of the underdog, they apply it to the study of overdogs. Radical sociologists want to study 'power elites', or the masters of men; liberal sociologists focus their efforts upon underdogs and victims and their immediate bureaucratic caretakers.[4]

This political and intellectual position announced the irruption of Marxism in the sociology of deviance that would take place between the end of the 1960s and the beginning of the 1970s.[5] In this context a new critical direction emerged in criminology, investigating on the one hand the historical trajectory through which the prison came to replace older forms of punishment and, on the other hand, the reasons for its persistence in the present, given its apparent failure. The aim became that of looking beyond the rhetorical legitimation of imprisonment, to unveil its latent functions. We see in this period the development of two main directions of analysis: the first is an ensemble of historically oriented works about the role of punitive

---

[3]   Alvin Gouldner, 'The Sociologist as Partisan: Sociology and the Welfare State', in *For Sociology* (Harmondsworth, 1975), p. 38.

[4]   Ibid., p. 51.

[5]   It would be a mistake to reduce to Marxism the many directions that emerged in this period in critical criminology (feminism, anarchism, black studies, etc.). But the object of this work is the political economy of punishment, an orientation that owes much to Marxist theory. Thus, I will focus more on this theoretical perspective. For an exhaustive reconstruction of the history of critical criminology (though limited to the European context) from its origins up to the 1990s, see René Van Swaaningen, *Critical Criminology. Visions from Europe* (London, 1997).

systems in the consolidation and reproduction of a capitalist economy. These works deconstructed the mainstream histories of punishment. Until that period this history had been represented as a continuous process towards more humane punishments: it was now rethought as a sequence of strategies whose main object was the imposition of class subordination.

The second direction of research focused on the present functions of social control and the prison: here the analysis concentrated itself on the impact of social control on contemporary capitalism and especially on the capitalist labour market. What these different perspectives had in common was the idea that punitive institutions could only be analysed under the point of view of the relations of production: a critical sociology of punishment had to uncover the role played by penality in the reproduction of these relations.

In the following pages I will offer a reconstruction of this 'materialist criminology', both in its historical and contemporary directions. First, it is necessary to introduce some theoretical assumptions of the political economy of punishment: this is why I start with an analysis of Rusche and Kirchheimer's works. Then, I review some recent works on the history of punishment and the prison in particular. This section is followed by an analysis of some contemporary perspectives within the political economy of punishment: that is, those works which investigated the relation between the economy and punishment in contemporary society. In the last section I will submit some critiques to this perspective, anticipating some arguments that will be developed in subsequent chapters. I suggest in particular that the contemporary materialist perspective appears inadequate to capture the deep transformations of the economy in contemporary societies: namely, the transition from a 'Fordist' to a 'post-Fordist' model of production and its implications for social control.

Penality and the Critique of Political Economy

The main assumption of the political economy of punishment is that it is possible to understand the evolution in the forms of punishment only if one separates them from the functions that have been historically assigned to them. Penality plays a role that is different from the control of criminality and from social defence: this role can be explained only if we put the evolution of social control strategies in the context of the economic dynamics of society and the corresponding contradictions. Both the historical emergence of peculiar punitive practices and their persistence in contemporary society should be connected to the relations of production and to the organisation of labour. The theoretical landscape in which the political economy of punishment can be situated is historical materialism as Marx presented it in the famous 'Preface' of 1859:

> In the social production which men carry on they enter into definite relations that are indispensable and independent of their will; these relations of production correspond to a definite stage of development of their material powers of production. The totality of these relations of production constitutes the economic structure of society – the real foundation, on which legal and political superstructures arise and to which definite forms of

consciousness correspond. The mode of production of material life determines the general character of the social, political, and spiritual processes of life.[6]

Thus, penality is part of those juridical, political and social institutions (the law, the state, the family, etc.) whose function is to preserve the hegemonic class relations. In order to describe the transformations of these institutions, it is necessary to link the ideological form of class power to the material power which dominates in the sphere of production:

> The ideas of the ruling class are in every epoch the ruling ideas, i.e. the class that is the ruling material force of society is at the same time its ruling intellectual force ... The ruling ideas are nothing more than the ideal expression of the dominant material relationships, the dominant material relationships grasped as ideas; hence of the relationships which make the one class the ruling one, therefore, the ideas of its dominance.[7]

The control of criminality, as an explicit legitimation of penal institutions, is a pure ideological representation through which the ruling class maintains the basis of its dominance. Punitive institutions are just one among the many expressions of the ideological power imposed on the subordinate classes. Through a symbolic legitimation of the existing social order, these institutions contribute to obscure the contradictions of capitalist society. In a class society criminal law is an expression of class power, not of a 'general interest':

> The would-be theories of criminal law that derive the principles of penal policy from the interests of society as a whole are conscious or unconscious distortions of reality. Society as a whole does not exist, except in the fantasy of the jurists. In reality we are faced only with classes, with contradictory, conflicting interests. Every historically given system of penal policy bears the imprint of the class interests of that class which instigated it.[8]

This is not to suggest that there is an automatic relation between structure and superstructure, as if the former produced the latter by necessity. For a long time, 'determinism' and 'economic reductionism' have been criticised both within Marxist theory in general and within the political economy of punishment in particular.[9] The complexity of the relations between the material structure of society and its punitive institutions was recognised by Georg Rusche. In 1933, in his first definition of the theory which would later be the core of *Punishment and Social Structure*, Rusche described this complexity:

> The dependency of crime and crime control on economic and historical conditions does not, however, provide a total explanation. These forces do not alone determine the

---

[6] Karl Marx, 'Preface' to 'A Contribution to the Critique of Political Economy', in Thomas Burton Bottomore and Maximilien Rubel (eds), *Karl Marx. Selected Writings in Sociology and Social Philosophy* (Harmondsworth, 1969), p. 67.

[7] Karl Marx, 'The German Ideology', in David McLellan (ed.), *Karl Marx: Selected Writings* (Oxford, 1977), p. 176.

[8] Evgenyi B. Pashukanis, *Law and Marxism. A General Theory* (London, 1978), p. 174.

[9] For an example of these critiques in criminology, see David Garland, *Punishment and Modern Society. A Study in Social Theory* (Oxford, 1990).

object of our investigation and by themselves are limited and incomplete in several ways.[10]

According to Rusche, the historical and materialist analysis of punitive systems was absent from the criminological literature of the time:

> These studies lack a foundation in the basic principles of sociological knowledge. They are neither connected to economic theory, nor are they historically oriented. Rather, they imply a fixed social structure which does not exist in reality, and they unconsciously characterise the social system as eternal and unchanging rather than as a historical process.[11]

The problem was how to overcome the concept of criminology as a science of criminality and as a *savoir* on the individual and social causes of deviance, and to produce a historical and economic knowledge of the evolution of punitive systems. But this implied that the history of punitive practices could no longer be represented as a linear evolution of legal institutions and practices. The history of punishment had instead to become an economic and social history of penality:

> Often, legal historians are guided not by an unprejudiced analysis of social laws, but by an evolutionary conception of the development of legal institutions: from barbaric cruelty to the humanitarianism of the relatively perfect legal system which we supposedly enjoy today. They overlook that we are dealing with a very long, now halting, now regressive movement.[12]

The transformations of punishment can be grasped following the evolution of economic relations in history and, in particular, the transition from pre-capitalist economies toward the capitalist mode of production: 'It is the history of the relations of the *two nations* ... that constitute a people – the rich and the poor.'[13]

Together with Otto Kirchheimer, Georg Rusche would write this history of the two nations and its title would be *Punishment and Social Structure*. However, the book (published in 1939) was almost ignored both by historians and criminologists for a long time. The political economy of punishment virtually disappeared from the landscape of criminological theory. Only with the second edition of *Punishment and Social Structure* in 1969, the theoretical program launched by Rusche would be continued by the emerging critical criminology. Both the initial oblivion and the subsequent renewed interest in the political economy of punishment are understandable: Rusche and Kirchheimer's book appeared in a historical period characterised by a strong adversity to Marxism in the US and to the social sciences in Europe. The emergence of totalitarian regimes, the Second World War, and later the post-war reconstruction with its faith in technocratic approaches to social problems (and criminality): all these factors conjured against *Punishment and Social Structure* and its critical perspective. It was in the changed context of the 1960s and 1970s that the intellectual and political space for a critique of repressive institutions reemerged. In this context the contribution by Rusche and Kirchheimer could be rediscovered and became a landmark in the political economy of punishment.

---

[10]   Georg Rusche, 'Labor Market and Penal Sanction: Thoughts on the Sociology of Criminal Justice', *Crime and Social Justice*, 10 (1978): 3.

[11]   Ibid., p. 3.

[12]   Ibid., p. 5.

[13]   Ibid., p. 5.

Georg Rusche and Otto Kirchheimer: *Punishment and Social Structure* and the Foundation of the Political Economy of Punishment

The starting point is Rusche's 1933 article. In this work (conceived as a research project for the *Institut für Sozialforschung* in Frankfurt), Rusche presented its main hypotheses, to be later developed in *Punishment and Social Structure*.[14]

Rusche's first hypothesis is that the criminal justice system is inspired by a logic of deterrence: the immediate function of punishment is to prevent people from breaking the laws. It is mainly against the subordinate classes that deterrence has to be directed, given that these classes share a tendency to commit the types of crime against which the system reacts more severely. The second hypothesis is that the ways in which deterrence works in practice change, depending on the conditions of the economy and the labour market:

> Now, experience teaches us that most crimes are committed by members of those strata who are burdened by strong social pressures and who are relatively disadvantaged in satisfying their needs when compared to other classes. Therefore, a penal sanction, if it is not to be counterproductive, must be constituted in such a way that the classes which are most criminally inclined prefer to abstain from the forbidden acts than become victims of criminal punishment.[15]

Rusche refers here to the various forms of social and economic subordination that Western societies experienced since the Middle Ages. In this sense, the history of punitive systems is the 'history of two nations': the history of the ways in which the rulers preserved their own social order against the threats posed by the ruled. Different penal policies emerged in modern history depending on the condition of the disadvantaged classes: in order to be effective, penal practices and institutions must impose upon those who violate social order worse living conditions than those experienced by law abiding people. In a capitalist economy, this means that the living conditions of the marginal proletarian class will affect criminal policies, and therefore also the conditions of those who are punished:

> One can also formulate this proposition as follows: all efforts to reform the punishment of criminals are inevitably limited by the situation of the lowest socially significant proletarian class which society wants to deter from criminal acts. All reform efforts, however

---

[14] After the publication of this article, Rusche worked on the manuscript of *Punishment and Social Structure*. The history of the manuscript and, in particular, its radical reworking by Otto Kirchheimer, suggest that here (more than in *Punishment and Social Structure*) it is possible to find Rusche's original ideas. It would be impossible here to offer a reconstruction of the dramatic history of this work (closely connected to Rusche's own life, to which he put an end in 1950): see Dario Melossi, 'Georg Rusche: A Biographical Essay', *Crime and Social Justice*, 14 (1980): 51–63. It should be remembered that in 1930 Rusche had written a first article on prison revolts and social policy in the US for the *Frankfurter Zeitung*, where some of his ideas were already clearly presented. This article has been reprinted as 'Prison Revolts or Social Policy: Lessons from America', *Crime and Social Justice*, 13 (1980): 41–44.

[15] Rusche, 'Labor Market and Penal Sanction', p. 3.

humanitarian and well meaning, which go beyond this restriction, are condemned to utopianism.[16]

What Rusche is criticising here is the traditional representation of the history of punishment as a linear progression toward civility. The evolution of punishment is not the result of ambitious progressive reforms: there is a clear limit to reform and civilisation, and this is given by the principle of *less eligibility*, to which any penal system must conform.

In pre-capitalist economies the material condition of marginal classes was connected to political factors which established the margins of exploitation of the labour force. Social stratification depended heavily on political and non-economic factors. But with the advent of capitalism, the situation of the proletarian class became a purely economic function. It is now the market (and the labour market in particular) that defines the situation of the working class. The dynamics of the market will establish the 'fair price' of the labour force, and the laws of the market drive this process: the more the supply of labour, the less the value of labour, and the worse the conditions of the labour force.[17] As a consequence, according to the principle of less eligibility, whenever there is a surplus of labour force punitive practices become harsher:

> Unemployed masses, who tend to commit crimes of desperation because of hunger and deprivation, will only be stopped from doing so through cruel penalties. The most effective penal policy seems to be severe corporal punishment, if not ruthless extermination ... In a society in which workers are scarce, penal sanctions have a completely different function. They do not have to stop hungry people from satisfying elementary needs. If everybody who wants to work can find work, if the lowest social class consists of unskilled workers and not of wretched unemployed workers, then punishment is required to make the unwilling work, and to teach other criminals that they have to content themselves with the income of a honest worker.[18]

The birth of the prison lies in the transition from a punitive regime oriented to the destruction of the body (so that in this destruction the political power of the monarch shines), toward a punitive regime aimed at preserving the body, because it can be exploited in the capitalist process of production.

The final section of Rusche's article presents a brief historical *excursus* where the author situates the origins of the penitentiary at the peak of a process that goes from the Middle Ages until the Industrial Revolution. The emergence of different punitive practices cannot be ascribed to the ideas of the reformers: it depends on the conditions of labour and, later, of the labour market. The secondary importance of those reformist arguments which offered a political legitimation to the transformation of punitive systems is evident here. In fact, as soon as economic conditions change again, humanitarianism leaves way to a renewed cruelty:

> This humanitarian system of punishment lost its utility when the Industrial Revolution, the replacement of the worker by the machine, at the turn of the eighteenth century removed the scarcity of workers, and the industrial reserve army came into existence ... Institutions

---

[16] Ibid., p. 4.

[17] Karl Marx, *Capital. A Critique of Political Economy, vol. I* (Chicago, 1918), p. 809.

[18] Rusche, 'Labor Market and Penal Sanction', p. 4.

of forced labour, penitentiaries became places of pure torture, suitable to deter even the most wretched.[19]

Rusche insists on the persistence of the principle of less eligibility: in fact, the material condition of society and its productive relations define the real content of penalties and penal regimes, because the economic and social value attached to the labour force drives the penal policies targeted at the marginal classes. Conversely, this value depends on the position of the proletariat in the labour market: this is Rusche's main hypothesis and the *leitmotif* of the political economy of punishment. *Punishment and Social Structure* develops these theories and applies them to the history of punishment from the late Middle Ages to the 1930s. In this work, the concept of less eligibility is more elaborated and is applied to a detailed analysis of crucial historical processes, as the transition from a feudal economy to mercantilism and later to the Industrial Revolution.

In the sixteenth century, Europe was affected by a dramatic demographic crisis (in part as a consequence of the Thirty Years War): as a result, labour force became scarce and wages started to grow. These circumstances induced many European states to change their policies toward the poor: those who were able-bodied had to be put to work. Through the imposition of work it would be possible to deal with two big problems: on the one hand, the social problem of beggars, and on the other hand, the reduction of profits caused by growing wages.

Inspired by this new philosophy of poverty, the first institutions for the containment of the poor were created around Europe: the *Bridewell* in England, the *Hopital General* in France, the *Zuchtaus* and the *Spinnhaus* in the Netherlands. Detention started to be considered as a viable alternative for the control of marginal classes: its utility went beyond the particular categories to which it could be applied (poor, beggars, prostitutes or criminals), and consisted in the fact that now the body of the deviant could be made productive through discipline. Control systems could now work on attitudes and morality, investing the soul of deviants: gradually, confinement emerged as the hegemonic system of punishment. Nevertheless, the principle of less eligibility continued to work: now it affected the treatment imposed on the incarcerated population. Again, humanitarian ideologies were of secondary importance: reforms retreated as soon as unemployment started to grow, reducing again the value of labour. An example is offered by nineteenth-century England: a surplus of labour force caused here a reversal in penal strategies and the re-emergence of those inhumane practices which had been so firmly criticised by the reformers:

> But the basis for the new system of punishment, the need for manpower, was disappearing during the same period. We have already indicated that the reform found fertile ground only because its humanitarian principles coincided with the economic necessities of the time. Now, when attempts were being made to give practical expression to these ideas, part of the base from which they arose had already ceased to exist.[20]

---

[19] Ibid., p. 6.
[20] Georg Rusche and Otto Kirchheimer, *Punishment and Social Structure* (New York, 1968), p. 85.

Thus, when the economic profitability of the new systems of punishment was over, the same innovations introduced by reformists were turned into cruel and inhumane treatments:

> Prison labour became a method of torture, and the authorities were expert enough in inventing new forms; occupations of a purely punitive character were made as fatiguing as possible and were dragged out for unbearable lengths of time.[21]

At this point, Rusche and Kirchheimer describe the transformations of the penitentiary (now the hegemonic form of punishment) through the nineteenth and twentieth centuries, but the hypothesis is still the same: both progresses and regresses can be explained through the connection between punishment and the labour market. This is the reason for the emergence and the later crisis of the Philadelphian model (based on solitary confinement), to be then replaced by the Auburn model (based on common labour during daytime and solitary confinement during night time). In the United States Auburn was preferred because of a scarcity of labour force in a period of rapid industrial development. In Europe the situation was completely different: there was a surplus of labour force and the punitive system abandoned any productive aim in favour of solitary confinement.

However, towards the end of the nineteenth century the situation changed again: the development of an organised working class movement and better labour market conditions improved the living standards of the proletarian class. This transformation had important effects on penal policies and on the treatment of prison population: social policies were implemented in order to deal with social conflicts and a new climate of leniency spread around European prisons:

> With the general improvement in living conditions, prison conditions also improved. The widespread substitution of prisons with an individual cell for each convict led to the construction of many new prisons and the abandonment of those regarded as unfit. Overcrowding with its moral and hygienic consequences was eliminated in part. Food was somewhat improved and attention was directed to problems of health.[22]

Incarceration rates started to fall and new theories of criminality appeared, which legitimated this shift in penal policy (for example, Ferri's sociological positivism).

The last section of the book hypothesises a further shift towards the replacement of incarceration by monetary penalties. But this section, much less convincing than the first part of the book, is the result of Kirchheimer's intervention on Rusche's manuscript.[23]

The Political Economy of Punishment and the New Histories of Punishment

In this section I shall review some critical histories of punishment which appeared in the second half of the 1970s. What follows is not a detailed reconstruction of these

---

[21] Ibid., p. 112.

[22] Ibid., pp. 149–150.

[23] Dario Melossi, 'Georg Rusche and Otto Kirchheimer: Punishment and Social Structure', *Crime and Social Justice*, 9 (1978): 73–85.

historical works on the prison; in fact, we have to deal with a literature (Melossi and Pavarini, Ignatieff, Foucault) whose analyses cover the whole historical period considered by Rusche and Kirchheimer, and it would be impossible to review these works for the whole period and to evaluate their historical accuracy.[24] For my purposes, it is important to see what these studies have to say regarding the actual relationship between the economy and punishment.

A Just Measure of Pain

In *A Just Measure of Pain*, Michael Ignatieff offers a socio-political history of the origin of the penitentiary. His work is a history of ideas concerning punishment, more than a history of punishment itself. Ignatieff analyses their emergence in the context of the class conflicts that took place in England between the end of the seventeenth and the beginning of the nineteenth century.

This work recognises an important influence to reformers like John Howard and Elizabeth Fry. According to the author, it would be impossible to understand the birth of the penitentiary by leaving the political and social debate of that period out of consideration: the role of reformers and philanthropists in the transition from corporal punishment to detention is relevant and cannot be reduced to an ideological legitimation of the existing social order. Thus, what Ignatieff offers is:

> ... A social history of these new ideas, focusing upon the fight to embody them in the penitentiary, the resistance they aroused among prisoners and political radicals, and the ironies of intended and unintended consequences that followed their triumph ...[25]

Ignatieff establishes a clear order of priority for the various factors which concurred to the emergence of the new punitive practices. In this sense, class relations in the English society at the time of Industrial Revolution were crucial. The intensity of class conflict turned them into a conflict within the political elites, in which different representations of social order and strategies for its preservation were debated. It is in this context that the ideas of the reformers can be situated: in other terms, the problem was how to protect social order in a society, like nineteenth-century England, that was discovering class conflict. But the role of the economy and of the relations of production is secondary in Ignatieff's analysis:

> Obviously, labour market conditions are only one of the factors determining punishment strategy. Other factors such as fluctuations in cultural estimations of the proper social distance between 'normality' and 'deviance' were not determined by labour market conditions.[26]

---

[24] For an exhaustive (and critical) analysis of this historical literature, see Michael Ignatieff, 'State, Civil Society and Total Institutions: A Critique of Recent Social Histories of Punishment', in Stanley Cohen and Andrew Scull (eds), *Social Control and the State* (Oxford, 1983), pp. 75–105.

[25] Michael Ignatieff, 'Preface', in *A Just Measure of Pain. The Penitentiary in the Industrial Revolution* (London, 1989).

[26] Ibid., p. 12.

The labour market and relations of production, which should stand at the core of what Ignatieff takes as the starting point of his analysis (class conflict), never become a primary object of interest; nor does the relationship between the penitentiary and the emerging capitalist economy. The connection between penal institutions (house of correction, workhouse and penitentiary) and productive institutions (manufacture and factory), as well as those between penality and labour market, are represented in terms of parallelism, not interaction.

Thus, the economy and the labour market have only an indirect importance: they represent a field whereby social disorder could proliferate (due to unemployment, refusal to work and crime) to which reformers and politicians wanted to put an end through penal policies. In this view, the penitentiary becomes a model of social order, the kind of social order endangered by the distortions of the labour market:

> The penitentiary, in other words, was more than a functional response to a specific institutional crisis. It exerted a hold on men's imaginations because it represented in microcosm the hierarchical, obedient, and godly social order, which they felt was coming apart around them.[27]

Ignatieff relates the stiffening of penal policy taking place in the first half of the nineteenth century to the effects of the Industrial Revolution and, in particular, to the growing unemployment. Masses of peasants who had been expelled from their lands following the *enclosures*, entered the urban centres producing an increase in criminality and social disorder: this social disorder explains the renewed terror imposed to the imprisoned population. Where Rusche and Kirchheimer saw a surplus-population which punitive practices contributed to turn into an 'industrial reserve army', Ignatieff sees potential criminals who endangered the traditional social order:

> Crime was interpreted as a sign of an ongoing crisis in labor market disciplines and class relations, especially in the agricultural districts of the south, but also in the manufacturing districts and in the juvenile labor market of the metropolis.[28]

Ignatieff seems to limit himself to a phenomenological description of class relations (indiscipline, revolts, social disorders and criminality), that leads him to leave the function of the prison (besides its apparent legitimation) unquestioned. He doesn't say, for example, what happened to these masses of marginal people to whom the new regime of hard discipline applied.

The emergence of the solitary system (Pentonville) is described as a result of the efforts by politicians to maintain order and to impose discipline on the rebellious poor. What Ignatieff does not say is whether this discipline answered somehow to the needs of the production system, which was undergoing a major transition from the manufacture to the factory system. In his view, the persistence of a 'social need' of order permitted the penitentiary to survive to its critiques: the survival of the prison is a result of the necessity to overcome the social crisis of the epoch. Reformers were able to interpret this crisis and to offer viable solutions:

---

[27]   Ibid., p. 84.
[28]   Ibid., p. 183.

... its support rested on a larger social need. It had appeal because the reformers succeeded in presenting it as a response, not merely to crime, but to the whole social crisis of a period, and as a part of a larger strategy of political, social, and legal reform designed to reestablish order on a new foundation.[29]

No matter if this social order was that of the emerging capitalist society. Ignatieff does not recognise that to make this order possible, it was necessary to transform the poor into a proletarian class: the relationship between punitive and productive institutions is thus reduced to a mere contingency. For Ignatieff, there is an analogy between, on the one hand, the prison, the mental hospital and the house of correction, and the factory on the other: but this is not due to a reciprocal interaction aiming to transform the criminal, the mad and the poor into proletarians. Instead, it is just a matter of ideological legitimation:

> It was just this resonance with the well-ordered manufactory, the workhouse, the asylum that made the penitentiary plausible, despite its evident failure to reform or deter ... By 1850 to challenge its logic was to challenge not just one discrete institution, but the interlocked structure of a whole encircling industrial order.[30]

In Ignatieff's work, the political economy of punishment is actually an 'economy of penal policies'. The object of this book seems to be a detailed description of the social and historical factors that allowed the reformers to succeed. The relations of production play a secondary role in this context: these are important only because they allow Ignatieff to situate the birth of the prison within a field of political struggle emerging around the issue of social order in a class-society. In other words, the relationship between economy and punishment becomes the relationship between social order (or disorder) and politics. The connection between relations of production and punitive systems is diluted in a whole complex of practices, ideas and policies: this leads Ignatieff to underestimate the historical importance of the emergence of the capitalist system of production.

Discipline and Punish

It would probably be inadequate to reduce Foucault's ideas on the political economy of punishment to what the author says in *Discipline and Punish*. In fact, this book is a systematisation of ideas Foucault was developing elsewhere, and it is often in non-systematic works that his most original insights can be found.[31]

Foucault's aim is to offer a genealogy of power technologies which would permit us to describe the internal economy and rationality of different control systems. The problem is: how did systems of social control change throughout history? And how did they develop, beside their negative and exclusive function, a positive and productive role?

---

[29] Ibid., p. 210.

[30] Ibid., p. 215.

[31] See in particular the courses held by Foucault at the *Collége de France* between 1970 and 1974 (whose 'summaries' are now published in English: see Paul Rabinow (ed.), *Michel Foucault. Ethics, vol. I* (London, 1997)).

The disciplinary technologies which Foucault describes in *Discipline and Punish* define the context within which the prison emerged. In turn, the emergence of the disciplinary society takes place within the process Foucault defines as 'governmentalisation of the State': that is, the transition from a model of power centred around sovereignty toward a power based on the 'science of government'. It was within governmental rationality that disciplinary techniques (and the prison in particular) found their peculiar place. In the Classic Age, a power which oriented its control practices to the protection of its own prerogatives was replaced by a governmental power which took the population and its productive dynamics as its main targets.[32]

The object of power is no longer the neutralisation of any threat coming from society through repressive practices, but to control social resources through technologies of government. In this respect, the individual and his/her role within a productive population become the focus of power technologies. As a consequence, power assumes a positive and productive role:

> The working out of this population-wealth-problem (in its different concrete aspects: taxation, scarcity, depopulation, idleness-beggary-vagabondage) constitutes one of the conditions of formation of political economy.[33]

This is a central point in Foucault's theory of power. Disciplinary technologies represent the productive site of a power whose philosophical foundation lies in the political economy, and the prison is an institutional form of this process. We can now understand how a political economy of the body could emerge from the prison: indeed, the invention of the penitentiary is embedded in the concept of the body as a productive entity.[34] If in Ignatieff's work detention is seen as a 'reaction' to the need for an efficient treatment of social disorder, Foucault describes the birth of the prison as the transition from a reactive to a productive model of power:

> We must show that punitive measures are not simply 'negative' mechanisms that make it possible to repress, to prevent, to exclude, to eliminate; but that they are linked to a whole series of positive and useful effects which it is their task to support ...[35]

Reclusion permits inclusion through exclusion. It is no longer a question of celebrating the strength of the king through a destructive exclusion of the tortured body (Damien), but of celebrating the rationality of governmental power through a constructive inclusion: detention aims to produce, to transform and to forge the inclusion of the disciplined subject. Foucault's analysis in *Discipline and Punish* is full of references

---

[32] On governmentality see Mitchell Dean, *Governmentality. Power and Rule in Modern Society* (London, 1999).

[33] Michel Foucault, 'Security, Territory, and Population', in Rabinow (ed.), *Michel Foucault. Ethics, vol. I*, p. 69.

[34] On the relation between governmentality, discipline and the control of the body see Barry Smart, 'On Discipline and Social Regulation: A Review of Foucault's Genealogical Analysis', in David Garland and Peter Young (eds), *The Power to Punish. Contemporary Penality and Social Analysis* (London, 1983), pp. 62–83.

[35] Michel Foucault, *Discipline and Punish. The Birth of the Prison* (London, 1977), p. 24.

to the structure of capitalist relations of production which emerged in the consolidation of disciplinary technologies. Indeed, the connection between discipline and capitalist organisation of work is much more than a contingency. When the author speaks of a 'political economy of the body', he refers to the fact that disciplinary techniques situate a productive body within peculiar spaces: the school, the barracks, the hospital, the prison and the factory. The docile body, once disciplined, can be inscribed in a productive context. No matter what kind of productivity (medical, scholastic, military or industrial), its rationality does not change.

Thus, discipline and governmentality are closely connected: the former is a technology for the government of the body, whereas the latter is a science for the government of a population in its own territory. Both are based on an economic *savoir* aimed at increasing social productivity. Disciplinary practices produce individuals who will form productive populations. In the section entitled *Panopticism*, Foucault is clear about the connection between the capitalist organisation of work and the disciplinary distribution of bodies:

> In fact, the two processes – the accumulation of men and the accumulation of capital – cannot be separated; it would not have been possible to solve the problem of the accumulation of men without the growth of an apparatus of production capable of both sustaining them and using them; conversely, the techniques that made cumulative multiplicity of men useful accelerated the accumulation of capital … The growth of a capitalist economy gave rise to the specific modality of disciplinary power, whose general formulas, techniques of submitting forces and bodies, in short 'political anatomy', could be operated in the most diverse political regimes, apparatuses or institutions.[36]

Ignatieff saw the similarity between the prison and the factory as an ideological device which legitimated detention as part of a larger complex of social institutions: in this context, to challenge the prison meant to challenge the whole industrial society and its institutions. However, Foucault goes beyond this parallelism and reveals the existence of a unitary logic behind the various apparatuses of the disciplinary society. They resemble each other not only because they answer in similar ways to similar social problems, but because they share the aim of transforming the bodies and organising them productively.

The prison develops a new concept of space and time, applied to bodies and populations. The synchronisation of gestures, the regulation of multitudes of individuals in the factory, the body-machine relationship: all these aspects exemplify a new and peculiar economic rationality taking form with the consolidation of industrial production.[37]

The importance of Foucault's work for the formation of a political economy of punishment cannot be underestimated. The birth of the prison becomes a matter of political economy because the political economy becomes itself the philosophy of the new science of government. Indeed, the relationship between disciplinary institutions and places of production is self-evident. Foucault's analysis of disciplinary techniques helps the political economy of punishment to overcome the limits of historical

---

[36] Ibid., p. 221.

[37] 'Discipline is no longer simply an art of distributing bodies, of extracting time from them and accumulating it, but of composing forces in order to obtain an efficient machine': Ibid., p. 164.

reconstructions like Ignatieff's one, which do not allow us to identify the deep connection between the prison and the factory. *Discipline and Punish* opens the field to an analysis of the economic and political history of penality which reveals the *structural* relation between the birth of the penitentiary and the emergence of capitalism.

The Prison and the Factory

Melossi and Pavarini's *The Prison and the Factory* is perhaps the most significant attempt to apply the Marxian paradigm to the history of the prison. This work situates the origin of the penitentiary in the complex transformation of Western societies which Marx described in the first volume of his *Capital*. Here, Marx deals with the so-called 'original accumulation', the stage when capitalism had to create the conditions for its own development. Capital had to destroy agricultural and handicraft-based economy and to turn its labour force into a working class. But the contradictory aspect of this process is quite evident: on the one hand capitalism liberated labour from political slavery and personal dependency; on the other, it subjugated it to a new kind of subordination – now a purely economic one. The 'liberation' of work took place through an expropriation of producers which imposed a different level of enslavement:

> Hence, the historical movement which changes the producers into wage-workers, appears, on the one hand, as their emancipation from serfdom and from the fetters of the guilds, and this side alone exists for our bourgeois historians. But, on the other hand, these new freedmen became sellers of themselves only after they had been robbed of all their own means of production, and of the guarantees of existence afforded by the old feudal arrangements.[38]

The masses of peasants expelled from the lands flew into the towns, enlarging the mob of vagrants and poor. At the beginning, this potential labour force was unable to find a place within the changed conditions of production and was reluctant to accept the new organisation of work emerging in the factories. Marx shows how this problem inspired a whole series of cruel punitive practices:

> The fathers of the present working-class were chastised for their enforced transformation into vagabonds and paupers. Legislation treated them as 'voluntary' criminals, and assumed that it depended on their own goodwill to go on working under the old conditions that no longer existed.[39]

The problem is here the production of a proletarian class through the transformation of labour into a variable capital, capable of producing a surplus value. The consolidation of the factory system gave birth to the process which Marx defined 'real subsumption of labour under capital'. This means that all the various typologies of pre-capitalist work are reduced under the general form of abstract labour: producers are turned into a social labour force and the 'collective worker' replaces the individual worker:

---

[38]   Marx, *Capital*, p. 786.
[39]   Ibid., p. 806.

First, with the development of the real subsumption of labour under capital, or the specifically capitalist mode of production, the real lever of the overall labour process is not the individual worker. Instead, labour-power socially combined and the various competing labour powers, which together form the entire production machine, participate in very different ways in the immediate process of making commodities, or, more accurately in this context, creating the product.[40]

Now, Melossi and Pavarini describe the role of punitive practices in the historical process of subsumption of work under capital. They show the contradiction on which this process is based (the liberation of work through its enslavement) and pose the question: which role did the prison play for the control of this contradiction? Their answer in *The Prison and the Factory* is that the role of punitive institutions was crucial: the penitentiary emerged as an institution ancillary to the factory, as a mechanism functional to the needs of the emerging industrial production system. The internal dynamics of the prison, both at the organisational and ideological level, cannot be separated from what happens at the same time in the field of production, and the concept of discipline acts as a medium between the prison and the factory. But the discipline described by Melossi and Pavarini is a technology for the control of individuals rooted directly in the universe of productive relations. All the segregating institutions which emerged toward the end of the seventeenth century shared the same disciplinary logic:

> Over and above their specific functions, one overall aim united them: control over a rising proletariat. The bourgeois state assigns to all of them a directing role in the various moments of the formation, production and reproduction of the factory proletariat: for society they are essential instruments of social control, the aim of which is to secure for capital a workforce which by virtue of its moral attitude, physical health, intellectual capacity, orderliness, obedience, etc. will readily adapt to the whole regime of factory life and produce the maximum amount of surplus labour.[41]

The prison appears indeed as an apparatus for the production and reproduction of subjectivity. A new category of individuals has to be shaped by the prison: eager to obey, execute orders and observe the rhythms of work by internalising a new concept of time and space. The task of the penitentiary is to inculcate these attitudes into the expropriated masses, thus contributing to the subsumption of work described by Marx. As in *Discipline and Punish*, we see here a political economy of the body. But here the body is not the 'generic' and unspecified one described by Foucault: it is a productive entity, treated as a source of surplus-value. This body, once associated with other bodies and subjected to the scientific organisation of work, has to become capital. Following Melossi:

> This discipline is the basic condition for the extraction of surplus-value, and is the only real lesson that bourgeois society has to propose to the proletariat. If legal ideology rules outside production, within it reign servitude and inequality. But the place of production is the

---

[40] Karl Marx, *Capital, vol. I* (Harmondsworth, 1976), p. 1039.

[41] Dario Melossi and Massimo Pavarini, *The Prison and the Factory. Origins of the Penitentiary System* (London, 1981), p. 42.

factory. Thus, the institutional function of the workhouses and later of the prisons was to teach the proletariat factory discipline.[42]

It is not just a question of describing the birth of the prison and showing its role in the formation of the industrial proletariat. The problem is how to identify the ancillary function of social control systems at large in the *reproduction* of the labour force. The borders of a historical enquiry are crossed here, and we are faced with the possibility to build a materialistic approach to the issue of the relationship between production and social control.

Having posed the question of the reproduction of the labour force, it becomes necessary for the two authors to take both the material and the ideological dimensions of the prison into account. The former allows them to shed light on the direct economic function of the penitentiary – that is, the creation of a disciplined labour force ready to be exploited. The latter, to grasp the reasons for the persistence of this institution beyond its direct profitability: the prison reproduces an ideal model of capitalist society. Melossi and Pavarini reveal the role of the prison in the ideological reproduction of capitalist relations of production, and illustrate how this process takes place through a deconstruction and reconstruction of individuals. In fact, the prison turns the poor into a criminal, the criminal into a prisoner and, finally, the prisoner into a proletarian:

> But once reduced to abstract subject, once his diversity is 'annulled' … once faced by those material needs which cannot be satisfied independently and thereby rendered dependent on the sovereignty of the administration, ultimately the product of the disciplinary machine has only one possible alternative to his own destruction, to madness: the moral form of subjection, that is the moral form of the proletarian. Better still: the moral form of the proletarian is here laid down as the only condition of existence in the sense of being the only way the property-less can survive.[43]

Thus, the prison is surely a repressive institution because it imposes on the prisoner an absolute deprivation which reduces them to a complete dependence on the administration. But it is also an ideological dispositive because it imposes submission to work as the only way to escape from this condition. In other words, Melossi and Pavarini expose the paradox of an institution which, while producing absolute deprivation, imposes its own disciplinary technologies as the only remedy to this

---

[42] Dario Melossi, 'The Penal Question in Capital', in Anthony Platt and Paul Takagi (eds), *Crime and Social Justice* (London, 1981), p. 195. See also Dario Melossi 'Institutions of Social Control and Capitalist Organisation of Work', in Bob Fine, *et al.* (eds), *Capitalism and the Rule of Law. From Deviancy Theory to Marxism* (London, 1979), pp. 90–99.

[43] Melossi and Pavarini, *The Prison and the Factory*, p. 163. The process of subjectivation through imprisonment described here by Melossi and Pavarini is reminiscent of Althusser's hypotheses on the *Ideological State Apparatuses*. For Althusser, ideology guarantees the reproduction of existing relations of production through the 'subjectivation of individuals': 'The individual is interpellated as a (free) subject in order that he shall submit freely to the commandments of the Subject, i.e. in order that he shall (freely) accept his subjection, i.e. in order that he shall make the gestures and actions of his subjection *all by himself*. There are no subjects except by and for their subjection. That is why they *work all by themselves*': Louis Althusser, 'Ideology and Ideological State Apparatuses', in *Lenin and Philosophy and Other Essays* (London, 1971), p. 169.

situation. The prison creates the prisoner and imposes at the same time labour, obedience and discipline (i.e. the elements constitutive of this condition) as the way to salvation. Finally, the deprivation imposed by the prison is powerfully represented as a natural consequence of the refusal of work discipline.[44]

Melossi and Pavarini describe these two dimensions of the prison in a coherent way. The material dimension is revealed through a description of punitive practices in relation to the conditions of the labour market: here the influence of Rusche and Kirchheimer and of their concept of less eligibility is clear. The ideological dimension emerges through the introduction of the contractual reason into the system of punishments. A new concept of time (as measure for value) makes possible the invention of a punishment based on the 'withdrawal of time'. Following Pashukanis:

> Deprivation of freedom, for a period stipulated in the court sentence, is the specific form in which modern, that is to say bourgeois-capitalist, criminal law embodies the principle of equivalent recompense. This form is unconsciously yet deeply linked with the conception of man in the abstract and abstract human labour measurable in time.[45]

The principle of the exchange of equivalents makes the prison ideologically acceptable in the same way as it makes a work contract 'fair': there is no abuse here, but only an exchange between equals and a 'just' retribution:

> The content of the punishment (the execution) is thus linked to its juridical form in the same way as authority in the factory ensures that exploitation can assume the character of a contract.[46]

Here we see at work the contradiction between formal equality and material inequality. This is visible both in the economic sphere where it emerges as the relation between the field of circulation (equality) and the field of production (inequality), and in the carceral institution where it is evident in the contrast between the principle of retribution and the practice of discipline. Thus, the penitentiary is at the same time an ideal representation of this contradiction and an example of the many ways in which it can be obscured.

In *Punish and Critique*, Adrian Howe suggests that in Melossi and Pavarini's work there is an incoherence between the analysis of the material and the ideological dimension of the prison.[47] In particular, Howe sees a contradiction between Melossi's more 'materialist' perspective (the first part of *The Prison and the Factory*) and Pavarini's emphasis on ideological aspects. I cannot see this contradiction; in fact, the material processes are legitimated by their ideological representation. The legalistic ideology conceals the reality of discipline and abuse within the prison in the same way as the ideology of the contract hides the reality of exploitation and

---

[44] See Althusser's definition of ideology: 'What is represented in ideology is therefore not the system of real relations which govern the existence of individuals, but the imaginary relation of those individuals to the real relations in which they live': Althusser, 'Ideology and Ideological State Apparatuses', p. 155.

[45] Pashukanis, *Law and Marxism*, pp. 180–181.

[46] Melossi and Pavarini, *The Prison and the Factory*, p. 57.

[47] Adrian Howe, *Punish and Critique* (London, 1994), p. 77.

subordination within the factory. Coherently, the common objective is to reproduce a working class who considers wage as the just value of its labour and reclusion as the just retribution for its crimes.

Political Economies of Contemporary Penality

The transition from the historical field to the analysis of the present condition raises some problems. The first is the 'translation' of the concepts introduced by Rusche and Kirchheimer: how can we adapt to contemporary reality some hypotheses conceived in a historical perspective? Rusche and Kirchheimer analysed the historical evolution of punishment through a period of time including different punitive systems. Instead, in a contemporary perspective the research focus has to be on the hegemonic punitive institution of contemporary society: the prison. But there is also a methodological issue, concerning the empirical analysis of the punishment-economy relationship. Here too, the utility of *Punishment and Social Structure* is limited: Rusche and Kirchheimer examined the evolution of capitalism through its various stages of development, whereas now we have to deal with one specific stage of capitalist economy.

A further problem, this time theoretical, is the necessity to overcome a heavy positivist heritage re-emerging also in some critical approaches to punishment. This can be summarised with the idea that the relation between the economy and punishment is mediated by criminality: the deprivation imposed to the subordinate classes (coupled with the capitalist ideology of individualism and property), would prompt the most deprived to commit 'crimes of survival'. At this point, the selectivity of the penal system would criminalise the poor, who are thus victimised twice: first, as victims of economic circumstances that deprive them of their basic means of subsistence; second, as victims of the criminal justice system and its selectivity.[48] This hypothesis had to be overcome, because it obstructed an analysis of the punitive system and of its relations to the economy independent of rhetorical legitimations such as social defence and the control of criminality.

Incarceration and Unemployment: The United States

The first important attempt to develop a contemporary perspective on the political economy of punishment is Ivan Jankovic's 1977 article 'Labour Market and Imprisonment'.[49] The most important aspect of this article is that Jankovic translated

---

[48] This perspective, exemplified by Willelm Bonger in *Criminality and Economic Conditions* (Boston, 1916), is present especially in the first stage of critical criminology. See Ian Taylor, Paul Walton and Jock Young, *The New Criminology* (London, 1973).

[49] Ian Jankovic, 'Labour Market and Imprisonment', *Crime and Social Justice*, 8 (1877): 17–31. Two other studies which appeared long before Jankovic's (but are almost forgotten) are worth mentioning here. The first one is Thorsten Sellin, *Research Memorandum on Crime in the Depression* (New York, 1937): this is important because, before the publication of *Punishment and Social Structure*, it takes into account Rusche's ideas (which Sellin knew from Rusche's 1933 article). Sellin considers here the concept of *less eligibility* as a useful tool for the study of the relation between economy and the penal system. The second study is by Sir Thomas Stern, 'The Effect of the Depression on Prison

Rusche and Kirchheimer's ideas into empirical terms. The author started from two hypotheses: the 'severity' hypothesis and the 'utility' hypothesis. The first holds that to a deterioration of economic conditions corresponds a stiffening of penal sanctions whose aim is to deter poor classes from committing crimes (*less eligibility*). The second hypothesis is that this process is also profitable: the increased severity of punishment would function to regulate the surplus labour force and to turn it into an industrial reserve army.[50]

Jankovic dealt with the problem of the empirical 'translation' of these concepts by adopting rates of unemployment as an indicator of the economic conditions, and incarceration rates as a measure of penal severity:

> This is a restatement of Rusche and Kirchheimer's 'severity' hypothesis: when the economy is bad, punishments are more severe. Unemployment is taken as an index of the state of the economy, and imprisonment as an index of severity of punishment ... The second hypothesis to be tested is that increased imprisonment functions to reduce unemployment. This 'utility' hypothesis asserts that the effect of changing penal policies is reflected in the conditions of the labour market.[51]

Jankovic clearly separated these hypotheses from the issue of crime rates. The starting assumption was in fact that the two trends could be observed independent of rates of criminal activity, and that the relationship between unemployment and imprisonment was indeed direct.[52] The author examined the case of the US between 1926 and 1974, obtaining ambivalent results. On the one hand, the severity hypothesis was in fact confirmed: incarceration and unemployment co-varied significantly, and this trend appeared to be constant after controlling for crime rates. On the other hand, it was impossible to find any significant impact of incarceration rates on the labour market: the 'severity' hypothesis was thus contradicted. Despite the partiality of results, the study by Jankovic supported Rusche and Kirchheimer's perspective and identified a possible way of applying it to contemporary penal systems:

Commitments and Sentences', *Journal of the American Institute of Criminal Law and Criminology*, 31 (1941): 696–711: Stern proposes an empirical test of Rusche's theories, verifying whether there was any relationship between the economic depression in the United States and Prison Sentences (Stern's case study was on two penitentiaries in Pennsylvania).

[50] If Jankovic is trying here to give an empirical concreteness to the concepts of Rusche and Kirchheimer, in the same period Richard Quinney opts for a theoretical actualisation. That is, Quinney doesn't enter into the empirical-quantitative field opened by Jankovic; instead, he works on a theoretical analysis of the role of punishment in the reproduction of a class-based society: 'Rather than being capable of absorbing the surplus population into the political economy, advanced capitalism can only supervise and control a population that is now superfluous to the capitalist system ... Criminal justice is the modern means of controlling the surplus population produced by late capitalism': Richard Quinney, *Class, State and Crime* (New York, 1977), p. 131.

[51] Jankovic, 'Labour Market and Imprisonment', pp. 20–21.

[52] This point separates Jankovic's work from other earlier studies which, though assuming the existence of a relationship between economy and imprisonment, suggested that criminality played an important role in it. For an example, see D.A. Dobbins and B.M. Bass, 'Effects of Unemployment on White and Negro Prison Admissions in Louisiana', *Journal of Criminal Law, Criminology and Police Science*, 48 (1958): 522–525.

Despite their shortcomings, the present findings lend some support to the Rusche-Kirchheimer severity hypothesis. Their greatest immediate contribution, however, may be that of putting current speculations about imprisonment and unemployment rates on a solid foundation ... Another contribution by the present study is in its demonstration that the relationship between unemployment and imprisonment is a direct one, independent of the changes in criminal activity.[53]

In the same years, David Greenberg applied the Marxist perspective to Canada and the US for the years 1945–1959 and 1960–1972, finding again a significant correlation between rates of unemployment and rates of imprisonment, independent of criminality.[54] This led Greenberg to criticise those authors who connected trends in incarceration rates either to rates of criminal activity or to 'homeostatic' dynamics of the criminal justice system: for Greenberg, variations in incarceration rates could only be explained by resorting to exogenous factors.[55]

A few years later, Greenberg tested the same hypothesis on Poland. The author considered two distinct periods: the years 1924–1939 – when Poland was a capitalist country – and the years 1955–1976 – when a system of socialist production had been established there. Greenberg found a connection between unemployment and imprisonment for the 'capitalist' period, but no correlation for the 'socialist' phase. These results seemed to confirm indirectly the validity of the materialist hypothesis (it worked when applied to capitalist social formations, not with socialist economies), and suggested an important theoretical innovation. In fact, Greenberg found that an important role was played by the amnesties established by the Polish Government in the years 1932–1969. These political measures explain, in part, the missing correlation between unemployment and incarceration, and suggest that political-ideological factors are at least as important as the economic ones:

> By pointing to amnesties as an explanatory variable, we are insisting on the partial autonomy of the political realm ... Marxists have not always felt comfortable in considering political and ideological factors as explanations, but to do so is necessary if reductionism is to be avoided.[56]

Between the 1970s and 1980s, many other US-based works appeared, whose aim was to verify the validity of Rusche and Kirchheimer's hypotheses as they had been initially 'translated' by Jankovic.[57]

Matthew Yeager examined the period 1951–1977, putting in relation rates of incarceration in federal prisons with unemployment rates in the US. As a control variable, however, Yeager did not select criminality (i.e. crime rates), but sentencing

---

[53] Jankovic, 'Labour Market and Imprisonment', pp. 27–28.

[54] David Greenberg, 'The Dynamics of Oscillatory Punishment Processes', *The Journal of Criminal Law and Criminology*, 68 (1977): 643–651.

[55] See Alfred Blumstein, Jacqueline Cohen and Daniel Nagin, 'The Dynamics of Homeostatic Punishment Process', *Journal of Criminal Law and Criminology*, 67 (1976): 317–334.

[56] David Greenberg, 'Penal Sanctions in Poland: A Test of Alternative Models', *Social Problems*, 28/2 (1980): 203.

[57] For a review, also covering some studies not considered here, see Ted Chiricos and Miriam Delone, 'Labour Surplus and Imprisonment: A Review and Assessment of Theory and Evidence', *Social Problems*, 39/4 (1992): 421–446.

trends of the American courts; but the result was the same: in fact, there seemed to be a direct correlation between the economic indicator and the punitive indicator. Similar results were found one year later by Don Wallace; but his analysis was more complex, given that he took many control variables into account, such as crime rates, welfare benefits and public police expenditures. The period considered by Wallace is quite short (1971–1976) and incarceration rates referred only to State prisons. As for the independent variable, instead of official unemployment rates (which often underestimate the real level of exclusion from the labour market), Wallace turned to a different measure: the rate of participation in the labour market defined as '(T)he proportion of the civilian, non-institutionalised population aged 16 or older which is economically active in a given year'.[58]

This study offered further support to Rusche and Kirchheimer's theory, but showed a more complex relationship between the labour market and various institutions of social control: according to Wallace, the connection involved also those welfare-based institutions whose social control practices were inclusive and non-segregative.

In 1985, Galster and Scaturo tested the severity hypothesis in the US for the period 1976–1981.[59] As measures of the severity of punishment, these authors adopted three different indicators besides incarceration rates: rates of prison readmission for probation violators, prison sentences, and conditional-unconditional release rates. Their article tested the relationship between unemployment and the three variables, for each year in the time series. In this way, Galster and Scaturo could disaggregate the measure of penal severity and overcome some of the statistical shortcomings produced by the adoption of incarceration rates as the unique indicator of punitiveness.[60] The authors did not find any relationship between unemployment and penal severity, however: none of the three possible correlations seemed in fact to follow Rusche and Kirchheimer's paradigm. But these findings concerned the US as a whole, without any geographical distinction: instead, the results changed after a geographical disaggregation was made – in fact, the severity hypothesis was strongly confirmed for the Southern States.

A few years later Michalowski and Pearson came to the same results, in a study which analysed the years from 1970 to 1990.[61] This study tested both the hypothesis of the severity of punishment and Scull's theory of the fiscal crisis.[62] The expectation was that there would be a direct relation between unemployment and incarceration rates, and that incarceration would follow some indicators of the fiscal condition of the States under consideration. In both cases, these trends were supposed to be observable independently from the rates of crime.

---

[58] Don Wallace, 'The Political Economy of Incarceration Trends in late US Capitalism: 1971–1977', *The Insurgent Sociologist*, 11/1 (1980): 60.

[59] George C. Galster and Laure A. Scaturo, 'The US Criminal Justice System: Unemployment and the Severity of Punishment', *Journal of Research in Crime and Delinquency*, 22/2 (1985): 163–189.

[60] For a critique of the use of incarceration rates as indicators of penal severity, see Richard A. Berk, *et al.*, 'Prisons as Self-Regulating Systems', *Law and Society Review*, 17 (1983): 547–586.

[61] Raymond J. Michalowski and Michaela A. Pearson, 'Punishment and Social Structure at the State Level: A Cross-Sectional Comparison of 1970 and 1980', *Journal of Research in Crime and Delinquency*, 27/1 (1990): 52–78.

[62] Andrew Scull, *Decarceration* (New Jersey, 1977).

However, none of the two hypotheses found confirmation in this study: the only variable to which incarceration rates seemed to be connected was the geographic one (Northern States versus Southern States). In the end, however, what Michalowski and Pearson concluded from these findings was not really a critique of neo-Marxist theories. In fact, they suggested that:

> Undifferentiated, official statistics on unemployment may be inadequate measures of the relationship between labor patterns and imprisonment practices ... The extent to which labour is segmented into different productive systems; characterised by markets split along ethnic, racial, or gender lines; or is dominated by high- or low-skill jobs may be as important as official levels of unemployment in shaping the size and character of the penal apparatus in different states.[63]

In other words, the problem was how to integrate the quantitative indicator (unemployment) with other qualitative factors, which interacted with the labour market and affected the relationship between economy and punishment. It was not so much unemployment in itself which produced an increase in penal severity, as the unemployment affecting *some* social strata, traditionally considered dangerous for the social order: ethnic minorities, immigrants and the young poor.[64]

Following these findings, a new tendency emerged in the American political economy of punishment toward a more qualitative perspective: since Greenberg's study of Poland (and his stress on the importance of amnesties as political factors), the quantitative study of statistical correlations between unemployment and imprisonment gave way to an analysis of those social indicators which seemed to play a role in the economy-punishment relationship: the ethnic structure of the population, gender and class relations, the transformations in the structure of the labour market.[65] As we will see, this qualitative revision of Rusche and Kirchheimer's perspective represents an important attempt to overcome some limits of contemporary materialist criminology. However, there are also some recent examples of a return to the initial orthodoxy and to a quasi-mechanistic analysis of the connections between the labour market and the prison.

---

[63] Michalowski and Pearson, 'Punishment and Social Structure at the State Level', p. 73.

[64] For interesting case-studies on the interaction between ethnicity and employment conditions in the United States, see Theodore G. Chiricos and William D. Bales, 'Unemployment and Punishment: An Empirical Assessment', *Criminology*, 29/4 (1991): 701–724; Gary T. Lessan, 'Macro-economic Determinants of Penal Policy: Estimating the Unemployment and Inflation Influences on Imprisonment Rate Changes in the United States, 1948–1985', *Crime, Law and Social Change*, 16 (1991): 177–198; George S. Bridges, Robert D. Crutchfield and Edith E. Simpson, 'Crime, Social Structure and Criminal Punishment: White and Non-white Rates of Imprisonment', *Social Problems*, 34/4 (1987): 345–361.

[65] Samuel L. Myers and William J. Sabol, 'Unemployment and Racial Differences in Imprisonment', *Review of Black Political Economy*, 16/1-2 (1987): 189–209. More recently, with particular reference to political factors as a mediating variable between economy and punishment, see David Jacobs and Ronald E. Helms, 'Toward a Political Model of Incarceration: A Time-series Examination of Multiple Explanations for Prison Admission Rates', *American Journal of Sociology*, 102/2 (1996): 323–357.

In a recent article, Bruce Western and Katherine Beckett hypothesise the existence of an immediate relation between penal policies and economic policies in the US.[66] Following the 'utility' hypothesis, these two authors suggest that incarceration rates exercised a considerable (quantitative) influence on unemployment rates in the US: in the short term, incarceration would reduce unemployment rates by subtracting a substantial portion of the unemployed population from official statistics. However, in the long term the reverse would happen: unemployment rates would increase, because people who have been in prison are less employable than the others. Therefore, according to the authors the low levels of US unemployment in the 1980s and 1990s cannot be ascribed to the flexibility of the labour market, but to the dramatic increase in incarceration that has taken place since the end of the 1970s.

On the other hand, the penalising effects of incarceration on employability imply that, in order to maintain their low unemployment rates, the US should incarcerate even more than they do at present.[67] The influence of Jankovic on Western and Beckett is clear:

> We also view incarceration as a kind of hidden joblessness, similar to an old tradition in Marxist criminology (cf. Jankovic, 1977). Unlike that work, hidden unemployment here is viewed as a consequence of incarceration, not a functional necessity of capitalism. Instead of recruiting replacement workers to the reserve army of labour, we also claim that incarceration tightens labour markets in the short run and makes workers more unemployable in the long run.[68]

After considering the class composition of the prison population in the US, the authors conclude that if official statistics also took this population into account, unemployment rates would increase automatically by two percentage points. These data become even clearer if we concentrate on the African American population: in this case, the increase would amount to more than seven points. In other words, mass incarceration of blacks has reduced unemployment rates among African Americans by almost one third.

However, the question is: how could Western and Beckett come to conclusions so different from Jankovic's ones, and be able to show the existence of such a strong influence of incarceration on the labour market? The answer lies in the dramatic shift in recent US penal policy:

> Jankovic studied the idea that prison removes part of the surplus labour pool from the labour market. His research for the period 1926–1974 found that the size of the incarcerated population in the United States did not markedly affect the size of the unemployed population. Recent effects may be different, however, because of growth in prison and jail populations over the past 20 years.[69]

Western and Beckett close their study with a comparison between public intervention in the labour market in the US and in Europe. Whereas European states

---

[66] Bruce Western and Katherine Beckett, 'How Unregulated is the US Labor Market? The Penal System as a Labor Market Institution', *American Journal of Sociology*, 104/4 (1999): 1030–1060.

[67] Ibid., p. 1031.

[68] Ibid., p. 1032.

[69] Ibid., p. 1040.

are still adopting public policies aiming to reduce social inequality, in the US social policies have been replaced by penal policies. The management of unemployment and social marginality is thus shifting from the domain of the welfare state to that of the criminal justice system.

Incarceration and Unemployment: Other Contexts

Since the beginning of the 1980s, the political economy of punishment has started to cross the American borders.[70] In 1980, John Braithwaite examined the case of Australia. Braithwaite's aim was to compare two perspectives: on the one hand, Quinney's hypothesis that increasing incarceration rates in late capitalism function to control a surplus labour force; on the other hand, Scull's idea that the fiscal crisis of post-industrial capitalist states would produce a reduction in segregative practices (incarceration rates) and a tendency toward decarceration and *community control*. Through an analysis of the relationship between unemployment and incarceration for the period 1840–1980 in the regions of Victoria and New South Wales, Braithwaite confirmed the validity of Rusche and Kirchheimer's (and Quinney's) hypothesis, observing at the same time some contradictory trends since the 1920s.

His conclusion was that in fact there is a relation between the economy and penality. However, this is not automatic, but mediated by social policies, public opinion and the mass media. On the other hand, Scull's hypothesis received some support too: Braithwaite found an alternation of incarceration and decarceration phases, depending on economic conditions and cultural factors.[71]

In the same years, Steven Box and Chris Hale inaugurated the British political economy of punishment. In a series of studies, the two authors argued for the existence of a direct connection between the labour market and punitive policies in the UK.[72] Periods of economic crisis (like the one which affected England from the end of the 1970s to the end of the 1980s) are also periods of growing incarceration. This relation is the result of an increased severity by the criminal justice system, unrelated to the crime problem. In 1987, Steven Box summarised these findings and formulated a general hypothesis:

---

[70] See, besides the studies reviewed here: for Switzerland Manuel Eisner, 'Cycles of Political Control: The Case of Canton Zurich, 1880–1983', *European Journal of Political Research*, 15 (1987): 167–184; Martin Killias and Christian Grandjean, 'Chomage et taux d'incarcèration: L'example de la Suisse de 1890 à 1941', *Dèviance et Sociètè*, 10/4 (1986): 309–322. For the Netherlands: Willelm De Haan, *The Politics of Redress. Crime, Punishment and Penal Abolition*, Unwin Hyman (London, 1990), pp. 36–63.

[71] John Braithwaite, 'The Political Economy of Punishment', in El Weelwright and Ken D. Buckley (eds), *Essays in the Political Economy of Australian Capitalism* (Sydney, 1980), pp. 192–208.

[72] Steven Box and Chris Hale, 'Economic Crisis and the Rising Prisoner Population in England and Wales', *Crime and Social Justice*, 17 (1982): 20–35; Steven Box and Chris Hale, 'Unemployment, Imprisonment and Prison Overcrowding', *Contemporary Crises*, 9 (1985): 209–228; Steven Box and Chris Hale, 'Unemployment, Crime and Imprisonment, and the Enduring Problem of Prison Overcrowding', in Roger Matthews and Jock Young (eds), *Confronting Crime* (London, 1986), pp. 72–99; Chris Hale, 'Economy, Punishment and Imprisonment', *Contemporary Crises*, 13 (1989): 327–349.

> The 'radical' view ... considers that unemployment and imprisonment are linked, but instead of looking at crime and conviction rates as the mediating factors, it has focused on the belief that 'unemployment causes crime' and how this belief directly or subtly affects judicial sentencing practice, probation officers' sentence recommendations, and police deployment, apprehension, arrest and prosecution policies.[73]

Unlike many other authors, Box and Hale suggested a non-orthodox explanation for the economy-penality relation: thus, they distanced themselves from those 'conspiracy theories' which represented the criminal justice system as a monolith and as an integrated system working to satisfy the 'needs of capital'.[74] Since Jankovic's failure to demonstrate any direct effect of penal practices on the labour market, the link between punishment and the economy could no longer be considered in terms of immediate functionality. Therefore, Box and Hale extended the political economy of punishment to include also ideological and cultural factors, because the punitive system is not separated from the wider cultural processes of society. Control institutions share those tendencies, common representations and stereotypes that are common in the society, and these are influenced in turn by the economic climate. The agents of the criminal justice system do not answer to any abstract needs of capital: they probably ignore these needs. Instead, they limit themselves to take decisions according to their own perceptions of the crime problem and to their ideas about how to cope with it. Among these representations lies the stereotype for which the economically deprived are more crime-prone than others. In this sense, the relationship between unemployment and imprisonment is not mediated by an increase in crime, as by a *representation* (hegemonic in periods of crisis) of social marginality as a threat to the social order:

> As the economic crisis deepens, the judiciary becomes increasingly anxious about the possible threat to social order posed by 'problem populations' particularly unemployed males rather than females, and unemployed young males rather than unemployed older males, and within the former group, young black unemployed males ... and it responds to this 'perception' by increasing the use of custodial sentences, particularly against property offenders, in the belief that such a response will deter and incapacitate and thus defuse this threat.[75]

---

[73]   Steven Box, *Recession, Crime and Punishment* (London, 1987), p. 158.

[74]   For some examples, see the works by Jankovic, Quinney and Wallace cited above. See also Richard Vogel, 'Capitalism and Incarceration', *Monthly Review*, 34/10 (1983): 30–41; Mark Colvin, 'Controlling the Surplus Population: the Latent Functions of Imprisonment and Welfare in Late US Capitalism', in Brian D. McLean (ed.), *The Political Economy of Crime* (Ontario, 1986), pp. 154–165. For a historical perspective: Christopher Adamson, 'Toward a Marxian Penology: Captive Criminal Populations as Economic Threats and Resources', *Social Problems*, 31/4 (1984): 435–458.

[75]   Box and Hale, 'Unemployment, Imprisonment and Prison Overcrowding', p. 217. This passage is reminiscent of Steven Spitzer's articulation of the *surplus* labour force in '*social dynamite*' and '*social junk*': the surplus labour force represents a problematic population which is at the same time useful for the reproduction of capital. This population can either become a treat, justifying the increase in punitiveness described by Box and Hale, or remain a resource manageable through ordinary punitive means or social policies. See Steven Spitzer, 'Toward a Marxian Theory of Deviance', *Social Problems*, 22/5 (1975): 638–651.

Here the concept of less eligibility re-emerged clearly. However, Box and Hale offered a complex explanation of its concrete functioning, without supposing that social control agents were the agents of a conspiracy: this was a first step towards a plausible causal framework.

The French case has been analysed by Thierry Godefroy and Bernard Laffargue. These authors also discovered a direct correlation between unemployment and imprisonment.[76] In their studies, they explained this connection through the concept of 'sub-proletariat' and the processes of selective penalisation targeting this fraction of social marginality. The hypothesis was that in periods of economic crisis some segments of the working class fell into a condition of sub-proletariat, producing an increase in social insecurity whose immediate consequence was an increase in institutional punitiveness. Therefore, the surplus labour force was perceived by public opinion (and treated by the institutions of social control) as a source of crime and as the main cause of public insecurity:

> The rise in unemployment and the fall of a fraction of the working class into the sub-proletariat during economic recession result in the extension of those 'target groups' affected by the punitive criminal justice circuit. This leads to an increase in prison populations, regardless of variations in recorded crime. The movement may be amplified by criminal justice policies and changes in attitude linked with a prevailing sense of insecurity.[77]

Here, too, instead of intentional strategies we find aggregate decisions taken at different levels of the criminal justice system (police, courts, probation offices), giving birth to a 'penal-penalising process' whose consequence is the criminalisation of whole categories of people.

In the same vein, Dario Melossi examined the relationship between economic cycle and incarceration rates in Italy, for the period 1896–1965. Melossi started from the assumption that this relationship could be described through three models: it was possible to hypothesise that the economy influenced crime rates and these had in turn an effect on incarceration; that shifts in sentencing (as affected by economic conditions) played a mediating role; or to imagine a direct connection between the economy and incarceration unmediated by sentencing practices or legislative reforms.[78]

In Melossi's work, the economic indicator was given by the average national income, whereas the punitive indicator was represented by prison admission rates. Melossi did not find any significant relation between economy and *crime*, nor between economy and prison *conviction* rates. On the other hand, there seemed to be a direct relation between the economic indicator and prison *admissions*:

> More specifically, the results show that a change of one unit in the business cycle indicator is associated with a change of -.1692 in prison admissions. This is not trivial. It amounts to

---

[76] Bernard Laffargue and Thierry Godefroy, 'Economic Cycles and Punishment: Unemployment and Imprisonment. A Time-Series Study: France 1920–1985', *Contemporary Crises*, 13 (1989): 371–404.

[77] Ibid., p. 373. See also Thierry Godefroy and Bernard Laffargue, *Changements Economiques et Repression Penale* (Paris, 1995).

[78] Dario Melossi, 'Punishment and Social Action: Changing Vocabularies of Punitive Motive Within a Political Business Cycle', *Current Perspectives in Social Theory*, 6 (1985): 169–197.

saying that a yearly increase of Lire 100 (1938) per capita in the national income would be associated with a decrease of 16 in prison admissions per 100,000 population.[79]

In other words, Melossi confirmed for Italy the existence of a link not mediated by crime rates, sentencing practices or shifts in legislation. However, he argued that to find a significant statistical correlation between economic and punitive indicators did not imply any explanation: in fact, a statistical correlation could not be taken as a causal model:

> This consistency merely pertains, however, to a common finding of a statistically significant association between business cycle indicators and imprisonment indicators. Is it possible to use the ascertained associations in order to build a causal model of the same relationships?[80]

By raising this question, Melossi seemed to criticise implicitly Box and Hale's explanatory model: though the two authors had raised the problem of the transition from a statistical correlation to a causal paradigm, in fact they limited themselves only to a critique of conspiracy theories. By suggesting that the relation between prison overcrowding and economic crisis was the result of 'unintended consequences', they didn't formulate a causal explanation: there was still a visible disconnection between *ideological* processes and *material* conditions of the economy. As we shall see, Melossi would reconnect these two dimensions and develop a research program whose guidelines were already clear in *The Prison and the Factory*.

Variations on a Theme

Before concluding this review of the 'quantitative' political economy of punishment, it is worth mentioning some 'heterodox' developments in the literature on the contemporary relationship between economy and punishment. Together with the geographic expansion of materialist criminology, there have been attempts at redefining the indexes used to verify the relation between the material structure of society and the punitive system. The idea is that both the economy and penality can be described in other ways than those suggested by Jankovic and Greenberg.

Michael J. Lynch, for example, argues for the substitution of the concept of unemployment with that of 'rate of surplus-value'. In a Marxist perspective, surplus value gives a better image of the level of exploitation of labour and is a better measure of economic conditions than the official rate of unemployment.[81] Lynch adopts the concept of surplus value in his analysis of the relation between economy and punishment in the US between 1950 and 1984. According to this author, in the whole period it is possible to observe a significant correlation both between the rate of surplus value and punitiveness (measured as incarceration rates), and between the rate of surplus value and predatory crimes. This second finding throws some doubts on Lynch's theoretical position: he seems in fact to reconnect what had been separated

---

[79] Ibid., p. 176.

[80] Ibid., p. 178.

[81] Michael J. Lynch, 'Quantitative Analysis and Marxist Criminology: Some Old Answers to a Dilemma in Marxist Criminology', *Crime and Social Justice*, 29 (1987): 110–127.

since Rusche and Kirchheimer: that is, the relationship between economy and punishment on the one hand, and criminal activity on the other. In fact, Lynch argues that when surplus value increases, levels of investment in capital and new technologies tend to grow; the diffusion of labour-saving technologies produces a surplus labour force and a general worsening of working conditions; in turn, this exclusion of whole segments of the working class is reflected both by an increase in crimes against property, and by an increase in punitiveness.[82]

To some extent, this model resembles the one proposed by William Bonger: in fact, the underlying assumption is that crime (seen as a consequence of social inequality) is the mediating factor between the economy and punishment: capitalism is seen here as a source of inequality and social injustice, which in turn produce an increase in (street) crime.

In this context of revision of economic indicators, also James Inverarity has offered an important contribution. In a first study, carried out with Daniel McCarthy, the author examines the US between 1948 and 1984, testing again the Rusche and Kirchheimer hypothesis. Here the aim is to verify the correlation between unemployment and imprisonment, but this time with an important innovation: the distinction between 'monopolistic' and 'competitive' labour markets:

> We hypothesise that the Rusche and Kirchheimer thesis may be more applicable to unemployment in the competitive sector, where market forces play more of a role in allocating labour power. Monopoly sector unemployment is more likely to be covered by unemployment insurance and other social welfare benefits.[83]

The two authors find a positive correlation between unemployment and incarceration, but no significant difference between the two segments of the labour market.

Finally, an emerging field within the 'heterodox' political economies of punishment is represented by those studies that make use of the (non Marxist) concept of *economic waves*.[84] The difference from traditional accounts is not trivial: here economy and punishment are conceived as cyclical phenomena. Thus, the transformations observable both in the economic and penal field, are not linear: periods of economic

---

[82] Michael J. Lynch, 'The Extraction of Surplus Value, Crime and Punishment: A Preliminary Examination', *Contemporary Crises*, 12 (1988): 332.

[83] James Inverarity and Daniel McCarthy, 'Punishment and Social Structure Revisited: Unemployment and Imprisonment in the United States, 1948–1984', *The Sociological Quarterly*, 29/2 (1988): 267. In a subsequent work, James Inverarity examines for the same period the relationship between the labour market and various institutional reactions to unemployment in the US (incarceration, hospitalisation, enlistment, welfare aid): see James Inverarity and Ryken Grattet, 'Institutional Responses to Unemployment: A Comparison of US Trends, 1948–1985', *Contemporary Crises*, 13 (1989): 351–370.

[84] On the theory of long waves in capitalist economy, see Joseph A. Schumpeter, *Business Cycle, vol. II* (New York, 1939); Nicolaj D. Kondratieff, 'The Long Waves in Economic Life', *Review of Economic Statistics*, 17 (1935): 105–115; Ernest Mandel, *Long Waves of Capitalist Development: The Marxist Interpretation* (New York, 1980). According to Kondratieff, each long wave of capitalist development lasts more or less 50 years. Each cycle is characterised by a first phase of economic expansion (high profits, low unemployment, high salaries); this is followed by a second phase, characterised by a sudden contraction of investments, increasing unemployment, and reduction of consumption. Each phase lasts more or less 25 years.

growth (with low unemployment, a strict proportionality between productivity and income, and labour market stability) are characterised by a contraction of the prison population and by lenient penal policies. Conversely, periods of economic crisis (with high unemployment, income insecurity and declining productivity) are characterised by tough punitive policies and growing incarceration rates: these economic-punitive cycles would alternate at regular intervals.[85]

David Barlow, Melissa Hickman-Barlow and Theodor Chiricos adopted the waves-paradigm in a study of the relations between economy and the criminal justice system in the US between 1789 and 1990. The main hypothesis was that in periods of economic recession, penal institutions became more severe: this increased punitiveness was due to the necessity (by the economic system) to re-establish those margins of control over the working class, necessary to propel economic growth and to start a new cycle of prosperity and profits. In this context, the relation between punishment and the economy would be part of what the authors define the *social structure of accumulation*: the complex of state policies, economic provisions, fiscal policies and social control practices though which public powers supported capitalist accumulation and productivity:

> The social structure of accumulation consists of all the societal institutions and processes which affect, either directly or indirectly, the accumulation of capital. The social structure of accumulation is made up of many different components which provide the necessary conditions for stimulation of the economy.[86]

Following the Marxist revision of the theory of long waves proposed by Ernest Mandel, the authors argued that institutions of social control were particularly active within the social structure of accumulation during periods of recession: in the concluding phase of the economic cycle, when social productivity and profits decreased, these institutions worked to support the valorisation of capital:

> The Criminal Justice System is a vital component of the social structure of accumulation in capitalist societies. As the capitalist state's most openly coercive form of social control, criminal justice plays a critical role in maintaining social order and, thereby, establishing a favourable business climate.[87]

The period considered in this study is very long: as a consequence, it is difficult to draw exact boundaries between one wave and the next. It is not necessary here to review the whole periodisation suggested by the authors. We can limit ourselves to the

---

[85] Besides the two works cited here, for some examples of the application of the long waves theory to the political economy of punishment see: Eisner, 'Cycles of Political Control: The Case of Canton Zurich, 1880–1983' and Melossi, 'Punishment and Social Action'.

[86] David E. Barlow, Melissa Hickman-Barlow and Theodore G. Chiricos, 'Long Economic Cycles and the Criminal Justice System in the US', *Crime, Law and Social Change*, 19 (1993): 145. See also David E. Barlow and Melissa Hickman-Barlow, 'Federal Criminal Justice Legislation and the Post-World War II Social Structure of Accumulation in the United States', *Crime, Law and Social Change*, 22 (1995): 239–267, where the authors evaluate the relationship between economic cycles and penal legislation at the Federal level in the United States for the period 1948–1987.

[87] Barlow, Hickman-Barlow and Chiricos, 'Long Economic Cycles and the Criminal Justice System in the US', p. 146.

most recent wave (1940–1990). This cycle can be divided into two further periods: an expansion phase (1940–1970) and a contraction phase (1970–1990). The first period is characterised by economic prosperity, high wages and low unemployment, and on the side of punitive policies we see here a limited use of incarceration. Rates of imprisonment are low, criminality is not at the centre of the American political debate and the correctional system is inspired by a philosophy of rehabilitation and treatment. In other words, the social structure of accumulation is based on a model of consent (the Keynesian pact between labour and capital), which limits the space available to repressive institutions. However, the situation changes dramatically as soon as this expansionist phase gives way to a period of recession (at the beginning of the 1970s). In this period we see a crisis of the labour-capital pact, a dramatic downturn in profits and an increase in inflation. At this point, a restructuring of the industrial economy starts, producing an increase in unemployment and a reduction in real wages. At the same time a reversal of social control policies takes place, and the social structure of accumulation shifts toward an authoritarian model. Incarceration rates grow, legitimated by moral crusades against crime and by populist vocabularies such as 'zero tolerance' and the 'war on drugs':

> As in other aspects of the social structure of accumulation, mechanisms for social control come to be seen as outdated and ineffective and state managers seek new mechanisms of control. They seek strategies which are more effective in stopping crime and social unrest, and which will, at the same time, legitimise the political economic system.[88]

The problem with this interpretation is that the authors do not offer any exhaustive hypothesis about the concrete functioning of these transformations. There is no analysis of how social control institutions come to change their role within the social structure of accumulation, once the expansionist phase comes to an end. These authors limit themselves to the idea (borrowed from Box and Hale) that during economic downturns a punitive ideology emerges among criminal justice professionals. Again, the increased punitiveness of the penal system would be an unintended consequence of scattered decision-making processes: still, we miss a causal explanation.

More recently, the paradigm of economic cycles and social structures of accumulation has inspired an important study by Raymond Michalowski and Susan Carlson.[89] There are two main elements of interest in this work: first, through this theory the authors try to overcome some limits of the traditional hypotheses about the economy and punishment. According to Michalowski and Carlson, one important limit to the traditional political economy of punishment is that many analyses look at undifferentiated periods of time. In other words, many studies consider time series which include various economic cycles and thus different configurations of the social structure of accumulation. The second interesting aspect of this article is that the authors adopt a qualitative perspective of analysis. In fact, the cyclical transformations of the social structure of accumulation (affecting the link between unemployment and incarceration) give a qualitative meaning to the economy-punishment relationship;

---

[88] Ibid., p. 163.
[89] Raymond Michalowski and Susan M. Carlson, 'Unemployment, Imprisonment, and Social Structures of Accumulation: Historical Contingency in the Rusche-Kirchheimer Hypothesis', *Criminology*, 37/2 (1999): 217–249.

only on the basis of a qualitative analysis it is possible to infer some quantitative implications:

> Each of these Social Structures of Accumulation consists of a distinct set of institutional arrangements based on qualitative social relations among capital, labour, and the state that, we hypothesise, influence the strength and the direction of the unemployment-imprisonment relationship as well as other quantitative social and economic outcomes.[90]

Michalowski and Carlson consider the US for the period 1933–1992. This historical period includes the development of an entire economic cycle (1933–1980) and the first phase of the subsequent one (1980–1992). The authors isolate three phases within the first cycle: exploration (1933–1947), consolidation (1948–1966) and decay (1967–1979); then a new phase of exploration follows (1980–1992), which opens the current cycle.[91]

The expectation is to discover a weak positive correlation between incarceration and unemployment during the first two phases of the Fordist cycle (exploration and consolidation: 1933–1966); this correlation should become stronger for the last phase of the cycle (decay: 1967–1979). Furthermore, the exploration phase of the new cycle (1980–1992) is expected to reveal a negative correlation between unemployment and imprisonment. The argument is clear: the Fordist cycle was characterised by an increase in social security and a widening of welfare provisions, which relegated repressive institutions to a secondary position. When this model started to crumble (in the final phase of the cycle), the social structure of accumulation embraced a more repressive philosophy, and incarceration rates grew with unemployment. This correlation came to an end at the beginning of the new cycle (phase of exploration: 1980–1992), but the dissociation between incarceration and unemployment was only a consequence of the fact that official statistics underestimated the rates of unemployment. In fact, the beginning of the new cycle is characterised by mass exclusion from work and the emergence of an underclass invisible to official statistics: due to the invisibility of the underclass, it is impossible to find a significant correlation between unemployment and imprisonment.[92]

Through a comparison between data on unemployment, prison admissions and rates of violent crimes, Michalowski and Carlson confirm the initial hypotheses. In fact, the relationship between unemployment and incarceration follows a cyclical trend (independent of crime) strongly affected by political, social and cultural factors: that is, by the social structure of accumulation:

---

[90] Ibid., p. 223.

[91] About this internal articulation of economic cycles, see the works by David Gordon and Samuel Bowles, and the theoretical positions which emerged from the *Review of Radical Political Economy*.

[92] 'While nonworkers have always been excluded from unemployment statistics, the simultaneous shortening of the period of unemployment eligibility and significant expansion of the underclass meant that structurally displaced workers were increasingly unrepresented in official unemployment data', Michalowski and Carlson, 'Unemployment, Imprisonment, and Social Structures of Accumulation', p. 231.

Our analysis indicates that the unemployment-imprisonment relationship may be more sensitive to heretofore less-examined qualitative changes in social-institutional relations. Based on this, we suggest that the relationship between punishment and social structure is indeed historically contingent as Rusche and Kirchheimer originally proposed, particularly if one considers the ways social-structural arrangements change within a given mode of production.[93]

As a conclusion to this section on the heterodox perspectives in the political economy of punishment, it is possible to suggest at least two remarks. First, the relationship between economy and punishment can no longer be reduced to a purely quantitative correlation between rates of unemployment and rates of imprisonment. The universe of the economy has to be represented in more complex terms: unemployment in itself – as statistical measure of official levels of exclusion from the labour market – is not enough for the construction of a sociological analysis of the connection between economy and social control. Thus, it seems necessary to develop an interpretation of the economy and of its relation to penality that takes into account those political, social and ideological factors which could provide a sociological and criminological meaning. Second, we need a causal explanation of the correlation between the economy and punishment: the following section reviews some criminological studies which put these questions at the core of the political economy of punishment.

A Return to Rusche and Kirchheimer?

I introduce now some perspectives which, starting from the theoretical problems emerging within neo-Marxist criminology, suggest some new interpretations of the economy-punishment relationship. These contributions attempt to overcome some limits intrinsic to the political economy of punishment, this time without adopting the heterodox perspectives described earlier. To the contrary, these works develop some neglected aspects of Rusche and Kirchheimers's hypothesis: therefore, it is from these two authors that I start again.

In the opening pages of *Punishment and Social Structure*, Rusche and Kirchheimer offer a general definition of the historical relationship between production systems and punitive practices:

> Every system of production tends to discover punishments which correspond to its productive relationships. It is thus necessary to investigate the origin and fate of penal systems, the use or avoidance of specific punishments, and the intensity of penal practices as they are determined by social forces, above all by economic and then fiscal forces.[94]

On the other hand, in his *Labor Market and Penal Sanction* Rusche explains the concrete functioning of this relationship within capitalist social formations. In those pages Rusche points to the structural limit intrinsic to any reform of the penal system, depending on the existing economic conditions:

---

[93]   Ibid., p. 242.

[94]   Rusche and Kirchheimer, *Punishment and Social Structure*, p. 5.

> All efforts to reform the punishment of criminals are inevitably limited by the situation of the lowest socially significant proletarian class which society wants to deter from criminal acts. All reform efforts, however humanitarian and well-meaning, which go beyond this restriction, are condemned to utopianism.[95]

Thus, the first fragment describes a historical correspondence between the economy and punitive systems, whereas the second clarifies how this relationship varies according to specific social-historical conditions: here Rusche is introducing the principle of *less eligibility*, which establishes the limits within which the living conditions of law-abiding citizens can still be preferable to the condition of those punished by the criminal justice system.

Three aspects deserve our attention here. First, in both cases the connection between social structure and penality is represented as a dynamic process: both in a historical and contemporary perspective, the relation lies within a process of continuous transformation. The object of Rusche and Kirchheimer's analysis is the relationship between punishment and social structure both in its macro-historical trajectories and in its micro-cyclical oscillations.[96]

If the analysis of social history allows Rusche and Kirchheimer to conclude that '*... every system of production tends to discover punishments which correspond to its productive relationships*', the analysis of a peculiar capitalist social formation makes it possible to follow the lines according to which this correspondence varies.

Second, in Rusche and Kirchheimer's definition, the relationship between economy and punishment is a complex tendency. Their aim is not to establish, once and forever, a definite and mechanical relation: in fact, political, social and cultural factors play an important role which cannot be overlooked. On the one hand Rusche speaks of a long-term *tendency* toward the correspondence between systems of production and punishments; on the other hand, he evokes the effects of various *social forces* on this correspondence.

Finally, the principle of less eligibility cannot be reduced to an immediate correspondence between penal and economic indexes, even less to a simple comparison between imprisonment and unemployment rates. Rusche says that it is the *situation* of the marginal proletarian class that defines the external limit to any reform of the penal system. This means that the borders, within which the principle of less eligibility operates, are given by a complex of social factors which define the condition of the proletarian class and the relationship between this condition and the punitive regime.

It is quite clear that, in a capitalist system, the social condition of individuals depends on their position in the labour market; however, in contemporary capitalism this is influenced also by a complex of social policies and public provisions whose impact on the relation between the labour market and the penal system is relevant.[97]

---

[95] Rusche, 'Labor Market and Penal Sanction: Thoughts on the Sociology of Criminal Justice', p. 4.

[96] On the importance of the distinction between macro- and micro-trajectories of the relationship between economy and punishment, see Melossi, 'Punishment and Social Action', p. 186.

[97] This point seems very important if one considers that the time in which Rusche and Kirchheimer lived was characterised by the emergence of Keynesian policies, public intervention in the economy and the idea of welfare state.

In their valuable introduction to the French edition of *Punishment and Social Structure*, René Levy and Hartwig Zander make this point clear:

> The central issue is not so much the category of 'penal regimes', as that of 'penal-reform'; not so much the notion of 'labour market', as the analysis of social policies connected to labour market crises.[98]

These arguments shed some light on the implicit reductionism of the quantitative analyses which tried to test the validity of Rusche and Kirchheimer's hypotheses by reducing the concept of social structure to the statistics of unemployment and penality to the statistical data on incarceration. On the one hand, this double reductionism undermines the possibility to analyse the complex interaction between social, economic and penal policies; on the other hand, it prevents a dynamic, political and social analysis of this interaction.

The fact is that the expression 'the situation of the lowest socially significant proletarian class' lends itself to a wider interpretation: it goes beyond unemployment and the labour market. In the definition of this 'situation', other aspects (such as the social composition of the labour force, the organisation of work and class-conflict in general) are as important as the position of the proletariat in the labour market.[99]

This permits to extend the concept of less eligibility and to situate it at the intersection between labour market, social policies and penal policies. The first two factors define the situation of the lowest proletarian class, which in turn draws the borders of punitive practices: at this point, the ideological side of the relationship between economy and penality can also emerge. In fact, it would be impossible to determine the 'social significance' of the 'lowest proletarian class' without taking into account those ideological and cultural processes which define the social value of each segment of the labour force (usually depending on its labour market-value). Now we have some elements for the construction of a complex explicative model, which can enable us to overcome statistical correlations and to think in terms of causality.

Dario Melossi's contributions follow this direction explicitly. In fact, his works put together an interest in the quantitative dimension of the political economy of punishment with an effort to formulate a complex explanatory theory.[100] The starting point of Melossi's work (as he had already clarified it in *The Prison and the Factory*) is the concept of *discipline*, conceived as the mediating factor between the economy and punishment. The concept of discipline is very important because it helps to make

---

[98] René Lévy and Hartwig Zander, 'Introduction' to Georg Rusche and Otto Kirchheimer, *Peine et structure sociale* (Paris, 1994), p. 56.

[99] In this sense, Lévy and Zander suggest that unemployment is for Rusche a 'virtual category', more than a real one. Once again, the two authors stress the importance of the social and political dimension, concerning both the historical transformations of the concept of less eligibility, and the tendential correspondence between relations of production and punitive systems. The result is a further confirmation of the limited validity of purely quantitative approaches to the political economy of punishment.

[100] Among Melossi's more quantitative works, see 'Omicidi, economia e tassi di incarcerazione in Italia dall'unità ad oggi', *Polis*, 12/3 (1998): 415–435, 'Punishment and Social Action', and 'Political Business Cycles and Imprisonment Rates in Italy: Report on a Work in Progress', *The Review of Black Political Economy*, 16/1-2 (1987): 211–218.

sense of the ancillary role of social control institutions in capitalist production. Disciplinary technologies, inside as well as outside the prison, satisfy a fundamental need of the capitalist system of production: the reproduction of the labour force. Thus, both the correspondence between production systems and modes of punishment in general, and the principle of less eligibility in particular, can be referred to this function of labour force reproduction.[101] The concept of discipline allows Melossi to extend his analysis beyond the relationship between incarceration and unemployment, and to consider the processes of transformation which take place both in the system of production and in punitive institutions. In this sense, Melossi criticises the inadequacy of categories like labour market and incarceration: they are of limited use for a description of the relationship between economy and penality. This relation is in fact variable and informed by political, ideological and cultural factors which cannot be reduced to the sphere of the economy.[102] Melossi agrees with some of the authors reviewed earlier, that this relationship follows a cyclical trend: but he introduces the concept of *political business cycle*, which also includes social and political factors:

> The host of social and political conditions that appear as accompaniments of the business cycle are not determined by it, or even subordinate to it. On the contrary, they make its unfolding possible. Put another way, the relation between the business cycle and its social and political accompaniments is not the outcome of the working of inscrutable economic 'laws' which determine the fluctuations in the values of other social variables. Instead, the relationship is a product of the activities of social actors whose interaction causes economic indicators to fluctuate in a roughly oscillatory fashion.[103]

Melossi's hypothesis is that these cycles influence both the terms of the relation between economy and punishment itself, and the forms of social construction and cultural perception of this relation.[104]

At this point, however, I would argue that the concept of discipline also shows some theoretical limits: in fact, it seems to imply a static conception of the relation

---

[101] Melossi, 'Georg Rusche and Otto Kirchheimer: Punishment and Social Structure', p. 81.

[102] Melossi analysed these problems especially in his 'Strategies of Social Control in Capitalism: A Comment on Recent Work', *Contemporary Crises*, 4 (1980): 381–419, where the author speaks of the 'crisis' (now we can say a 'temporary crisis') of the prison's role in disciplining the labour force. Under the influence of Scull's decarceration hypothesis, in this article Melossi argued that the relation between economy and punishment was abandoning the prison and shifting toward the urban environment (where it was taking the form of *community treatments*). In a subsequent article, Melossi specified his analysis of social control in the city, suggesting that the urban *ghetto* was turning itself into a new social control institution inspired by the principle of less eligibility. See Dario Melossi, 'Oltre il Panopticon. Per uno studio delle strategie di controllo sociale nel capitalismo del ventesimo secolo', *La questione criminale*, 6 (1980): 277–361.

[103] Melossi, 'Punishment and Social Action', pp. 179–180.

[104] 'Times of depression are times for punishment. Politicians decry the wasteful and immoral behavior of the past age, the frightening increase in criminal and deviant activities, the shattering of society's institutional and moral bonds. Their words are echoed in media reports ... Workers are said to have been wasting their fat paychecks and are now asked to repent in the dull austerity of their new unemployment status. It is now time to draw the line. It is time to punish': Melossi, 'Punishment and Social Action', p. 181.

between punitive institutions and the economic structure, thus shifting indirectly toward those conspiracy theories so much criticised within the political economy of punishment. Therefore, the final question is: why is there a correspondence between political business cycles of economic depression and the growth in social and institutional punitiveness? Melossi argues that the new 'penal climate' observable in periods of depression is not limited to an increase in incarceration or to a worsening of prison conditions, but is also reflected in a growing social demand of punitiveness and penal severity. According to Melossi, this is neither a consequence of the 'needs of capital', nor an unintended consequence of institutional decision-making: what changes is the social construction of deviance and of the means for controlling it. Hegemonic social representations of crime and punishment change according to economic trends.

In other words, a new 'morality' appears during periods of economic crisis, worsening conditions of work and growing unemployment: this new morality is more rigid toward deviance, more punitive and favourably disposed toward 'law and order' campaigns. This 'moral climate' shapes and gives a new meaning to the relationship between economic cycles and penal policies:

> The relationship between the economy and imprisonment should not be seen as directly causal. Rather, one should connect economic change to the changing moral climate that usually accompanies it, assuming that the attitudes developed by participants in the conflicts of economic life are deeply related to more general, historically specific, social attitudes.[105]

The punitive moral climate emerging during political business cycles of recession permeates the public opinion as well as punitive institutions, intellectuals as well as the mass media and political elites: thus crime becomes a privileged theme for public discussion. In these periods a moral panics emerge, diverting public opinion from the deeper causes of insecurity and fear.[106]

These arguments seem close to those suggested by Box and Hale. In both cases, the mediation between economy and penality is found in the changing social representations of deviance and social control. In other words, both Melossi and Box and Hale suggest that periods of economic crisis are characterised by the emergence of a social intolerance (shared by the agents of the criminal justice system), whose consequence is an increase in punitiveness and penal selectivity. However, there are at least two important differences which make Melossi's argumentation more convincing. First, whereas Box and Hale explain the increase in incarceration rates as an unintended consequence of the fact that the criminal justice officials perceive the unemployed as a dangerous class, Melossi analyses this process by referring to a complex theoretical model which he defines 'a grounded labelling theory'.[107]

---

[105] Dario Melossi, 'Introduction' to *The Sociology of Punishment. Socio-Structural Perspectives* (Aldershot, 1998), p. XXIV.

[106] Ibid., pp. XXV-XXVI. Concerning the effects of these cyclical shifts on criminological theories, Melossi speaks of a 'criminology of revenge', which becomes hegemonic in periods of economic and social crisis: see Dario Melossi, 'Changing Representations of the Criminal', *The British Journal of Criminology*, 40 (2000): 308.

[107] 'A "grounded labelling theory" concerns itself also with the way in which variable social-structural elements, like e.g. "the political business cycle", impinge upon the variable degree of probability

The forms of rationalisation of their own activities which criminal justice agents offer both to themselves and to the public, change dramatically during cycles of economic recession: rationalisations of the crime issue based on respect for diversity, the importance of social integration and the rehabilitative role of punishment, give way to rationalisations based on social defence, the neutralisation of public enemies and the need to reduce levels of public tolerance toward deviance:

> Within the (empirically determinate) boundaries delineated by the vocabulary of the law on the books, public officials who are in charge of law enforcement account for their behaviour by using vocabularies of punitive motive in a manner which is roughly oscillating over time, and is a response, among other things, to variations in the mood of the public, which in turn is connected to roughly cyclical economic indicators.[108]

This means that a 'discursive chain' links together the social perception of the political business cycle and the rationalisations of the crime problem adopted by social control agencies.

The second important difference between Melossi and Box and Hale is that Melossi does not consider unemployment as the qualifying aspect of a political business cycle: he refers to a complex set of factors pertaining to the economic sphere but not reducible to unemployment. In this respect, the author adopts the concept of *performance*, by which he refers to the general conditions of work and income inequalities, to the standard of life and the levels of exploitation of the labour force; taken together, *all* these aspects define a political business cycle.

Political business cycles affected by a punitive moral climate and by an increasing criminalisation of marginal classes, are also cycles characterised by a growing economic pressure on the working class: people work harder, for longer and with less social rights. Thus, the notion of 'performance' permits a qualitative interpretation of the concept of less eligibility: in this sense Melossi appears to be much closer to Rusche's original hypothesis than the other authors examined here. In fact, the concept of performance reminds that *situation of the lowest socially significant proletarian class* to which, according to Rusche, the principle of less eligibility conforms. Melossi is clear on this point:

> The connection that should be established through research is not therefore between an indicator of punishment, that is rates of imprisonment, and an indicator of unemployment, based on the (faulty) assumption that imprisonment functions to control a Marxian 'industrial reserve army'. Rather, a direct connection should be established between increased performance demands applied to the working class and increased penal pressure on the bottom strata of society (the 'underclass'). Such pressure creates a sort of 'social whip' effect that makes everybody work harder, especially those who are close enough to the bottom to hear the howling and moaning of the ones being hit.[109]

---

that a certain behaviour will be defined as normal or deviant': Dario Melossi, 'An Introduction: Fifty Years Later, Punishment and Social Structure in Comparative Analysis', *Contemporary Crises*, 13 (1989): 320. See also Dario Melossi, 'Overcoming the Crisis in Critical Criminology: Toward a Grounded Labelling Theory', *Criminology*, 23 (1985): 193–208.

[108] Melossi, 'An Introduction: Fifty Years Later', p. 320.

[109] Dario Melossi, 'Gazette of Morality and Social Whip: Punishment, Hegemony and the Case of the USA, 1970–1992', *Social & Legal Studies*, 2 (1993): 263.

Here we can make sense of the ancillary role of punitive institutions: through the threat of harsh punishment the principle of less eligibility sustains and reinforces the demand of performance which the elites put on the working class. Today as in the early stages of capitalist development, the aim is the disciplining of that *lowest socially significant proletarian class* who appears reluctant to conform to the new conditions of economic exploitation.

Beyond the Political Economy of Punishment?

In these pages I offered a review of the political economy of punishment, both in its historical and contemporary orientations. I tried to describe the various phases that characterised this field of critical criminology: from the historical works on the origin of the prison to the first attempts at actualising the Marxist perspective, from the 'orthodox' approaches (Jankovic and Greenberg) to the 'heterodox' ones, concluding with the 'grounded labelling theory' formulated by Melossi. The aim was to show the extreme variety of perspectives and hypotheses which characterise materialist criminology: my impression is that some theoretical and empirical problems could be overcome through a revision of Rusche and Kirchheimer's original ideas. I refer to what could be defined as the 'internal' limits to the contemporary political economy of punishment: the translation of Rusche's concepts; the relationship between historical reconstruction and the analysis of the present; the relationship between long and short economic waves; the empirical validity of these relations and the definition of a causal model.

However, I would suggest that together with these internal limits, the political economy of punishment is confronted today also by important 'external' limits. External, because they do not concern so much methodology or the connection between a theoretical paradigm and an empirical model, as the very capacity to take into consideration the social and economic transformations which are taking place in Western societies since the 1970s.

The political economy of punishment reviewed here describes contemporary social structure by referring to a specific socio-economic paradigm: Fordist capitalism and the welfare state. When I speak of Fordist capitalism, I refer to the enormous expansion of mass industrial production which took place between the end of the Second World War and the early 1970s. It was a period in which the labour market was stable and unemployment was a limited phenomenon. A period in which the institutions of social control shared with those of the welfare state a program of social inclusion for those segments of the working class who remained outside the labour market: citizenship was still imagined as a complex of social rights, and crime was widely seen as a consequence of economic deprivation. In addition, the unemployment which this political economy of punishment linked to the (already growing) incarceration rates, was still a contingent phenomenon: that is, unemployment rates could decrease again, following new public interventions on the labour market, on the demand-side or on the distribution of welfare provisions.

However, at some point this cyclical trend came to a conclusion: the cycle appeared to end with a stable tendency toward the mass-expulsion of labour force from the labour market – at least from stable and guaranteed work. It was in this period that the term *underclass* was reintroduced in sociological discourse.[110] This 'surplus' population was in fact excluded from a territory of work whose boundaries were more and more restricted: a structural marginality emerged, produced both by the capitalistic restructuring of production and by the neo-liberal assault on the Welfare State.

However, materialist criminologists failed to consider the deeper consequences of these transformations.[111] The 'underclass' was described as a segment of a working class still considered hegemonic in the field of capitalist production: a full perception of the qualitative dimension of the transition was missing. What many critical criminologists seemed to underestimate is that the underclass is what remains of the working class after the reorganisation of work and the neo-liberal 'reform' of welfare; it is not a small population of permanently disadvantaged people, but the result of a process of structural transformation which turned a significant segment the working class into new (working) poor.

Furthermore, what the political economy of punishment has interpreted as a temporary crisis of the balanced universe of Fordism, represents instead the result of that crisis. The emergence of a new configuration of the relations between economy and society, between labour and social citizenship and between production and social control, reveals the capitalist reaction to a crisis of productivity produced by the social movements of the 1960s and 1970s and by the fiscal crisis of the welfare state. The capitalist power elite launched a true 'counterrevolution' in order to preserve the production of surplus value and margins of profit. Thus, the Fordist and Keynesian social pact (in which punitive institutions were also included) came to an end, and in its place a different configuration of relations of production emerged: *post-Fordism*. In the next chapter I will describe some significant transformations implied by the transition to post-Fordism. However, the analysis will not be limited to economic aspects: as Melossi argues, the social and political dimension of this transition cannot be underestimated and further aspects should be also taken into account: the productive process, the transformations of the labour market, the emergence of neo-liberal social policies and the end of the welfare state.

A new paradigm might be emerging, whose future developments are still difficult to foresee: but a renewed political economy of punishment cannot overlook these transformations and their social and political consequences.

---

[110] At the same time, also the very old equation between *underclass* and *dangerous class* (together with the related distinction between deserving and undeserving poor) re-emerged. And this happened both in criminological and political discourses. See Lydia Morris, *Dangerous Class. The Underclass and Social Citizenship* (London, 1999).

[111] For an exception, see Loic Wacquant, 'The Rise of Advanced Marginality: Notes on its Nature and Implications', *Acta Sociologica*, 39 (1996): 121–139.

Chapter 2

Post-Fordism and the Emergence of the Multitude

Imperial power is the negative residue, the fallback of the operation of the multitude; it is a parasite that draws its vitality from the multitude's capacity to create ever new sources of energy and value. A parasite that saps the strength of its host, however, can endanger its own existence. The functioning of imperial power is ineluctably linked to its decline.

(Michael Hardt and Antonio Negri, *Empire*, Cambridge MA, 2000, p. 361)

Post-Fordism: A Regime of Surplus

Before proceeding further into my analysis of the recent transformations of capitalist production and trying to investigate the relationships between these transformations and the new emerging strategies of social control, I should submit two preliminary warnings concerning definitions.

The first is methodological, and refers to the meaning of the term 'post-Fordism', so frequently used in this study. As I said in the 'Introduction', post-Fordism is a concept currently adopted both in the economic literature (at least by some less 'orthodox' authors) and more generally in sociological and political discourse. However, the wide diffusion of a term does not imply a particular explicative efficacy or descriptive adequacy. The prefix 'post' (as in 'post'-modern, 'post'-industrial and indeed 'post'-Fordism) always refers to a *process*. In this sense, it defines some tendencies and the indefinite space spanning between a 'no longer' and a 'not yet', more than the consolidation of a clearly defined paradigm.

The second warning concerns the need to 'clarify' in what meaning the term 'post-Fordism' is used in this context. Given that it refers to some emerging features of contemporary Western economies – rather than to any precise theoretical model – the term can be (and has been) used to describe diverse (and sometimes even contradictory) phenomena.[1] Some theorists insist on the disruptive effects produced on a global scale by the emergence of a neo-liberal economy, pointing in particular to the

---

[1]   For a synthesis of some socio-economic perspectives in which this term has been adopted in the last decade, see Werner Bonefeld and John Holloway (eds), *Post-Fordism and Social Form. A Marxist Debate on the Post-Fordist State* (London, 1991); Roger Burrows and Brian Loader (eds), *Toward a Post-Fordist Welfare State?* (London, 1994); Ash Amin (ed.), *Post-Fordism. A Reader* (Oxford, 1994). For an empirical study testing some of the assumptions of the 'post-Fordist' debate, see Denise Thursfield, *Post-Fordism and Skill. Theories and Perceptions* (Aldershot, 2000). An overview of the debate around post-Fordism within the Critical Management Studies can be found in the 1990s issues of the *Academy of Management Review* and the *Journal of Management Studies*.

increasing inequalities between 'First-World' and 'Third-World' countries;[2] others consider mass unemployment and the transition from 'production' to 'consumption' as the main features of contemporary economy, and illustrate the dramatic impact they have on local communities;[3] others insist on the technological revolution which took place in production, arguing for its positive effects for a labour-force that would be approaching a stage of freedom from work.[4] Finally, scholars working within the French 'School of Regulation', describe post-Fordism as the convergence of diverse phenomena such as the emergence of a trans-national financial economy, the crisis of the nation-state as the main economic actor on the global scene, the end of the Keynesian social pact between labour and capital which regulated industrial and economic relations in the 30 years following the Second World War, and the emergence of a new 'regime of accumulation' based on the crisis of the wage-labour relation.[5]

For my purposes, the term post-Fordism will be used to analyse some recent transformations of work and production, as they have been debated in the 1990s within the Italian 'Autonomist Marxism'. This is a neo-Marxist (and to some extent a 'post-Marxist') stream of thought which emerged during the 1960s and 1970s as an alternative to more 'orthodox' Marxist approaches. Influenced by Marx's *Grundrisse* rather than by *Capital*, and by Althusser's structuralism rather than by Antonio Gramsci's concept of 'hegemony', Autonomist Marxism played an important role in the class struggles of the late 1960s and early 1970s, both in Italy and in continental Europe. It would be impossible to offer here a full account of its theoretical assumptions; however, we can identify at least some relevant aspects which distinguish this one from other Marxist traditions, and characterise it as an original perspective.

The first assumption is that capitalist processes of transformation are always linked to class conflict: the transformations of production, and particularly the introduction of new technologies and new systems of work organisation are seen as capitalist attempts to neutralize class resistance and to overcome workers' insubordination. Each new form of struggle in the field of production gives birth to new forms of capitalist control over the labour process. In this context, the contradiction between capital and labour is a structural feature of the capitalist economy: it can be displaced, softened, regulated and even repressed, but it will never be eliminated.[6]

Second, the traditional Marxist distinction between 'structure' and 'superstructure' is deeply revised: indeed, no rigid separation between the two spheres of social life can be identified. And this is not just because 'ideologies' play an important role in society (as the 'mainstream' critiques of Marxism hold), but because in the transition

---

[2] See for example the works by Immanuel Wallerstein (on the 'World System') and Samir Amin (on the 'Third-World').

[3] For an example see Zygmunt Bauman, *Work, Consumerism and the New Poor* (Buckingham, 1998).

[4] Jeremy Rifkin, *The End of Work. The Decline of the Global Labour Force and the Dawn of the Post-Market Era* (New York, 1995).

[5] For a detailed reconstruction of the ideas of the 'Regulation School' (whose most representative authors are Michel Aglietta and Alain Lipietz), see Robert Brenner, and Mark Glick, 'The Regulation Approach: Theory and History', *New Left Review*, 188 (1991): 45–119; Bob Jessop, 'Regulation Theories in Retrospect and Prospect', *Economy and Society*, 19/2 (1990): 153–216.

[6] For an application of this perspective to the history of the working class see Edward P. Thompson, *The Making of the English Working Class* (London, 1963).

from Fordism to post-Fordism, capitalist relations of production have extended themselves beyond the walls of the factory, thus affecting previously untouched spheres of life (such as reproduction, communication, biology, culture, language and desire): therefore production has become a truly 'social' process and the working class has been turned into a 'socialised labour force'.

Third, technological development is not seen only as a capitalist instrument to increase productivity and to enforce the extraction of surplus value from the labour process. Technology is not just another weapon in the hands of the capitalist class: it can be also a resource for the new 'socialised labour force', through which freedom *from* work (not only freedom *of* work) becomes possible, at least in theory. Finally – in contrast with many 'neo-Hegelian' interpretations of Marx – any philosophy of history is rejected here, because there's no teleology to be detected in the course of history. In other words, the supposed decline of capitalism is not seen as the consequence of some rigid 'laws' (such as the 'falling rate of surplus value'). What determines 'accumulation crises' (propelling also capitalist reactions to them) is the growing contradiction between capital and labour, and between capitalist relations of production and the increasing socialisation of productivity.[7]

Autonomist Marxism is just one among several interpretations of contemporary socio-economic conditions, and it is characterised by an explicit political orientation. However it seems more adequate than others – because it puts social conflict at the core of economic transformations – to shed light on those aspects of the transition to post-Fordism which seem to affect more significantly the field of social control: social inclusion and exclusion, labour mobility through international migrations, capitalist strategies to maintain control over the labour force, changing patterns in the division of labour, etc.[8]

---

[7] Some useful reconstructions of 'Autonomist Marxism' have been published in English: Harry Cleaver, *Reading Capital Politically* (Brighton, 1979); Nick D. Witheford, *Cyber-Marx. Cycles and Circuits of Struggle in High-Technology Capitalism* (Urbana, 1999); Steve Wright, *Storming Heaven. Class Composition and Struggle in Italian Autonomist Marxism* (London, 2002). Some writings of Italian authors who belong to this tradition have been translated into English: see in particular Antonio Negri, *Marx Beyond Marx: Lessons on the Grundrisse* (New York, 1984), *The Politics of Subversion: A Manifesto for the Twenty-First Century* (Cambridge, 1989), *Revolution Retrieved: Selected Writings on Marx, Keynes, Capitalist Crisis and New Social Subjects* (London, 1988), 'Interpretation of the Class Situation Today: Methodological Aspects', in Werner Bonefeld, Richard Gunn and Kosmas Psychopedis (eds), *Open Marxism, vol. II: Theory and Practice* (London, 1992), pp. 69–105; Raniero Panzieri, 'The Capitalist Use of Machinery: Marx Versus the Objectivists', in Phil Slater (ed.), *Outlines of a Critique of Technology* (Atlantic Highlands, 1980), pp. 44–69. More recently some anthologies of 'Autonomist Marxism' have also appeared: see for example Paolo Virno and Michael Hardt (eds), *Radical Thought in Italy: A Potential Politics* (Minneapolis, 1996); Red Notes Collective (ed.), *Immaterial Labour, Mass Intellectuality, New Constitution, Post-Fordism and All That* (London, 1994). In particular on the thought of Antonio Negri – one of the founding fathers of 'Autonomist Marxism' – see Nicholas Thoburn, 'Autonomous Production? On Negri's "New Synthesis"', *Theory Culture & Society*, 18/5 (2001): 75–96.

[8] In order to clarify the arguments which follow in the next pages, I would like to synthesise here the main features identified by 'Autonomist Marxism' as characterising the transition from 'Fordism' to 'post-Fordism': (1) The growth of tertiary economic sector at the expense of industrial production; (2) The gradual replacement of industrial factories by 'virtual' enterprises; (3) A growing decentralisation of production; (4) The replacement of the assembly line by flexible technologies

According to this critical perspective, at a global level we witness a process of transformation of the economy characterised by the decline of the industrial (Fordist) model and by the emergence of new relations of production. This affects all the different levels around which Western capitalism has developed since the end of the Second World War. On the one hand – in the context of production in a strict sense – we see the 'explosion' of the Taylorist paradigm of labour organisation: the big factory is disappearing gradually from the landscape of the post-modern city. The 'global cities' of contemporary capitalism are no longer theatres of heavy industrial productions, but virtual territories where fluxes of information, images, finance and symbols circulate along decentered networks.[9]

The mass-industries – those 'monuments to productivity' inspired by a panoptic utopia of total control over the labour force, which were taken as models of a perfect organisation and synchronisation of work – are now losing most of their appeal – at least in the most advanced (post-industrial) capitalist economies. The majority of the emerging productive sites tend to be either 'immaterial' (the small, automated and hyper-technological factory) or 'invisible' (the many sweatshops where the residual material labour is performed, often without any regulation and even more often by an immigrant, hyper-exploited and female labour force). The process of production is thus becoming increasingly dispersed, molecular and diffused.[10] No longer does any rigid organisation of the labour process (such as Taylor's 'scientific management') seem to be eligible here: mobility, flexibility and decentralisation replace the fixity, rigidity and centralisation of the Fordist factory.[11]

At the same time, the Fordist strategy of wage regulation suffers a dramatic crisis: the collapse of the factory regime produces the dismissal of the virtuous political-economic circle which in the second half of the twentieth century allowed Western industrial systems to keep workers income, social productivity and mass consumption together, in an apparent commonality of interests.[12] And this happens because a

---

and organisations based on the 'network' model; (4) A growing importance of communicative activities, personal relations, language and social creativity within the process of capitalist production; (5) The emergence of new types of work which put under question the traditional distinction between time of work and time of non-work, society and factory, production and reproduction, etc.; (6) A technological revolution that makes it possible to reduce the need for human labour to a minimum, thus liberating time and resources for human development.

[9] For some examples, see Saskia Sassen, *The Global City: New York, London, Tokyo* (Princeton, 1991).

[10] A good example of this trend toward a 'small is beautiful' economic rationality is to be found in the Italian 'industrial districts', concentrated mainly in the North-Eastern regions of the country (Emilia Romagna and Veneto). Particularly in Italy – but comparable situations can also be found in Germany, France and Spain – these new productive sites are characterised by a high level of 'informal work' (which means that workers do not enjoy their full economic and social rights), and by a considerable employment of immigrant labour force. These two features appear strictly connected: small factories need flexible and disposable workers, and immigrants satisfy this need perfectly – especially if they are kept in a condition of irregularity and precarious citizenship, as is currently the case in Europe. See Fabio Quassoli, 'Migrants in the Italian Underground Economy', *International Journal of Urban and Regional Research*, 23/2 (1999): 212–231.

[11] Robert Reich, *The Work of Nations. Preparing Ourselves for 21st Century Capitalism* (New York, 1991).

[12] On the development of Western welfare systems as a compromise between capital and labour see Gosta Esping-Andersen, *Social Foundations of Postindustrial Economies* (Oxford, 1999).

fragmented labour force, disseminated through small and de-unionised factories, has lost much of its power over labour conditions: 'work flexibility' is synonymous with the loss of contracting power, especially considering that the new labour force has to compete with the growing army of the 'unemployed' and underemployed, who exercise a strong pressure on wages, working conditions and safety regulations.[13] Last but not least, to all this we must add the process of 'reform' of the Keynesian policies developed in the second half of the twentieth century: those measures which – by sustaining public spending and state intervention – kept market imbalances and their social consequences under control.[14]

Meanwhile, the geographies of the global economy are being completely rewritten; globalisation means that capital is no longer just trans-national, mobile and quick to expand across the borders of the nation-states: it is becoming a truly global entity. In the last 30 years or so, it has defined its own unlimited space of valorisation in which borders, sovereign institutions or territorial delimitations can no longer be successfully maintained. Financial power is free to circulate, taking full advantage of the real-time information technologies now available.[15] The new territory of capital is indeed a 'smooth' global space in which fluxes of money, information and labour force circulate under a diversified regime of control – namely: money and information are virtually free, whereas the labour force is constrained by restrictive immigration laws limiting workers' freedom to move and settle.[16] Taking all these aspects into account, I would follow Antonio Negri and Michael Hardt, who recently defined this new territory of capitalist development as an 'Empire': this definition – surely more 'evocative' than descriptive – seems nonetheless to be an effective metaphor for the present condition. This concept suggests that the full globalisation of capital and capitalist relations of production leads to a dramatic crisis of the institutions of sovereign power (nation-state, territorial boundaries, the First World/Third World divide, and the distinction between colonising and colonised areas), and to a reconfiguring of the entire global space.[17]

---

[13] I bracket the terms 'unemployment' and 'unemployed' on purpose. As I will try to clarify in the following pages, one of the most important transformations implied by the transition from a Fordist to a post-Fordist model of production is the fact that official labour statistics are less and less able to capture material economic conditions. The terms 'unemployment' and 'unemployed' are considered here as 'labels' attached to the labour force according to an image of 'employment' and 'the employed' that is becoming very distant from contemporary economic realities. Trying to simplify: someone can perform three or four part-time works for a total of 40 weekly hours – but all of them in the informal economy – and figure as 'unemployed', whereas someone else might be working just ten hours a week, but with a regular contract defining him/her as 'employed'. Both conditions are very frequent today, and this has to do with the total work-flexibility imposed by the de-regulation of labour markets in a neo-liberal economy.

[14] On this aspect see the classic book by Frances Piven and Richard Cloward, *Regulating the Poor. The Functions of Public Welfare* (London, 1972). On the crisis of the welfare state see James O'Connor, *The Fiscal Crisis of the State* (New York, 1973).

[15] See Kenichi Ohmae, *The Borderless World: Power and Strategy in the Interlinked Economy* (New York, 1990).

[16] Zygmunt Bauman, *Globalisation. The Human Consequences* (Cambridge, 1998).

[17] Hardt and Negri, *Empire*, pp. 221–222.

The transition from a regime of full employment to a condition in which unemployment is becoming a 'structural' problem; from an economy of production to an economy of information; from industrial work to immaterial production, and from the centrality of the working class to the emergence of a post-industrial labour force: all these features of post-Fordist production cannot be confined to the 'dominant' economies, nor to some fractions of their labour force. The huge differences between the various regimes of production prevailing in different areas of the 'Empire' are not signs of the coexistence of different stages of capitalist development, as if there were a post-Fordist model in the 'First World', a Fordist model in the 'Second World' and a pre-Fordist model in the 'Third'.[18] Michael Hardt and Antonio Negri argue that a unique global labour force is indeed emerging, disseminated in different corners of the world, and hierarchically organised within the global division of labour, but always under the same frame of production: the globalised, post-industrial economic system. Some fractions of this global labour force are highly mobile, others are constrained by restrictive immigration laws; some perform an immaterial labour, others are confined to the service sector; some experience a condition of 'vulnerability' whereas others live in conditions of plain 'exclusion' from the formal economy; some are defined as 'employed' according to the official statistics, others figure as 'unemployed' even if they are involved in the over-exploitative circuits of informal production. Nonetheless, they are all part of the same labour force and contribute to the valorisation of the same globalised capital, because they are all inside the same global circuit of production and consumption:

> Today all economic activity tends to come under the dominance of informational economy and to be qualitatively transformed by it. The geographical differences in the global economy are not signs of the co-presence of different stages of development but lines of the new global hierarchy of production.[19]

In other terms, what inscribes hierarchical differences on the body of the labour force is global capital, which imposes different conditions of exploitation to its diverse fractions, and thus reshapes the meaning of 'development' and 'underdevelopment', 'centre' and 'periphery': growing portions of the so called 'Third World' are now to be found in the global cities of the 'First World' – often in the form of over-exploited immigrant workers – whereas 'central' economic and financial powers can 'migrate' to the peripheries of the world, where they find cheap labour and deregulated markets. It is precisely in this sense that Negri and Hardt speak of the end of 'imperialism' and the birth of a post-modern 'Empire'.[20]

In these pages I would like to concentrate on two peculiar sides of the transformations under way. The first, which I would refer to as 'quantitative', concerns the progressive reduction in the level of direct 'employment' of the labour force, and thus the

---

[18] For an example of this perspective, see Samir Amin, *Accumulation on a World Scale: A Critique of the Theory of Underdevelopment* (New York, 1974).

[19] Hardt and Negri, *Empire*, pp. 287–288.

[20] 'The passage to Empire emerges from the twilight of modern sovereignty. In contrast to imperialism, Empire establishes no territorial centre of power and does not rely on fixed boundaries or barriers. It is a *decentred* and *deterritorialising* apparatus of rule that progressively incorporates the entire global realm within its open, expanding frontiers': Ibid., p. XII.

reduction of the demand for 'Fordist' (i.e. 'industrial') labour expressed by the production system since the second half of the 1970s. The second can be defined as 'qualitative' – because it concerns the transformations taking place in the mode of production and in the composition of the labour force within post-Fordist capitalism. The interaction between these two streams of transformation leads me to define the transition from Fordism to post-Fordism as the shift from a regime of production characterised by *scarcity* – and by the development of a complex of strategies whose aim was to *discipline* this scarcity – toward a regime characterised by *surplus* – and by the emergence of strategies aiming to *control* this surplus.

It would be inappropriate to think of these two processes – the reduction in the amount of productive labour directly 'employed' on the one hand, and the qualitative transformations of work on the other – separately. Instead, both affect the same post-Fordist labour force, only at different levels of the productive hierarchy: and one of the most important effects of this paradigmatic shift is precisely the blurring of traditionally distinct economic realities such as 'work' and 'non-work', 'production' and 'reproduction', 'employment' and 'unemployment'. Quality and quantity overlap here, so that – for example – 'unemployment' cannot be analysed without referring to the informatisation of work; the growth of the 'informal' economy has to be examined by taking labour migrations into account; the worsening of working conditions must be connected to the availability of an 'industrial reserve army' of labour, and so on.

I will now try to describe these processes (and their consequences) more in depth: first, because I should clarify in what sense post-Fordism can be defined as a 'regime of surplus'; second, because we need to investigate the 'subject' of this surplus: the new socialised labour force – the productive *multitude*, as I will define it[21] – to which new strategies of social control seem to be directed.

Social Surplus: 'The New Excluded'

We can start with the assumption that post-Fordist economies develop in a condition of relative independence from the *amount* of labour *directly employed* in the process of production. I use the terms 'amount' and 'directly' on purpose: in fact, 'amount' refers to the total number of *formal workplaces* rather than to the bulk of work that is actually required by the system. In other terms, the fact that fewer people can get 'employed' does not mean that the total labour performed in the production process has been reduced. Put very simply: less people work for longer and harder, and more people are either formally 'out of work' or prisoners of the 'informal economy'. As a consequence:

> ... working hours have lengthened even as unemployment remains high and stubbornly resists (slow) economic growth. The double shift has become a routine part of the lives of many women ... Millions of men and women hold two or more jobs in order to earn what one good industrial job yielded a decade earlier.[22]

---

21 Here the concept of 'multitude' is borrowed from *Empire*. A definition of the concept is offered in the final paragraph of this chapter.

22 Stanley Aronowitz and William DiFazio, *The Jobless Future* (Minneapolis, 1994), p. 314.

According to Juliet Schor, for example, in the US between 1969 and 1987, rates of unemployment and underemployment almost doubled (from 7.2 percent to 16.8 percent), with a substantial decrease in the number of (full-time) employed people. At the same time, however, the total amount of work performed (as measured by yearly hours of work) has increased dramatically and overtime has been widely extended, almost to become the rule. How can we interpret these contradictory data? In fact, it would seem that there has been simultaneously a sharp decrease in 'employment' and a significant growth in the rate of 'workforce participation':

> Workers struggled at first from a traditional ideology of 'timelessness' against the very idea of time. They resented employers' attempts to impose time and time discipline. As decades passed they struggled over the ownership of time – how much was theirs, how much the boss's. And today, many fight for overtime – the right to sell as much time as they can.[23]

Now I can specify the meaning of the term 'directly': this concept offers a further specification to the hypothesis that 'employment' has decreased. 'Directly' employed labour means here industrial, full time, productive work. In other terms, what is decreasing is labour employed in industrial activities, in the production of commodities.[24] But at the same time, we witness a steady increase in the number of (traditionally out-of-the-market) activities now being more and more marketised. I refer here to those 'reproductive' activities (care, education, 'affective' labour in general) that were once confined within the boundaries of the family and are now industrially organised and exploited in the service-economy.

However, a crucial point is that these activities are only *seldom recognised as real 'employment'*. In fact, it is precisely here that precarisation and insecurity reach their peaks, and the 'working poor' (especially poor women) concentrate more. Consider for example the field of domestic labour. Here work is often as un-guaranteed, insecure, hidden, unregulated and sometimes invisible as are indeed the undocumented immigrant women who often perform it. Thousands of domestic workers appear as 'unemployed' in official statistics, not to mention those who do not appear at all, because they are 'illegal' and thus virtually non-existent.[25] In this respect, rather than being abolished (as Jeremy Rifkin has argued), work is being fragmented, segmented and 'destroyed'

---

23 Juliet Schor, *The Overworked American. The Unexpected Decline of Leisure* (New York, 1992), p. 140.

24 Here I follow the Marxist definition of the difference between 'productive' and 'unproductive' work. This has been widely debated over the last century. Marx considered 'productive' only those activities whose end-result is a commodity: only in this case, Marx argued, the extraction of surplus-value – the unique indicator of 'productivity' – is possible. Today this position is being gradually revised also in mainstream economic literature, in order to include the production of services and information. An important role in this revision was played by the feminist critiques to the gendered division of labour: 'reproduction', feminists argued, is as 'productive' as production. This debate is becoming even more central now that, with the expansion of the informational economy, wealth depends less on the manufacturing of material commodities and more on the production and exchange of information and symbols. See Manuel Castells, *The Rise of the Network Society* (Oxford, 2000).

25 On the growing involvement of immigrant workers in the 'informal economy', see the special issue of the *International Journal of Urban and Regional Research*, 23/2 (1999), on 'Immigrants and the Informal Economy in European Cities'.

by the massive introduction of new technologies (information technologies) into the production system and by the transformations of the labour market:

> Technological development does not extend production, but restructures and modifies it through a constant increase in flexibility. This does not create new employment, but destroys it. Thus, unemployment is no longer a purely conjunctural phenomenon: it is becoming a structural feature.[26]

In all Western industrial countries, between the 1960s and the 1990s there has been a reversal in the relationship between the amount of labour force employed in 'goods handling' and in 'information handling'. Let us offer just a few examples. According to Manuel Castells, in the US between 1950 and 1991, the percentage of labour force employed in 'goods handling' declined from 69.3 percent to 51.7 percent. In the same period 'information handling sectors' witnessed a sharp increase in employment: from 30 percent to 48.3 percent. And the same holds for Japan, France, Germany, Italy and the United Kingdom – though in varying proportions. In the meantime, in these same countries, the number of part-timers and insecure workers has almost doubled, due to the flexibilisation of labour markets and to the long wave of deregulation which characterised the past three decades.[27] These processes started in the early 1970s: in part as a capitalist reaction to workers' refusal of the factory discipline and to their absenteeism and insubordination (especially in the late 1960s), and in part as an adjustment to overproduction and to the saturation of domestic markets.[28]

Already in the early 1980s, the Fordist factory looked much like a 'desert' in which the noisy machineries of mass production had been replaced by silent and 'cleaver' machines requiring only the surveillance of few technicians.[29] As a consequence, a growing portion of the working class was expelled from the restructured productive sectors, thus joining the ever-growing army of the 'unemployed', underemployed, part-timers and flexi-workers. Many of them found a place in the emerging 'third sector', in those economic niches complementary to the industrial production, in which slavery-like working conditions often prevail.[30] Meanwhile, the neo-liberal assault on welfare produced the abatement of social guarantees, spreading those

---

[26] Andrea Fumagalli, 'Aspetti dell'accumulazione flessibile in Italia', in Sergio Bologna and Andrea Fumagalli (eds), *Il lavoro autonomo di seconda generazione. Scenari del postfordismo in Italia* (Milan, 1997), pp. 137–138. Stanley Aronowitz and William DiFazio put it very simply: 'The paradox is that even when business investors pour substantial parts of their capital into machines and buildings, these investments do not significantly increase the number of new permanent, full-time jobs. Computerised machines employ very little direct labor; most of it is devoted to setup, repair, and monitoring ... The more investment in contemporary technologies, the more labor is destroyed': Aronowitz and DiFazio, *The Jobless Future*, p. 6.

[27] Castells, *The Rise of the Network Society*.

[28] For a comprehensive analysis of these diverse factors see Michel Aglietta, *A Theory of Capitalist Regulation* (London, 1979).

[29] A fascinating description of the process of restructuring which took place in the Italian FIAT since the late 1970s – and its devastating effects on the local working class – can be found in Marco Revelli, *Lavorare in FIAT. Da Valletta ad Agnelli a Romiti. Operai sindacati robot* (Torino, 1989).

[30] On the re-emergence of slavery in Western economies see André Gorz, *Reclaiming Work. Beyond the Wage-Based Society* (Cambridge, 1999).

situations of vulnerability, total flexibility and new poverty representing now a paradigmatic condition of the post-Fordist labour force.[31]

This process of replacement of *welfare* with *workfare* was anticipated, 30 years ago, by Frances Piven and Richard Cloward when they wrote that:

> Publicly subsidised work tends to be used during business depressions, when the demand for labour in the private markets collapses. Conversely, arrangements to channel paupers into the labour market are more likely to be used when rapid changes in markets or technology render a segment of the labour supply temporarily maladapted.[32]

Restrictions in the access to regular, full time and guaranteed employment, together with the political assault on social rights and the 'culture of dependency' they were supposed to foster, produced a hypertrophy of the hidden economies and of those productive circuits where 'the new excluded' had to search for alternative sources of income.[33] Whole productive sectors rely now on deregulated, un-guaranteed markets, often on the border between legal and illegal economy. More and more the philosophy of 'just in time' and 'lean production' pushes toward the externalisation of production: from the factory to the small sites of decentralised production.[34] The restructuring of the industrial sector leads to the delocalisation and decentralisation of production, to outsourcing and downsizing. The main consequence of all this is the transition from a 'work' individually perceived (and socially represented) as a biographic event capable of narration, toward a 'work' experienced as a fragment (or a 'life in fragments' in Bauman's words), a necessity of the day, an urgency of the moment: it is precisely here that the process of 'corrosion of character' described by Richard Sennett finds its roots.[35]

We get here to a very important point: if it is true that what we are witnessing is not really the disappearance of 'employment', but rather its fragmentation, its uneven diffusion throughout the whole society and its explosion into an archipelago of regular and irregular, guaranteed and un-guaranteed, part-time and overtime jobs; if it is true that production and reproduction are overlapping, with the former being recognised as proper 'work' and the latter being exploited and yet often deprived of any guarantees and social rights; if it is true that an increasing portion of the poor are actually working poor and that a significant fraction of (once guaranteed) workers are now becoming poor; if all these assumptions share some degree of plausibility, then the question arises: can we still maintain that the term 'unemployment' refers to the absence of *work* and to a condition of individual inactivity?

---

[31] For an interesting case study on precarisation and the condition of 'working poor', see Barbara Ehrenreich, *Nickel and Dimed. On (Not) Getting by in America* (New York, 2001).

[32] Piven and Cloward, *Regulating the Poor*, p. 23.

[33] To these aspects we should add the legal and political discrimination of immigrants in Europe and the US, which turns them into a fully disposable labour force: being constantly denied citizenship rights, these workers must accept any condition of work, because it appears preferable to detention and deportation. For them, workfare translates into a plain regime of 'less eligibility', as we will see in chapter 5.

[34] See Michael J. Piore and Charles F. Sabel, *The Second Industrial Divide: Possibilities for Prosperity* (New York, 1984).

[35] Richard Sennett, *The Corrosion of Character. The Personal Consequences of Work in the New Capitalism* (New York, 1998).

Perhaps what economic language (and especially the language of statistics) defines as 'unemployment' is undergoing a process of radical change. Once the concept is situated within the post-Fordist condition described so far, unemployment seems to define something different from the mere condition of non-*work*. I would suggest that 'unemployment' is the loss of a regular *job*, where 'job' means a productive activity characterised by stability, access to some legal guarantees, entitlement to a complex of social rights: all those elements the labour force has been systematically deprived of, in the transition from Fordism to post-Fordism.[36] André Gorz synthesises this process when he argues that 'unemployment' is the abolition of:

> ... the specific 'work' peculiar to industrial capitalism: the work we are referring to when we say 'she doesn't work' of a woman who devotes her time to bringing up her own children, but 'she works' of one who gives even some small part of her time to bringing up other people's children in a playgroup or a nursery school.[37]

In this respect, 'unemployment' is no longer necessarily associated to inactivity (as was the case in the Fordist economy) and becomes instead something like an official measure of the gap existing between the many and diversified productive 'activities' in which people are actually involved, and the conditions – imposed by the system – under which these activities obtain social recognition as 'work'. Thus, more than measuring people's exclusion from the field of production, official rates of unemployment show the growing inadequacy of official statistics to capture the contemporary economic reality, and in particular people's involvement in large sectors of the post-Fordist economy.

This is why I would argue that what we see here is a *social surplus*: a complex of productive activities (and workers performing them) not captured by the concept of 'employment' as it is ordinarily adopted (in statistics, political discourses and everyday language). And this surplus (which is synonymous with social exclusion, economic marginality, individual insecurity and poverty) is a consequence of the artificial separation between 'work' and 'job' imposed by the dominant, neo-liberal economic rationality.[38] Again, the disappearance of jobs does not imply the disappearance of work. Instead, the crisis of the Fordist factory and the fragmentation of production means that work (conceived as an ensemble of productive actions), covers now ever-growing fields of life – because the contemporary economy based on insecurity, precariousness and total flexibility requires a total mobilisation of the 'self', as a condition to obtain some kind of social inclusion, and this mobilisation involves every aspect of life.

What we witness is thus a radical disjunction between 'work' as it is experienced by 'the new labour force', and a system of citizenship rights still rooted firmly in the

---

[36] On this aspect – with an exclusive reference to continental Europe – see Ulrich Beck, *Schoene Arbeitswelt. Vision: Weltbürgergesellschaft* (Frankfurt am Main, 1999).

[37] Gorz, *Reclaiming Work*, p. 2.

[38] For an extensive philosophical analysis of the differences between Work, Labour and Action, see Hannah Arendt, *The Human Condition* (Chicago, 1958). Arendt argues that there has been a historical development in Western societies, for which 'work' (organised industrial production) has supplanted older forms of 'labour' (activity for the production of durable goods), and 'action' (public engagement and political activity).

Fordist concept of work as a job and as a full-time, life-long employment. Therefore, what André Gorz refers to as the 'exit from the wage-based society', represents a new configuration of the 'work-income-social citizenship' complex. The fragmentation of 'work' excludes from social citizenship a growing fraction of the population (immigrants, precarious workers, 'mc-jobbers') whose productive activities (in the broadest sense) are not socially recognised as a gateway to inclusion and full social integration.[39] A dramatic contradiction emerges here: the right to income, social inclusion and citizenship is based on a model of work that was hegemonic during the Fordist era, but is gradually disappearing from the landscape of Western societies.[40] In fact, according to Guy Standing, Fordist social citizenship:

> ... while never powerfully redistributive, was mostly universalistic in principle, linked firmly and unequivocally to the performance of labour ... Social security was based firmly on the image of an industrial society in which the working class was expected to remain or become the overwhelming majority of the population and the norm for social behaviour.[41]

Therefore, whereas until the second half of the twentieth century it was reasonable to conceptualise citizenship as an ensemble of rights 'of' work grounded on a generalised right (and duty) 'to' work,[42] this seems no longer to be the case in our societies. A paradigmatic example of the process of disjunction of citizenship from work is offered again by the condition of immigrants in Europe and the US: on the one hand these people are employed almost exclusively in those informal and flexible sectors of the economy where an unskilled and disposable labour force is needed. On the other hand, the right to circulate and settle is granted only to those who can give evidence of a stable employment and sufficient income.[43]

---

[39] See for example André Gorz, *Critique of Economic Reason* (London, 1989). It should be remembered, however, that the issue of what should be recognised as 'work', with all the consequences this implies for the labour force, has been a field of constant struggle between labour and capital. I refer here again to the feminist struggles over the gendered division of labour and the recognition of 'domestic' labour as proper work. See Silvia Federici, *Wages Against Housework* (London, 1975).

[40] Some champions of conservatism argue that even the right to 'dignity' is linked to the performance of a job: 'In our society having a job is a necessary condition of what has been called social dignity – maintaining the respect of one's fellow citizens (having a job of course includes being a homemaker in a family where others have a job outside the home). The point is not merely that having a job shows that you can take care of yourself; more important, it shows that you are carrying your share of the social burden. What your fellow citizens think of you in this sense should matter': Amy Gutmann and Dennis Thompson, *Democracy and Disagreement* (Cambridge, 1996), p. 293.

[41] Guy Standing, *Beyond the New Paternalism. Basic Security as Equality* (London, 2002), p. 13.

[42] This is the picture we get from T.H. Marshall's 1950 classic essay on 'Citizenship and Social Class', now republished in Thomas H. Marshall and Tom Bottomore, *Citizenship and Social Class* (London, 1992), pp. 3–51.

[43] In Italy this situation has been further aggravated by the latest legislation on immigration. The so called 'Bossi-Fini' law (from the names of the two proponents) states that immigrants can enter the country legally only if they possess a stable job, and they lose their residence permit if they lose the job. Here it is not difficult to see the contradiction between the ideology of flexibility, which dominates public discourse, and the rigidity of the practices regulating the legal status of migrants.

I can now submit a preliminary description of what was defined earlier as a regime of 'surplus'. *Social surplus* means here that the contemporary dynamics of production are disconnected from the institutional practices for the recognition and government of social citizenship. The crisis of the Fordist-Keynesian pact and of the welfare state (which was based on that pact), imply that the institutions for the (economic) government of society are unable to guarantee social inclusion through work. The dissociation between the 'material' constitution of society (its productive dynamics) and the 'formal' constitution of citizenship (its 'mode of regulation') becomes structural here.

In the Fordist age it was reasonable to consider unemployment and social exclusion as consequences of an individual deficit, resulting from the incapacity of some parts of the population to find a proper place within a system that was able to guarantee a universal condition of inclusion and citizenship. The situation looks very different today, however, because those instruments of social regulation are gradually disappearing, and there seems to be neither a social order to be re-established, nor any individual deficit to be readjusted through discipline. Rather, we see only a growing surplus of labour force – easily depicted as a 'dangerous class' – to be governed at distance. Following Zygmunt Bauman we could say that the relation between capital and labour is shifting from a condition of reciprocal 'engagement', to a situation in which the former is gradually 'disengaging' itself (both economically and politically) from the latter.[44] Economic forces operate in a condition of relative independence from work, and work is becoming a dependent variable.

Assuming the 'point of view' of capitalist development, we could say that the welfare state belongs to a historical period in which the labour force had to be disciplined in order to be adjusted to the industrial organisation of work. In a system characterised by full-employment, in which 'waged work' was an effective gateway to social citizenship, the disciplinary aspects of welfare could be conceived as tools for the constitution of an adequate labour force. Indeed, the historical development of Fordism needed some apparatuses for the government of the population and some dispositives of social control which would attune a reluctant labour force to the system of production.

Put differently, in that condition the *surplus* was on the side of capital, whose requirements had to be imposed to the labour force: a surplus of organisation, discipline, scientific management and productivity. In that context, the labour force was inadequate, unprepared and thus in need of discipline in order to reach the level of cooperation and economic efficiency required by capital; and those who remained outside (or 'behind') had to be re-integrated through the penal-welfare complex. This process was described in Chapter 1, where I analysed the role of the prison in the production and reproduction of the working class. The prison functioned there as a *disciplinary* machine whose aim was to defeat the resistance of the labour force, to fill its deficits, to enforce its cooperation within the production system and to promote individual self-control. In the same scenario I would situate the *disciplinary logic* of the welfare state: a complex technology for the reproduction of the labour force.

Here comes the question: is this logic still operating in our post-Fordist economies?

---

[44] Zygmunt Bauman, *Liquid Modernity* (Cambridge, 2000), pp. 121–149.

Productive Surplus: 'The Immaterial Labour Force'

The 'qualitative' side of the transformations under way is represented by the process of informatisation, automation and post-industrialisation which is taking place in growing sectors of production. This technological revolution is affecting the forms of work as well as the organisation, management and material content of labour. As a consequence of automation and informatisation, this is becoming more and more 'cognitive', 'immaterial' and 'symbolic'. This transformation does not concern only a minor fraction of the labour force. Even if the number of workers directly involved in the handling of information is still a minority of the total labour force, it should be noted that all economic sectors – agricultural, industrial, services, etc – are being transformed as a consequence of informatisation.[45]

'Immaterial' means that work is based increasingly on the elaboration of symbols, on the construction of new languages, on a *savoir-faire* which can never be repetitive, and on the management of signs. Labour tends to become de-materialised in the sense that it is no longer related to a specific object: it is becoming a communicative performance, an act of creation. Immaterial labour *creates* a second nature (the virtual world of information) rather than just *transforming* nature, as was the case with industrial production. Thus, based on his observation of a knowledge-intensive workplace, Stanley Deetz can speak of an increasing 'difficulty of observing the work process and ... of measuring specific product characteristics'.[46]

We can see here how far we are getting from Taylorism: that system of management was in fact based on a rigid separation between creation, programming and execution of the task. The condition for this system of management to function was a perfect knowledge of the productive process by the management:[47] a knowledge which could then be translated into a total power over the labour force. In this respect, the Taylorist factory clearly needed (and also reproduced) a disciplinary order:

> Under Taylor the reorganisation of work was to optimise efficiency. First and foremost this requires the construction of knowledge. One of Taylor's first concerns was the importance of placing order on what was viewed as a confused mass. He did this by constructing norms and standards. In essence, Taylorism was the application of disciplinary power to greater organisational depths.[48]

---

[45] On this aspect see Castells, *The Rise of the Network Society* (particularly Chapter Four, 'The Transformations of Work and Employment').

[46] Stanley Deetz, 'Discursive Formations, Strategized Subordination and Self-surveillance', in Alan McKinlay and Ken Starkey (eds), *Foucault, Management and Organisation Theory. From Panopticon to Technologies of Self* (London, 1998), p. 155.

[47] 'Under scientific management the 'initiative' of the workmen (that is, their hard work, their good-will and their ingenuity) is obtained with absolute uniformity and to a greater extent than is possible under the old system; and in addition to this improvement on the part of the men, the managers assume new burdens, new duties and responsibilities never dreamed of in the past. The managers assume, for instance, the burden of gathering together all of the traditional knowledge, which in the past has been possessed by the workmen, and then of classifying, tabulating, and reducing this knowledge to rules, laws, and formulae which are immensely helpful to the workmen in doing their daily work': Frederick W. Taylor, *The Principles of Scientific Management* (New York, 1967), p. 36.

[48] Barbara Townley, 'Beyond Good and Evil: Depth and Division in the Management of Human Resources', in McKinlay and Starkey (eds), *Foucault, Management and Organisation Theory*, p. 195.

The repetition of tasks, the synchronic coordination along an assembly-line designed from above, the hierarchical subordination of each worker: all these basic aspects of the Taylorist factory lose their appeal in the flexible post-Fordist factory, because they become obstacles to the growth of knowledge-driven productivity. Thus, 'what *tends* to disappear through integral automation are the routine, repetitive tasks that can be precoded and programmed for their execution by machines. It is the Taylorist assembly line that becomes an historic relic ... It should not be surprising that information technologies do precisely that: replace work that can be encoded in a programmable sequence and enhance work that requires analysis, decision, and reprogramming capabilities in real time at a level that only the human brain can master'.[49]

While according to Taylor's *principles of scientific management* nothing within the cycle of production had to be left to the 'initiative and incentive' of the workers (last but not least because their intellectual abilities, Taylor argued, were comparable to those of an ox[50]), in the post-Fordist factory growing areas of production must be left 'unmanaged':

> Maintaining an unmanaged space for worker activity is a necessary precondition if teamworking regimes are to deliver their promised flexibility and innovation. For this unmanaged space is where workers' intimate understanding of production can be articulated and refined in a continuous process of incremental innovation without fear of managerial appropriation.[51]

The Taylorist factory was *silent*: workers in fact should not talk. They did not need to share any information about the production process, because this was totally planned and driven from above: they had to execute orders and to perform clearly defined tasks. The post-Fordist factory looks quite different. New figures of work emerge here: multi-skilled workers whose productivity lays in the capacity to perform new tasks, avoid repetitions and communicate; according to the Italian Autonomist Marxist Paolo Virno:

> In the age of manufacture, and then during the apogee of the Fordist factory, working activity is mute. The worker is silent. Production is a silent chain, in which only a mechanic and exterior relation between antecedent and consequent is admitted, whereas any simultaneous interaction is forbidden ... In post-Fordist production, instead, the material productive process can be empirically described as a complex of linguistic acts, a sequence of assertions, a symbolic interaction. In part, because the activity of living labour consists of the regulation, surveillance and coordination of the system of machines. But also because the production process has as its 'raw material' knowledge, information, culture and social relations.[52]

---

[49] Castells, *The Rise of the Network Society*, pp. 257–258. On this aspect see also: Taiichi Ohno, *Toyota Production System. Beyond Large Scale Production* (Cambridge, 1988); Benjamin Coriat, *Penser à l'envers. Travail et organisation dans l'enterprise japonaise* (Paris, 1991).

[50] 'As we have before stated, the pig-iron handler is not an extraordinary man difficult to find, he is a man more or less of the type of the ox, heavy both mentally and physically', Taylor, *The Principles of Scientific Management*, p. 137.

[51] Alan McKinlay and Phil Taylor, 'Through the Looking Glass: Foucault and the Politics of Production', in McKinlay and Starkey (eds), *Foucault, Management and Organisation Theory*, p. 175.

[52] Paolo Virno, 'Lavoro e linguaggio', in Adelino Zanini and Ubaldo Fadini (eds), *Lessico Postfordista* (Milan, 2001), p. 181.

Thus, labour becomes a linguistic activity so far as communication becomes a commodity, and intellect – conceived as an ensemble of communicative, expressive and inventive faculties – becomes the new instrument of post-Fordist production. Therefore, the times and spaces which in the Fordist system separated the universe of production from the sphere of reproduction, gradually lose their meaning: work and productivity extend beyond the walls of any closed institution:

> Work has even less to do with the factory. The latter is no longer recognized or considered to be the specific site of the consolidation of labouring activity and its transformation into value. Work abandons the factory in order to find, precisely in the social, a place adequate to the functions of concentrating productive activity and transforming it into value. The prerequisites of these processes are present in, and diffused throughout, society.[53]

This means that productivity does no longer depend so much on a rational and economically efficient management of resources *within* the factory (its immediate productive factors – fixed and variable capital): it depends rather on the entrepreneurial ability to intercept and de-codify fluxes of knowledge and concentrations of social experience (such as fashions, languages and images), in order to exploit them as sources of value. In this respect, it is becoming increasingly difficult to establish a rigid distinction between times of work and times of non-work, in what Manuel Castells describes as a 'timeless time'.[54] On the one hand, the time of 'reproduction' of the immaterial labour force becomes itself 'productive', because the post-Fordist enterprise exploits competences, abilities and attitudes that are produced during time of non-work (in leisure, entertainment, social life, affective experiences and so on). On the other hand, immaterial labour can be defined precisely as the process of production of those very linguistic relations, communicative events, and social experiences within which the social competences, abilities and attitudes to be later exploited by capital can emerge.

Thus, immaterial labour takes the form of a *production of meaning*, communication and social networks. In this very peculiar sense, it is possible to agree that the traditional Marxist distinction between 'structure' – as the universe of the capitalist valorisation of subjectivities – and 'superstructure' – as the universe in which those subjectivities are formed and reproduced – has been dissolved:

> The superstructure is put to work, and the universe we live in is a universe of productive linguistic networks. The lines of production and those of representation cross and mix in the same linguistic and productive realm. In this context the distinctions that define the central categories of political economy tend to blur. Production becomes indistinguishable from reproduction; productive forces merge with relations of production; constant capital tends to be constituted and represented within variable capital, in the brains, bodies, and cooperation of productive subjects.[55]

The point is not just that the 'superstructure' is more important than Marx had suggested, or that it has a life in itself: to the contrary, I am suggesting that also the

---

[53] Negri, *The Politics of Subversion*, p. 89.

[54] Castells, *The Rise of the Network Society*.

[55] Hardt and Negri, *Empire*, p. 385.

'superstructure' is becoming part of the 'structure' of production – it is put to work, and is becoming the main field of production.

A good example of the processes I am describing here is offered by the meaning of the 'logo'. In the post-Fordist 'economy of signs and space',[56] the logo is no longer just a label helping consumers to distinguish one product from another. Today, the logo represents the 'linguistic' or 'immaterial' value of a product, which makes it part of a lifestyle and a medium of social communication. The logo expresses a 'relational experience', a social meaning, a linguistic code: it produces and spreads new forms of (consumerist) subjectivity.[57] However, what turns the logo into a device for the production of social meanings and identities is precisely the fact that it is in itself the result of the commodification of social relations: in order to be effective – that is to say profitable – the logo must be able to catch, intercept, and codify some forms of social relation, and to represent them as features of a particular product.[58] Just to give an example, Nike does not produce only shoes, it produces also a new way of life, whose main symbol is Nike's logo. However, its actual content is only 'packaged' and offered to the public by Nike, through the economic valorisation of languages, gestures, images and musics to be found in everyday life – be it the subculture of the African-American ghetto or the slogans of anti-global demonstrations (Nike's recent TV spots are very eloquent in this respect). It is in this sense that the post-Fordist enterprise can be described as an engine for the valorisation of fluxes of language, symbols and communication through their commodification and marketisation. But this means that the enterprise marketises the sphere of reproduction, non-work and communication itself. To continue with the same example, the economic success of Nike depends less on the rational organisation of its production sites than from the ability of its 'cool hunters' to infiltrate in discos, basket-fields, ghettos, mass demonstrations, etc.

On the other hand, the whole life is now put to work, because the most intimate (and 'social') among the human faculties are directly exploited in the production process: language, imagination, communication and desire. All these faculties are in fact inseparable from the individual 'being': they are part of the very concept of 'subjectivity'. This was not the case in the Taylorist factory, however, in which human individuality (conscience, thoughts, desires, etc.) had to be left outside the walls of the factory (this was an explicit requisite of 'scientific management') because it represented an 'impediment' to the rationality of the system. Reflecting on these peculiar aspects, André Gorz argues that while the human condition within the Taylorist factory could be described as 'alienation', the condition of many post-Fordist workers resembles a form of 'prostitution':

---

56 Scott Lash and John Urry, *Economies of Signs and Space* (London, 1994).

57 Following Bauman, we can say that the 'logo' plays a fundamental role in setting out the (symbolic) rules we have to follow in order to (per)form our 'consumer identity'. According to this author, this is a weak and volatile identity, resulting in the shift from the 'work ethic' to the 'aesthetic of consumption'. Nevertheless, it is the identity (or better, the set of ever changing identities) on which the post-Fordist production is based. See Bauman, *Work, Consumerism and the New Poor.*

58 In this respect, see Naomi Klein's *No Logo* (London, 2000), where the author describes the function of the logo in the new global economy, and the role of 'cool hunters' in post-Fordist production.

> Selling oneself, and particularly selling 'the whole of oneself', including what is most common to human beings ... is not simply the behaviour of a 'servant': it is the very essence of prostitution. For prostitution is not simply 'the sale of one's body', since body and sexuality are not separable from the whole person, and their sale is always a sale of self.[59]

Now, the capitalist valorisation of these attitudes and faculties cannot take place within those spaces and times defined as a 'job' by a contract: the producers of symbols are always at work, because what is actually exploited is their ability to capture profitable aspects of social life, and social life is what takes place outside the office, the factory, etc.

It is thus understandable in what sense the process of production is becoming less dependent on individualised performances to which capitalist command can impose a rational organisation from above, as was the case in the Taylorist factory: productive cooperation inside the post-Fordist labour force refuses any disciplinary logic which would compel it to a repetitiveness, to a synchronisation and to a rigid order which is antithetical to the processes of communication.

Therefore, the organisational form required by the new immaterial production is not the rigid assembly line, but the flexible network. The networked enterprise catches and valorises processes of cooperation emerging from below: this cooperation is based on linguistic and symbolic exchanges that would be frustrated by any pre-coded model of organisation. This new development is what makes post-Fordist enterprises so profitable, but it raises also some problems: in this condition, to what extent (and in what forms) is capitalist control over the labour force still possible? If any type of organisation seems to be dysfunctional to the free flux of communication and cooperation (on which productivity is based), how can capitalist management still be exercised? The issue is further aggravated by the fact that in this context, any precise measurement of individual productivity becomes problematic, given that post-Fordist productivity is based on performances which seem to escape any clear definition in terms of time and space. Following Stanley Deetz:

> The three primary forms of 'capital' for knowledge-intensive companies are 'intellectual' (skills and knowledge unique to specific employees), 'relational' (networks and trust relations with clients), and 'artefactual' (data bases and files containing technical data and client data). All these forms of capital are highly symbolic, thus need constant reproduction and secondary systems of justification, and are highly mobile. Further, each is more a property of the employee than anyone else.[60]

If it is plausible that the productivity of work depends mainly on the valorisation of what has traditionally been defined as the universe of non-work, and if cooperation is the material prerequisite of this system of production, then I would argue that – together with the traditional economic categories mentioned before – also the concept

---

[59]   Gorz, *Reclaiming Work*, p. 43.

[60]   Deetz, 'Discursive Formations, Strategized Subordination and Self-surveillance', p. 156. On the problem of measurability and predictability of the post-Fordist labour force see also Barbara Townley, 'Foucault, Power/Knowledge, and its Relevance for Human Resource Management', *Academy of Management Review*, 18/3 (1993): 518–545.

of 'value' (conceived as the amount of labour necessary to the production of a commodity) is under question. Marxist theory describes the concept of 'value' as the capitalist project of measuring the social productivity of work through time. However, my point here is that it becomes problematic to establish an economic quantification of the time and resources necessary for the reproduction of the most important form of capital in post-Fordist production: intellect. Let's follow Marx:

> On the one side, then, it [capital] calls to life all the powers of science and nature, as of social combination and of social intercourse, in order to make the creation of wealth independent [relatively] of the labour time employed on it. On the other side, it wants to use labour time as the measuring rod for the giant forces thereby created, and to confine them within the limits required to maintain the already created value as value.[61]

As can be argued from the quoted passage, Marx foresaw many of the transformations we witness today, in particular the irruption of science into the sphere of production and the consequent reduction in the amount of living productive labour directly employed in the process. In his *Grundrisse*, Marx defined the new labour force emerging from the application of technology to production as a 'general intellect':

> The development of fixed capital indicates to what degree social knowledge has become a distinct force of production, and to what degree, hence, the conditions of the process of social life itself have come under the control of the general intellect and been transformed in accordance with it.[62]

The realisation of the productive potentialities of the general intellect depends on processes of cooperation and communication that are external and potentially in conflict with the organisational rationality of the capitalist enterprise. Whereas capitalist organisation is based on *competition*, these potentialities are grounded in *cooperation*. Where the capitalist sees 'human capital', immaterial workers express 'human intellect'. Therefore, capitalist command imposes itself to the labour force as an exterior power and as a regimentation of productive abilities: in the very act of commanding over social cooperation, it limits their potential for production.[63]

In other words, capital's control over this new labour force operates *a posteriori*: no longer as a predetermination of the organisational requisites which permit to increase production, but as an expropriation of social productivity, so that 'the result is usually a very loose work arrangement with managerial control concentrated at the outcome rather than the work process'.[64]

Obviously, this expropriation still takes places successfully: I am not suggesting here that the socialised post-industrial labour force is now materially free from capitalist power. In fact, what I am investigating is precisely the emergence of new

---

[61] Karl Marx, *Grundrisse* (Harmondsworth, 1973), p. 706.

[62] Ibid., p. 706.

[63] 'The exchange of labour power is no longer something that occurs, in determinate quantity and specific quality, within the process of capital; rather, an interchange of activities determined by social needs and goals is now the precondition, the premise of social production ... Work is now an immediate participation in the world of social wealth': Negri, *Revolution Retrieved*, pp. 117–118.

[64] Deetz, 'Discursive Formations, Strategized Subordination and Self-surveillance', p. 157.

forms of control over the post-Fordist labour force. However, at the present stage I would suggest that these forms of control are no longer related to a capitalist rationality 'intrinsic' to the process of work, being instead rooted on a power that is becoming more and more 'external' to the production process. Following Antonio Negri again, this is more a 'political' than an 'economic' form of power which:

> ... over-determines the organisation of social labour, imposing its reproduction according to lines of inequality and hierarchy. Exploitation is the production of political lines of over-determination of social production. This is not to say that the economic aspect of exploitation can be negated: on the contrary, exploitation is precisely the seizure, the centralisation and the expropriation of the form and the product of social cooperation, and therefore it is an economic determination in a very meaningful way – but its form is political.[65]

In the Fordist factory, capitalist valorisation was based on a scientific organisation of work which permitted to maximise productivity from *inside* the production process. Instead, today this maximisation seems to depend on the possibility to control productivity from the *outside*, by turning cooperation into competition, and this happens through the market: by marketising the immaterial products of post-Fordist production, capital reinstates 'value' as the measure of work, and thus regains its control over the whole system. But this control, let us repeat again, is external to the process of work, because it does not concern so much the organisation of production as its end-result: the market is what turns social cooperation into economic competition.

We can see here another side of what was defined as post-Fordist *surplus*. Surplus appears here as a growing contradiction between productive potentialities, relations of cooperation, forms of communication on the one hand, and a capitalist rationality reduced to purely external command on the other. No longer able to govern social productivity from inside, capital appears only as a power of control exercised through the violence of the market, as an external limit imposed to a social cooperation whose potential for freedom has increased out of control.

The Post-Fordist Labour Force as a *Multitude*

The arguments presented so far could suggest that there is a deep fracture between what I have defined as 'the new excluded' and 'the immaterial labour force'. It could be argued that these concepts refer to different sections of the workforce and thus describe contradictory aspects of the transition to post-Fordism. Indeed, we find on the one hand a labour force which has been expelled from the (formal) circuits of production as a consequence of industrial restructuring, and on the other hand the hyper-integrated, high-income workers of immaterial production. In between – in conditions of high insecurity, precariousness and exploitation – a growing portion of the new labour force: in particular women and immigrants.

In other words, on one side there are growing masses of people whose work is needed less by a restructured post-industrial economy; on the other, a new aristocracy of work whose performances are highly valued and represent the power-center of the

---

[65] Negri, 'Interpretation of the Class Situation Today', p. 74.

system. We could even say (as indeed some commentators do) that the increasing importance and centrality of immaterial, cognitive and high-tech labour is deepening the exclusion and marginalisation of those strata of the working class now dismissed (or rendered more vulnerable) by the post-Fordist economy. Thus, a renewed hierarchy of work would be emerging, whose features are well synthesised by Manuel Castells when he argues that:

> The prevailing model for labour in the new, information-based economy is that of a core labour force, formed by information-based managers and by those whom Reich calls 'symbolic analysts', and a disposable labour force that can be automated and/or hired/fired/offshored, depending upon market demand and labour costs.[66]

Following this perspective, we should reach the conclusion that with the transition to post-Fordism, the labour force has been 'defeated' by the neo-liberal rationality – as seems to have happened in other periods of the history of capitalism, according to a 'cyclical' approach to economic processes.[67] It would seem, in fact, that by restructuring the economy in the name of flexibility, precariousness, insecurity and competition, capitalist power has imposed a neo-Hobbesian condition of 'war of all against all' among the labour force itself: growing fractions of the workforce find themselves excluded because they fail in the competition against other sections of the same labour force. Thus, the conflict between work and capital would have been turned into a conflict among workers. On a global scale, the same could be said about the international composition of the labour force: here, the argument would go, the growing informatisation of production taking place in the dominant countries causes (or at least contributes to and is based on) a dramatic deterioration of living and working conditions in those areas of the 'Empire' in which automation is still absent, thus forcing masses of people to migrate.

This point of view is not entirely new, and represents the main argument of those theorists and commentators who refuse the concept of post-Fordism, or at least put under question its capacity to describe the transformations affecting the contemporary labour force. When we speak of post-Fordism, these theorists argue, we are referring only to a small èlite of high-tech, immaterial and communicative workers, leaving aside both a growing portion of the labour force in advanced economies and, above all, whole economic systems of the so called 'developing' countries. André Gorz seems to follow this argument when he says that '… it is crazy to present a form of work which ensures that there is less and less work and wages for everyone as the essential source of autonomy, identity and fulfilment for all'.[68]

It is not my aim here to criticise this perspective: indeed, on the surface some of its arguments are convincing. It is unquestionable, for example, that the current technological revolution is depriving of work growing fractions of the population, and that this does not imply, for those who suffer this deprivation, any 'liberation

[66] Castells, *The Rise of the Network Society*, pp. 295–296.

[67] In this respect, see the recent work by Dario Melossi, *Stato, controllo sociale e devianza* (Milan, 2002), where the author further specifies his 'cyclical' approach to the political economy of punishment, already presented in some earlier works mentioned in Chapter 1.

[68] Gorz, *Reclaiming Work*, p. 46. A number of articles and essays dealing with this apparent contradiction of post-Fordism can be found in the latest issues of the journal *Capital & Class*.

from work', but only unemployment, vulnerability, insecurity and social exclusion. It is also true that the lives of the majority of the working population – especially immigrants – are characterised by insecurity and precariousness and that there are important economic sectors to which informatisation simply does not apply. Furthermore, it is meaningful to say that some areas of production could never become 'immaterial' if other sectors of the economy did not remain absolutely 'material', and that immaterial labour is to some extent the form of work that exercises more control and power over the others. Finally, it would be difficult to deny that some economic distinctions such as employment/unemployment, production/reproduction, time of work/time of non-work, however inadequate they can appear at the level of theoretical analysis (as I have argued before), are nonetheless experienced as real, from the point of view of individual experience, and can produce very material consequences on individual lives. On a factual level, being an 'unemployed', an immigrant domestic worker or a part-timer has real, concrete and perceptible consequences.

However, what I would suggest is that these arguments refer to what can be defined as the 'surface' of labour: they describe the immediate and visible features of the contemporary condition, and seem to rely on the very economic rationality they try to put under question and to criticize. Again, this is not to argue that 'unemployment', 'social exclusion' or 'insecurity' are empty concepts. What I am suggesting here – based on the arguments presented earlier – is that we should attempt to 'deconstruct' these concepts, and to insist that their current meaning in the public discourse is not neutral: in fact, it is driven by the hegemony of an economic rationality which imposes its own hierarchies to the labour force as a whole, discriminating between those 'inside' and those 'outside', those who 'can get by' and those who 'can't get by'. Concepts like the ones mentioned before (and the critical perspectives which take them for granted) do not offer an explanation for the contemporary condition: in a sense, they are part of the problem. Because the problem is: do these differences maintain any explanatory efficacy in a post-Fordist economy?

A critical analysis of the post-Fordist condition requires terms like 'work', 'employment' and 'unemployment', to be deeply problematised, in order to show – for example – that 'productive' is not necessarily synonymous with 'marketised', and that 'work' (as an activity) is not the same as 'job' (as a 'condition'). It is not at the level of capitalist rationality – and by taking its hierarchical and exclusionary concepts for granted – that we can make sense of the intrinsic contradictions of contemporary economy. Instead, we should try to overcome this very rationality by adopting a language that makes use of new terms, new critical concepts which can help us to catch some under-perceived aspects of the condition of the post-Fordist labour force. Here, I would follow the post-modern feminist thinker Rosi Braidotti who – in a different context – defines these critical concepts as 'figurations', which:

> … evoke the changes and transformations which are on-going in the 'g-local' context of advanced societies. Figurations are expressive of cartographic readings of the subject's own embedded and embodied position.[69]

---

[69]   Rosi Braidotti, *Metamorphoses. Towards a Materialist Theory of Becoming* (Cambridge, 2002), p. 173.

In the contemporary global economy, the post-Fordist labour force appears as a unified productive entity, an ensemble of cooperative and productive subjects who escape any kind of rigid economic organisation: in this sense, we can refer to it by adopting the 'figuration' of the 'multitude', recently reintroduced in political and sociological debates by Antonio Negri and Michael Hardt.

This concept leads us back to classical political theory. In that context, the concept of multitude was defined against that of 'People'. In his *De Cive*, Hobbes states that the incapacity to establish a proper distinction between 'the People' and 'the Multitude' leads to sedition and to the falling of any government. The People is an entity capable of expressing a general will through the will of a single individual synthesising everybody's will. On the contrary, the multitude is an undifferentiated ensemble of subjects, to whom no single will and no particular action can be ascribed. Sedition, Hobbes continues, takes place not when the people rebel against the sovereign but when the citizens revolt against the 'city', and this happens when the multitude rises up against the People:

> It is a great hindrance to civil government, especially monarchical, that men distinguish not enough between a people and a multitude. The people is somewhat that is one, having one will, and to whom one action may be attributed; none of these can be properly said of the multitude. The people rules in all governments. For even in monarchies the people commands; for the people wills by the will of one man [however it seems a paradox] the king is the people.[70]

Here I adopt the term 'multitude' only in a metaphoric sense, as a 'figuration' which allows me to make sense of some peculiar features of the post-Fordist labour force, as opposed to the industrial working class of the Fordist age. Referred to the contemporary productive reality, the concept of multitude describes thus a diversified labour force, whose characteristics seem to escape any disciplinary project of individualisation and unification. Multitude means that the productivity of the post-Fordist labour force is based on activities which cross the traditional borders between production and reproduction, employment and unemployment, labour/work/action.[71] But the concept also refers to the fact that neither any hegemonic subject, nor any single political 'project' or 'action' seems to be in the condition to express and to represent the intrinsic complexity of this new labour force. In this respect, the concept of multitude puts in question – and to some extent overcomes – the concept of 'class': not so much because the old working class is now losing its (economic and political) centrality; rather, because in the new conditions of dispersed, fragmented and diffused production, it is no longer possible to define a specific place in which the subjects of work are formed, their productivity is expressed and their conflicts take place – as was the case for the working class inside the Fordist factory:

> On the one hand, the relations of capitalist exploitation are expanding everywhere, not limited to the factory but tending to occupy the entire social terrain. On the other hand, social relations completely invest the relations of production, making impossible any

---

[70] Thomas Hobbes, *De Cive* (New York, 1949), Chapter XII, Section 8, p. 135. The concept of 'Multitude' as opposed to that of 'The People' appears also in Baruch Spinoza's *Theological-Political Treatise* (Indianapolis, 2001), III, 2,6,9.

[71] Arendt, *The Human Condition*.

externality between social production and economic production ... The very qualities of labour power ... can no longer be grasped, and similarly, exploitation can no longer be localized and quantified. In effect, the object of exploitation and domination tend not to be specific productive activities but the universal capacity to produce, that is, abstract social activity and its comprehensive power.[72]

The 'new excluded' and the 'immaterial labour force' appear, thus, to be part of the same productive complex. Inclusion and exclusion, employment and unemployment, are indeed real situations; however they are imposed to the post-Fordist 'multitude' by the hegemonic rationality of capitalist exploitation and by the mechanisms (and discourses) of control which contribute to its reproduction. The crumbling of those boundaries which – by 'enclosing' individual and collective action – defined the space of disciplinary control over the labour force in the Fordist age, gives way to a smooth post-Fordist 'non-place'.[73] Here, the aim of social control seems no longer to be the discipline of individuals, but rather the development of effective strategies (and the market is one of these) by which the social productivity embodied in the multitude can be captured and controlled. Following Gilles Deleuze and Felix Guattari:

> Capitalist organisation in its entirety operates less and less by the striation of space-time corresponding to the psycho-social concept of work. Rather, it is as though human alienation through surplus labour were replaced by a generalised machinic enslavement, such that one may furnish surplus value without doing any work.[74]

The concept of multitude conveys a great utility if we employ it to define a social labour force whose productivity and capacity for cooperation is formed independently from any capitalist rationality. Multitude is thus what comes before command and is potentially opposed to it: it is the 'many' (subjects of the same global labour force) who are increasingly 'out of disciplinary control'. Whereas the employed and the 'unemployed', the part-timer and the full-timer, the included and the excluded represent what remains of the multitude once the (neo-liberal) institutions of social government have successfully deployed their strategies of hierarchy and subordination, the multitude expresses the growing irreducibility of the 'social' to economic categories.

With this, I am not proposing an undue shift from political to economic theory, linking the concepts of 'People' and 'multitude' to the transition from Fordism to post-Fordism. Again, the use of the term is here figurative and metaphorical. And continuing with this metaphor, I would suggest that there is a parallelism between, on the one hand, the decline of the *People* and the *working class* – both unitary entities, susceptible of *reductio ad unum*, capable of representation, located in specific territories (the nation-state and the factory), and subject to a disciplinary regime of power – and, on the other, the emergence of the *multitude* and the *socialised labour force* – both multiple entities, irreducible to a unitary representation, unbounded to

---

[72]   Hardt and Negri, *Empire*, p. 209.

[73]   The term 'non-place' is borrowed from Marc Augè, *Non-Places. Introduction to an Anthropology of Supermodernity* (London, 1995).

[74]   Gilles Deleuze and Felix Guattari, *A Thousand Plateaus: Capitalism and Schizophrenia* (Minneapolis, 1987), p. 492.

any specific territory and subject to a new, post-disciplinary regime of control. Negri and Hardt seem to have this in mind when they argue that:

> Imperial command is exercised no longer through the disciplinary modalities of the modern state but rather through the modalities of bio-political control. These modalities have as their basis and their object a productive multitude that cannot be regimented and normalised, but must nonetheless be governed, even in its autonomy. The concept of the People no longer functions as the organised subject of the system of command, and consequently the identity of the People is replaced by the mobility, flexibility, and perpetual differentiation of the multitude.[75]

The transition from Fordism to post-Fordism is thus reflected in the crisis of the nation-state and its regulatory powers – defined primarily as a complex of disciplinary strategies for the normalisation of the working class – as well as in the emergence of new forms of bio-political control of the multitude. However – contrary to the disciplinary project – these strategies of control seem to be increasingly external to the productive dynamics of the new labour force, presenting themselves (as we will see) as a purely punitive and repressive power, without any productive role. It is here that the dissociation between bio-politics and discipline, mentioned in the 'Introduction' as one of the most significant features of contemporary social control strategies, clearly emerges; and to this problem I turn in the next chapter.

---

[75] Hardt and Negri, *Empire*, p. 344.

Chapter 3

The Government of Surplus –
Preliminary Incursions in the Field
of Post-Fordist Social Control

From the 'Discipline of Scarcity' to the 'Government of Surplus'

In this chapter I will outline some emerging features of contemporary social control, and try to interpret them in the light of the transition toward a post-Fordist economic order. As I argued in Chapter 1, my points of reference are, on the one hand, the political economy of punishment (as originally developed by Georg Rusche and Otto Kirchheimer and later by Ian Jankovic, David F. Greenberg and many other materialist criminologists) and, on the other hand, the Foucauldian hypotheses about discipline and the disciplinary society. My analysis will start from the emergence of what I described earlier as a 'post-Fordist surplus', and the basic idea will be that 'post-disciplinary' technologies for the social control of the contemporary labour force – the 'post-Fordist multitude' – are converging toward a new configuration of control which I would define as the 'government of surplus'. This argument is based on the one hand on the exhaustion of the productive role of capitalist management observable in the field of production (as was suggested in Chapter 2) and on the other hand, on the hypothesis that a similar process can be detected also in the field of social control. In other words, if at the level of production we are witnessing the withering away of a 'disciplinary' capitalist organisation of the labour force – together with a dramatic crisis of the mechanisms of social regulation attached to it, especially the welfare state – it is possible to argue that also the strategies of social control are shifting to the 'outside' of the post-Fordist multitude, configuring a 'post-disciplinary order'.

At this point, I would emphasize that my hypotheses do not configure a 'new paradigm', neither are they led by the pretention to offer an exhaustive description of the current processes of transformation. As was the case with the post-Fordist economy, also in the field of social control, together with some processes of radical change, we discover also the persistence of strategies, practices and institutions of social control showing some continuity between past and present: after all, the police, tribunals and prisons are still (and almost everywhere) the main institutions of (formal) social control. In this respect, it could be argued that there is nothing entirely new about contemporary penal strategies – at least in a long-term and historical perspective; that any predilection for 'catastrophic' accounts in criminological theory is more a consequence of distorted perceptions than a result of real social transformations, and that quite often new rhetorics are deployed only to 'cover' old practices.[1]

However, this should not deter us from attempting to analyse what seems to be changing under the apparently unmodified surface of the present condition, and to identify some logics behind these transformations. Before I submit my arguments, however, it is worth going back for a moment to that complex of strategies and rationalities which, under Fordism, defined the relationship between social control and the capitalist form of production. This is necessary because, as we have seen, the process of development of industrial capitalism – from the phase of 'primitive accumulation' to the apogee of Fordism – saw the technologies of control playing a vital role in the disciplinary rationalisation of production and in the subjugation of the labour force to capitalist rationality: now, it is precisely the crisis affecting this 'productive' role of social control that stands at the core of my hypothesis.

Let us turn again to Michel Foucault and in particular to his theories about *governmentality, discipline* and *bio-power*. These are in fact the basic conceptual coordinates through which Foucault 'mapped' Western modernity and its apparatuses of power, thus forging an important tool for reconstructing the various relationships between disciplinary control and the industrial system of production; and this map inspired also some influential perspectives within the political economy of punishment.[2]

The mind goes inevitably to *Discipline and Punish*. In fact, it is here that Foucault deals explicitly with the issue of penality and of its historical configurations, devolving great attention to the processes of transformation of the capitalist economy and to their effects on the universe of punishment. It should be noted, however, that his research on the 'birth of the prison' represents only a systematisation of analyses and reflections which the French philosopher had been conducting for several years (I refer here in particular to the courses held at the *Collége de France* between 1970 and 1974[3]). In this respect, Foucault's less systematic works also deserve consideration, because in these materials quite often we find his most interesting insights about the relationships between systems of production and modes of social control.[4] Broadly speaking, the aim of the Foucauldian project is to reconstruct a genealogical map of contemporary technologies of power. According to Foucault, this map permits a de-codification of the intrinsic economies and rationalities of the various systems of penal control which have emerged through the history of Western societies. The main question is: how could these systems shift from a 'sovereign' logic based on the destruction of deviance, toward a new rationality grounded on the productivity of power?

---

[1] As suggested, among others, by Pat O'Malley. This author, though very attentive to the transformations of penality implied by the transition to a neo-liberal order, warns about the importance of politics, rhetoric and narratives in the penal field. See for example Pat O'Malley, 'Criminologies of Catastrophe? Understanding Criminal Justice on the Edge of the Millennium', *The Australian and New Zealand Journal of Criminology*, 33/2 (2000): 153–167.

[2] For a general reconstruction of the influence of Foucauldian and Marxist theories on the sociology of punishment see in particular David Garland, *Punishment and Modern Society: A Study in Social Theory* (Oxford, 1990).

[3] Michel Foucault, *Dits et écrits. Tome II: 1970–1975* (Paris, 1994).

[4] For an example, see Michel Foucault, 'Questions of Method', in Graham Burchel, Colin Gordon and Peter Miller (eds), *The Foucault Effect. Studies in Governmentality* (Chicago, 1991), pp. 73–86.

The disciplinary technologies described in *Discipline and Punish* define the context in which we can locate the transition from the torture to the prison; that is, from a *destructive* power to a *transformative* one. Conversely, we can understand the emergence of the disciplinary universe only if we situate it within a much wider political process: the 'governmentalisation' of power.[5] As I mentioned in the Introduction, this means the transition from a rationality based on the religious image of the 'pastoral power', toward a practice of power inspired by a secularised 'science of government': the science of government determined a radical redefinition of the 'knowledge-power' complex, within which the new disciplinary techniques – and the prison in particular – could emerge. In the Classic Age, a sovereign power deploying its resources and punitive techniques in order to preserve its own absolute prerogatives, was gradually replaced by a governmental power affecting the population and its potential for productivity. Thus Foucault defines governmentality as:

> The ensemble formed by the institutions, procedures, analyses and reflections, the calculations and tactics that allow the exercise of this very specific albeit complex form of power, which has as its target population, as its principal form of knowledge political economy, and as its essential technical means apparatuses of security.[6]

In other words, governmentality means the irruption of the 'political economy' into the *raison d'état*: that is, into the complex of *savoirs* concerning the proper management of a territory and of its population. This event involves a deep change in the practices, institutions and strategies of government: from that historical moment, to govern a State would mean to maximise the productive potentialities of the population, to enhance its welfare and to set up appropriate mechanisms for the scientific measurement of results – social statistics, census, national accounting, and so on.[7]

The idea that it was possible to exert an influence on the population and its economic processes by constructing rational strategies of government, gave birth to new 'regimes of practices': that is, to a system of power and knowledge defined by the new objects of government – economic production, public health, sexuality and hygiene. A power inspired by the principle of self-perpetuation, whose practices were shaped by the idea that a sovereign should always be able to neutralise whatever danger is posed to its own existence, was thus replaced by a power acting as a positive agent in the transformation of reality. And this happened through a continuous exchange of knowledge, practices and technologies between the political system and the emerging biological and social sciences.[8] The concept of 'power' referred now to the capacity to regulate a population and to govern a 'social body': a productive

---

[5] On the concept of 'governmentality' and its many applications to the field of social science and social history, see Mitchell Dean, *Governmentality. Power and Rule in Modern Society* (London, 1999).

[6] Michel Foucault, 'Governmentality', in Burchell, Gordon and Miller (eds), *The Foucault Effect*, p. 102.

[7] For a clear synthesis of the importance of the 'governmentality' hypothesis in the criminological context (though in a critical vein), see David Garland, '"Governmentality" and the Problem of Crime: Foucault, Criminology, Sociology', *Theoretical Criminology*, 1/2 (1997): 173–214.

[8] Dario Melossi reconstructs the emergence of this 'transformative power' in his study of the concept of 'social control' in the United States (as an alternative to the concept of 'State', hegemonic in European history). According to Melossi, 'social control' summarises power's ability to shape a

government, capable of insinuating itself deeply inside the complex interactions between social phenomena, productive processes, and vital fluxes. These interactions should no longer be blocked or repressed, but directed, channelled and organised efficiently. It is in this context that 'the social' (whose 'death' was already announced in the late 1970s by Jean Baudrillard) emerged as a new field of power.[9] Grounded as it was in the emerging political economy, the transition from *sovereignty* to *governmentality* marked the definitive absorption of a capitalist economic rationality by the science of government. Again in Foucault's words:

> The working-out of this population-wealth problem (in its different concrete aspects: taxation, scarcity, depopulation, idleness-beggary-vagabondage) constitutes one of the conditions of formation of political economy. The latter develops when it is realized that the resources-population relationship can no longer be fully managed through a coercive regulatory system ... [10]

Thus, the transcendence of a sovereign power standing outside and above the reality over which it ruled, gave way to the immanence of a government embedded in the very processes it regulated. No longer would the coordinates of this new power be 'territory' – as the geographical delimitation of the monopoly over violence – 'sovereignty' – as the transcendental legitimation of that monopoly – and the 'People' – as the target of that violence. Instead, the field of exercise of this new governmental power would be the triad 'territory-population-wealth': a complex organism, a social body with its own dynamics of production and reproduction, consumption and waste, health and disease – a social realm whose resources are scarce and must be governed according to the principles of liberal political economy.

   Together with this new rationality, Foucault also describes the formation of those dispositives and practices of 'security' whose function was to guarantee the correct functioning of the governmental apparatus and to preserve the principle of economic maximisation. Foucault refers here to various practices for the control and the surveillance of the population, but also to public education, social insurance and national health: in sum, all the technologies necessary to enhance and perpetuate the productivity of a population.[11] Social control and the field of penality belong to this set of apparatuses of security, and here, following Foucault, the 'analytics of governmentality' meshes with the 'microphysics of disciplinary power'. Indeed, the

---

society, to inform its relations of production, its cultural phenomena and the formation of a 'public oipinion'. Dario Melossi, *The State of Social Control* (Cambridge, 1990).

[9] On the 'death of the social', see Jean Baudrillard, *In the Shadow of the Silent Majorities or 'the Death of the Social'* (New York, 1983). More recently: Nicholas Rose, 'The Death of the Social? Refiguring the Territory of Government', *Economy and Society*, 25/3 (1996): 327–356.

[10] Michel Foucault, 'Security, Territory, and Population', in *Essential Works of Foucault 1954–1984, vol. I*, Edited by Paul Rabinow (New York, 1997), p. 69.

[11] This is Foucault's definition of the 'apparatuses of security', formulated during a lecture at the *Collége de France* in 1978: 'The setting in place of mechanisms of security ... mechanisms or modes of state intervention whose function is to assure the security of those natural phenomena, economic processes and the intrinsic processes of population: this is what becomes the basic objective of governmental rationality' (quoted in Graham Burchell, 'Governmental Rationality', in Burchell, Gordon and Miller, *The Foucault Effect*, p. 19).

disciplinary technologies are not precedent to governmentality, something like a middle stage between the death of the sovereign power and the birth of the new science of government. Disciplinary control is instead immanent to governmentality and bio-power: governmentality deals with the productive government of the population as a whole, whereas disciplines concentrate on the individual body as a peculiar component of that population.

In this context, penality – one of the most significant concretisations of the disciplinary logic – plays a completely different role from the one it had in the age of sovereignty: it takes part in the process of diffusion of a productive and economic conception of power. In fact, only at this stage could modern society witness the sunset of torture with its ritual of physical destruction, and the dawn of a silent and discrete penality operating with systematic regularity in the penumbra of the total institutions. Punishment became a process through which subjects could be *produced, not destroyed*: subjects whose utility – both as individuals and as parts of a productive population – would be realised in the process of work.[12]

Again, at the centre we find the body. The various technologies of power act on the body and imprint their traces on it: on the body was consumed the spectacular violence of Damien's torture in the opening pages of *Discipline and Punish*; on the body are now grounded the disciplinary technologies announcing the end of those public torments. The same body on which the unlimited destructive violence of the sovereign power was exercised, becomes now the peculiar object of the new disciplinary practices. It catalyses the new regulatory knowledge (biology, statistics, medicine, psychiatry, social psychology, criminology); the new regulatory institutions (schools, hospitals, asylums, prisons, barracks); the new regulatory practices (inquiry, survey, exam, therapy, sentence):

> The factory, the school, the prison, or the hospitals have the object of binding the individual to a process of production, training, or correction of the producers. It's a matter of guaranteeing production, or the producers, in terms of a particular norm. This means that we can draw a contrast between the confinement of the eighteenth century, which excluded individuals from the social circle, and the confinement that appeared in the nineteenth century, which had the function of attaching individuals to the producer's apparatuses of production, training, reform or correction.[13]

As I said earlier, the rationality of disciplinary and governmental bio-power is clearly based on the idea of a productive power. However, in order to interpret this productivity a very important aspect needs to be clarified: the dispositives of power and control had to be activated because there was a socially diffused un-productivity to be remedied for, a latent dispersion of resources to be contained and a deficit of productive cooperation to be filled. Here, *the capitalist relations of production stood above and beyond the labour force*, they had to force it to forms of cooperation for

---

12   'The body no longer has to be marked; it must be trained and retrained; its time must be measured out and fully used; its forces must be continuously applied to labour. The prison form of penality corresponds to the wage form of labour': Michel Foucault, 'The Punitive Society', in *Essential Works of Foucault 1954–1984, vol. I*, p. 35.

13   Michel Foucault, 'Truth and Juridical Forms', in *Essential Works of Foucault 1954–1984, vol. III*, Edited by James D. Faubion (New York, 2000), p. 78.

which it appeared inadequate, unprepared, insufficiently socialised and often explicitly reluctant.[14]

The prison and the other disciplinary institutions materialised a new concept of space and time applied both to the individual bodies and to the population as a whole. The synchronisation of movements, the regulation of masses of individuals within the factory, the connection between the body and the machine: all these were aspects of a peculiar economic rationality initially shaped by the emergence of the industrial production and consolidated later by the development of Fordist capitalism. The disciplinary technologies of control were an expression of this rationality, once it could be translated into specific models of punishment.[15] The lines of this evolution would develop simultaneously both inside the factory – where Taylor's *Principles of Scientific Management* would enhance and govern the productivity of labour – and outside it – where Keynesian policies would regulate the relation between economy and society through the state's intervention in the social processes.[16]

Economic management, state regulation and the social control of deviance: in all these strategies we detect a governmental rationality which reacts to the workforce's insufficiencies, losses and lack of cooperation: these were all strategies for the disciplining of the labour-force within a capitalist model of production. The factory had to be governed 'scientifically' in order to limit the lack of productivity; the social body had to be governed 'scientifically' in order to reduce the lack of inclusion caused by the anarchy of the market; deviance had to be treated 'scientifically' in order to contain the lack of socialization which derived from the failure of the other practices of government:

> The proper treatment of offenders required individualized, corrective measures carefully adapted to the specific case or the particular problem – not a uniform penalty tariff, mechanically dispensed. One needed expert knowledge, scientific research, and flexible instruments of intervention, as well as a willingness to regulate aspects of life which classical liberalism had deemed beyond the proper reach of government. The normative

---

[14] I would agree with Barry Vaughan that 'The development of the prison, as an alternative to capital punishment, is the story of how the burgeoning middle class tried to impose their own standards of behaviour upon those who were thought to be worthy of inclusion within society but not yet able to take their place voluntarily': Barry Vaughan, 'Punishment and Conditional Citizenship', *Punishment & Society*, 2/1 (2000): 28. In other words, criminals were 'incomplete citizens', who could be 'completed' through discipline and rehabilitation. This idea synthesises the 'inclusive' project of modern penal institutions.

[15] 'People's time had to be offered to the production apparatus; the production apparatus had to be able to use people's living time, their time of existence. The control was exerted for that reason and in that form': Foucault, 'Truth and Juridical Forms', p. 80.

[16] On the 'disciplinary-governmental complex', in which we find both the Taylorist organisation of production and the welfarist regulation of society, writes Maurizio Lazzarato: 'Inside the factory, Taylorism radicalises scientifically the reduction of the body to an organism (its reduction to mechanic schemes). On the other hand, the welfare state articulates and diffuses the population through reproduction, multiplying the figures of subjugation (control over the family, the women, the children, health, education and old age)': Maurizio Lazzarato, *Lavoro Immateriale. Forme di vita e produzione di soggettività* (Verona, 1997).

system of law had to give way to the normalizing system of science, punishment had to be replaced by treatment.[17]

From a point of view internal to the political economy of punishment, this is an effective description of the symbiosis between economic production, social processes and institutional practices of control which characterised in particular the Fordist age. What these diverse fields of State intervention had in common was an ideology which saw the social body as affected by a structural scarcity, a permanent disadvantage, a deficit to which the power to punish (and more generally the governmental 'power to regulate') could oppose effective remedies. David Garland defines this as the 'modernist project', whose expected result was – reversing Jock Young's definition – an 'inclusive society'.[18] However, what both Garland and Young seem to overlook is the fact that these policies of (at least in principle) universal inclusion were inextricably linked to the development of the mass industrial production, to the Fordist organisation of work and to a coherent model of citizenship based on waged labour. They aimed at maximising the productive capacity of a labour force deemed to be in need of socialisation and discipline, whose productive deficits emerged in the form of deviance, criminality, illness, unemployment or poverty. Only within such a paradigm of social citizenship can we make sense of the relationship between welfare and penality, the prison and the factory, discipline and capitalist production: the transformative project of disciplinary control was inscribed in a broader project of (potentially) universal citizenship, and the role of the disciplinary prison was to produce 'good citizens', by producing efficient workers.[19]

Therefore, the question is: what technologies of control and rationalities of power are emerging from the crisis of Fordism and of its systems of social regulation? What technologies of control follow the end of the industrial phase of capitalist development? Is any disciplinary project still meaningful, given the emergence of a post-Fordist, post-industrial labour force? In other words: what new governmental rationalities are announced by the transition from a regime of social *scarcity* toward a regime of social *surplus*?

---

[17] David Garland, *The Culture of Control. Crime and Social Order in Contemporary Society* (Oxford, 2001), p. 40. For an accurate description of the central themes of 'welfarist criminology' and its correctional ideology, see also David Garland, *Punishment and Welfare: A History of Penal Strategies* (Aldershot, 1985).

[18] Jock Young, *The Exclusive Society* (London, 1999).

[19] 'Punishment is used against those who have fallen below the standards which are expected of all citizens but is also used to mould them into citizens – hence punishment is not only a deterrent but is also deployed as a device for character-transformation. It is used on those who are conditional citizens, people who may be moulded into full citizens but who are, at present, failing to display the requisite qualities expected of citizens': Vaughan, 'Punishment and Conditional Citizenship', p. 26. The term 'universal citizenship' should be taken with some caution: modern Western citizenship has never been a truly 'universal' system, as many feminist and post-colonial theorists have shown. Nonetheless, we can agree that its underlying 'logic' was inclusive, though this inclusion was tailored around the hegemonic image of the male, white, working subject.

Control as 'Non-Knowledge'

In the history of Western capitalism, dramatic economic transformations have always been characterised by huge contradictions, social conflicts and changes in the institutions and practices of social regulation. When new 'regimes of accumulation' – to borrow the terminology of the 'regulation school' – appear, the whole realm of social life is profoundly reshaped. The transition from Fordism to post-Fordism, and in particular the process of transformation of the contemporary labour force into a productive *multitude* quite distant from the industrial 'working class', do not seem to make an exception to this rule. In fact, significant changes can be observed in the field of contemporary governmental rationality and its 'apparatuses of security'.

What I defined in Chapter 2 as the 'social surplus', can be described as a complex of subjectivities that are *beyond the reach of the disciplinary technologies*: their condition of poverty, marginalisation and social exclusion is the sign of a widening contradiction between a model of citizenship still based on the Fordist paradigm of work, and a sphere of production that is abolishing precisely that kind of work – through the imposition of flexibility, precarisation, deregulation, and so on. On the other hand, the 'productive surplus' can be defined as a complex of subjectivities *beyond the reach of the capitalist rationality*: in fact, their experience of work shows a growing contradiction between a potentially free and cooperative productivity, and a structure of production nonetheless enforcing competition and the exploitation of labour.[20]

By referring to social exclusion, unemployment and marginality as conditions of 'social surplus', I try to show two poles of a structural contradiction of our times. On the one hand we live in a society whose dynamics of inclusion are mediated by work conceived as 'job' – as a full-time, guaranteed and stable employment in the formal economy: a society which confers the right to citizenship only to those individuals who can be defined as proper 'workers'. On the other hand however, we witness the emergence of a structure of production that is based exactly on the precarisation and fragmentation of work.[21] In other words, access to income, citizenship and social integration is linked to a requisite that is disappearing from the landscape of the post-Fordist 'material constitution'.[22]

Here I would identify a first side of a contradiction which the contemporary strategies of control try to contain, repress or inhibit, because of its potentially subversive consequences for the social order: the contradiction between the requisites which the formal constitution of our society requires people to satisfy, and the resources offered by the post-Fordist material constitution. In this context, the old dichotomy for which the poor, the marginalised and the excluded were at once 'threats' to and 'resources' for capitalist development, takes a different tone: when

---

[20] This aspect will become clearer in the final section of this chapter, particularly in the paragraph entitled 'The Bridled Net'.

[21] For a paradigmatic example of this paradox, see the condition of immigrants in Europe described in chapter 5.

[22] On the concept of 'material constitution' – the productive structure of a society – as opposed to the 'formal constitution' – the juridical formalisation of that economic structure – see Antonio Negri, *Insurgencies. Constituent Power and the Modern State* (Minneapolis, 1999).

social exclusion becomes an existential condition for a growing fraction of the post-Fordist labour force, new strategies of control become necessary, because any economic 'resource' can easily turn itself into a potential 'threat' to the stability of the whole system.[23]

On the other hand, when I speak of immaterial labour, intellectualisation of production, linguistic work and the 'general intellect', and define these as the emerging features of a new 'productive surplus', I try to outline a further (and complementary) contradiction: the contradiction between a labour force possessing the instruments, capacities and productive attitudes which could allow it to overcome the capitalist control over (and organisation of) work, and a system of production which nonetheless imposes itself from the outside as a parasitic command. Following Hannah Arendt, this could be synthesised as the contradiction between *activity* – social cooperation – and *work* – production of surplus value.[24] What we see here is a conflict between a social productivity which, being grounded in the human intellect itself (communication, invention, creativity), tends to escape any capitalist direction, and a managerial rationality which nonetheless must impose itself.[25]

In other words, the emergence of a 'social surplus' (the underclass, the permanently unemployed, working poor, informal workers, etc.) suggests that the old disciplinary technologies (based on the industrial work-ethic and work-organisation) become useless, because the economic structure on which they were grounded is disappearing. As regards the growing 'productive surplus' (immaterial labour, creative work, hi-tech production, etc.), on the other hand, those technologies appear to be dysfunctional, because immaterial production is based precisely on the refusal of any rigid disciplinary logic. All this said, in order to trace the coordinates of the new relations between production and control we must start from the transition which sees the industrial labour force – the working class – being transformed into a fully socialised labour force – the multitude – whose potential productivity escapes the rationality of capitalist direction. This means that we should analyse the new geographies of control starting from the crisis of the disciplinary rationality: that is, from the crisis of a model of power inscribed in the body of a labour force that was located within the times and places defined by industrial production.

This transition cannot be overlooked. The model of power which informed the disciplinary technologies was grounded on an individualised knowledge about the bodies, the individuals and the forms of cooperation to which they had to be forced. The knowledge-power complex on which disciplinary control was based, shaped a process of individualisation and produced an exact cartography of the productive dynamics of the population. This is a framework which Foucault discovered in the prison but also in the factory, the hospital, the school, the asylum, the barrack, and society at large. Knowledge had to be scientifically extracted from the human body to be later applied to it reflexively (in the form of disciplinary

---

23   See Christopher Adamson, 'Toward a Marxian Penology: Captive Criminal Populations as Economic Threats and Resources', *Social Problems*, 31/4 (1984): 435–458.

24   Hannah Arendt, *Labor, Work, Action* (Trustee, 1987).

25   On this aspect of the 'post-Fordist condition' see Romano Alquati, *Lavoro e attività. Per un'analisi della schiavitù neomoderna* (Rome, 1997).

practices of control), when a multiplicity of bodies had to be organised within the field of production:

> In an institution like the factory, for example, the worker's labour and the worker's knowledge about his own labour, the technical improvements – the little inventions and discoveries, the micro-adaptations he's able to implement in the course of his labour – are immediately recorded, thus extracted from his practice, accumulated by the power exercised over him through supervision. In this way, the worker's labour is gradually absorbed into a certain technical knowledge of production which will enable a strengthening of control. So we see how there forms a knowledge that's extracted from the individuals themselves and derived from their own behaviour.[26]

However, what seems to be vanishing with the transition toward a regime of surplus is precisely the possibility to gather this knowledge from the productive body of the post-Fordist multitude. In fact, this 'knowledge of production' remains now in the hands of the labour force; the multitude escapes the dispositives of control and what Deleuze and Guattari defined 'apparatuses of capture',[27] and appears irreducible to the categories through which capitalist rationality imposes its own hierarchies on work: 'labour' and 'value', 'employment' and 'unemployment', 'time of work' and 'time of non-work', 'production' and 'reproduction'. This knowledge cannot be expropriated because it is grounded on the most 'human' among human faculties – language, affect, communication, creativity, thought: something which cannot be measured by economic categories – as was instead the case with the industrial production, where time was a proper measurement of individual productivity and space defined the borders within which labour exploitation could take place.

If the *regime of scarcity* can be defined – in Foucauldian terms – as the universe in which a 'power-knowledge' operated, perhaps we can describe the regime of the post-Fordist surplus as the field of exercise of a power characterised by a condition of *non-knowledge*. In fact, the concrete peculiarities of the multitude, its constitutive features, its potential behaviours and the many unforeseeable interactions to which it can give birth escape any precise definition. In other words, the post-Fordist labour force – flexible, mobile and permanently on the border between inclusion and exclusion, work and non-work, formal and informal economies, legal and illegal activities – does not offer itself to the full knowledge of the mechanisms of power and control. As we will see, it seems to be precisely this incapacity to make a clear distinction between 'threats' and 'resources', between the 'dangerous' and the 'labourious' classes or, to follow another sociologically successful dichotomy, between 'social junk' and 'social dynamite', which compels the institutions of social control to regroup whole sectors of the post-Fordist labour force as 'categories at risk', and to deploy consequent strategies of confinement, incapacitation and surveillance.

No longer constrained within any specific time and place; no longer organised in those 'total institutions' that were the Fordist factories; no longer homogeneous and predictable as the industrial working class was, the multitude defies power's technologies of knowledge and capitalist rationality. This condition of non-knowledge seems to

---

[26]   Foucault, 'Truth and Juridical Forms', pp. 83–84.
[27]   Gilles Deleuze and Felix Guattari, *A Thousand Plateaus. Capitalism and Schizophrenia* (Minneapolis, 1987).

push the dispositives of control toward a post-disciplinary order, in which individuals and their concreteness disappear as objects for social control. As I will show in the next pages, the new emerging model of control is therefore incorporating risk based strategies, whose aim is to reduce a social complexity that is going out of control. Unknowable individuals are thus replaced by artificially constructed categories.

The Panopticon and Beyond: Signs of a Post-Disciplinary Order

After being 'popularised' by Michel Foucault, Jeremy Bentham's *Panopticon* has been considered for a long time the most significant image of the disciplinary technology. Its architecture melts knowledge and power in the same plastic structure, thus offering a suggestive historical metaphor of the emergence of strategies aiming to organise the bodies in a defined space and time. However, the Panopticon is not a peculiar historical institution: in fact, it symbolises a broader rationality which gave birth to a project for the maximisation of social forces. The Panopticon allows the techniques of disciplinary power to operate from inside the social body, discretely and without interfering with the various social practices (production, correction, education, care, religion, etc.), to which they are applied. Here, the project of a productive power is visually materialised: panoptic power regulates, ordinates and organises the bodies in order to enhance their normalisation, productivity, rationality and efficiency.

In this respect, the Panopticon is a concretisation of the modern capitalist utopia of a continuous and total visibility of the subordinates by the eye of power: the 'one' can observe the 'many' because they know exactly where and when to watch; the many conform meticulously to the norm because they never know exactly from where and in which moment they will actually be observed. The exercise of panoptical power is automatically also an act of knowledge: power knows everything about the observed people, and its gaze is at the same time the source and product of knowledge. On the other hand, the many who are observed never know enough about the power that is watching them. It is exactly around this imbalance between a power that knows and a mass that doesn't know, that the internal economy and rationality of disciplinary power can establish itself successfully. In turn, it is this rationality that allows for the progressive constitution of a disciplinary society: a society defined by the diffusion of this 'unequal knowledge' (and of its main protagonist: the 'expert') across various fields of power: the school (where pupils are exposed to the eye of the teacher); the hospital (where patients are scrutinised by the eye of the doctor); the factory (where workers are put under the surveillance of 'scientifically organised' supervisors); the prison (in which guards, officers and the correctional personnel concentrate their eyes on the prisoners).

Now, it seems that this concatenation of power and knowledge – synthesising in fact the whole 'political economy' of the disciplinary system – is undergoing a process of disarticulation. No longer grounded on a detailed knowledge about the subject, technologies of control seem to be shifting towards a regime of preventive surveillance and containment of whole categories of individuals. What appears as increasingly difficult at the individual level – a disciplinary knowledge, a scientific treatment of individual 'abnormalities' and a clear distinction between the 'normal' and the 'pathological' – is nonetheless necessary at an aggregate level. The disciplinary knowledge about individuals thus gives way to the artificial construction of categories defined by risk.

The metaphor of Panopticon has been recently rediscovered in some suggestive analyses of the transformations of social control in post-modern societies. For instance, Thomas Mathiesen has argued that contemporary strategies of control are converging toward the constitution of a post-panoptical regime called *Synopticon*.[28] In what Guy Debord defined as a 'society of spectacle', it is no longer the 'few' who observe the 'many' to make sure that they will conform to the rules, but the many – constantly transformed into a docile and uncritical 'public opinion' – who watch the gestures of the few (mainly through the mass media) thus internalising those models, attitudes, behaviours and values through which they will become responsible individuals and trustable consumers. The couple 'power-knowledge' which defined the rationality of disciplinary power is replaced here by the couple 'spectacle-image', whose aim is not the *production of disciplined producers* (as was the case with the panoptical technology) but the *reproduction of enthusiastic consumers*.

Mathiesen grounds this analysis of social control on the transition from a 'producer society' towards a 'consumer society'.[29] Clearly, the importance of this transition cannot be overlooked. The 'aesthetic of consumption' pervading contemporary society is something very distant from – and to some extent even in contradiction with – the 'ethic of work' which shaped industrial society. Whereas the reproduction of a work *ethic* had to be enforced by a complex of disciplinary strategies oriented to the normalisation of individuals, the instillation of a consumerist *aesthetic* requires something very different: perhaps a system of control which leaves the individual – at least in theory – as free (to choose what and how to consume) as possible. If the panoptical model struggled to generalise conformity, the *synoptical* strategy has to allow for different lifestyles to express themselves freely – and to channel them into the theatre of consumption.[30]

Another suggestive analysis sees the panoptical model as being replaced by an *Oligopticon*: that is, by a rationality of control for which some restricted social

---

[28] Thomas Mathiesen, 'The Viewer Society: Michel Foucault's Panopticon Revisited', *Theoretical Criminology*, 1–2 (1997): 215–234.

[29] See for example, Zygmunt Bauman, *Work, Consumerism and the New Poor* (Milton Keynes, 1998).

[30] We are warned by David Garland not to take the rhetoric of 'responsibility', 'freedom' and 'agency' surrounding current penal technologies too seriously. The concept of 'agency' presupposes fixed boundaries within which some behaviours are deemed acceptable as far as they satisfy some predefined expectations (which in our society tend to correspond to the 'aesthetic of consumption' mentioned earlier). Freedom denotes a condition of self-determination not linked to any particular set of expectations: Garland, '"Governmentality"' and the Problem of Crime', p. 192. The pervasive character of consumerism, and its effects on crime control strategies are made particularly visible both by the privatisation of security and by the fact that experiences of consumption and leisure are increasingly turned into unobtrusive 'crime control' scenarios. On these aspects, see in particular Clifford Shearing and Philip Stenning, 'Private Security: Implications for Social Control', *Social Problems*, 30/5 (1983): 493–506 and 'From the Panopticon to Disney World: the Development of Discipline', in Anthony Doob and Edward Greenspan (eds), *Perspectives in Criminal Law* (Ontario, 1985), pp. 335–349.

groups exercise a power of surveillance on other selected social groups.[31] This perspective is based in particular on Zygmunt Bauman's distinction between the 'repressed' (those groups whose lack of material resources excludes them from consumption), and the 'seduced' (those people who are in the condition to have access to the temples of leisure, consumption and social inclusion): in contemporary segmented societies, the former exercise a power of surveillance, seclusion and confinement on the latter.[32]

However interesting these accounts might be, they do not seem to give a substantial contribution to my effort at reconfiguring the territory of the political economy of punishment. In fact, they concentrate on the concept of consumption, whereas at the core of my analysis stands the category of *production*. It is thus at the transformations of work – more than at those changes affecting the styles of consumption – that we have to look if we are to understand the transition from Fordism to post-Fordism and its influences on the field of social control. It must be said, however, that both the image of the *Synopticon* and the *Oligopticon* point to a crisis of the disciplinary utopia. The shared assumption is in fact that this grand narrative of modernity is leaving way to technologies of control which explicitly reject that disciplinary project.

If we follow the traces of this rejection, we discover the diffusion of technologies of control based on three peculiar practices: *generalised surveillance, selectivity of access* and *mass confinement*. However, not always do these practices imply the creation of new institutions of control. As I will try to show in the next pages, the post-panoptical order is often characterised by the persistence of old institutions (and especially the 'panoptical institution' *par excellence*: the prison), whose rationality, however, seems to be undergoing a process of transformation inspired by the emergence of new objectives. In order to offer a more precise description of this rationality, I will select some peculiar settings in which it is becoming more visible. In the remainder of this chapter I submit some ideas concerning two of them – the *metropolis* and the *internet* – whereas the next chapter will concentrate more deeply on the *prison*, to end in chapter 5 with an analysis of the *immigration detention centre*.

At first sight, it would seem that each of these 'social control-scenarios' displays the prominence of one kind of practices in particular. Thus, the prison and the immigration detention centre would offer clear examples of mass-confinement; the urban landscape would be the field of new practices of generalised surveillance, and the internet represents a public sphere increasingly affected by strategies of privatisation and selectivity of access. However, the point of view presented here is quite different: I selected these examples because they seem to be paradigmatic (for their strategic role in the neo-liberal order) of the current transformations of social control, but the three mentioned technologies of control characterise to some extent all of them simultaneously. Just to offer a few examples: the task of confining the 'social waste' produced by the neo-liberal economy and the downsizing of the welfare state, is performed by the prison and the immigration detention centre as well as by the urban ghettoes – and this seems true in particular for the American cities where,

---

[31] Robert Boyne, 'Post-Panopticism', *Economy and Society*, 29/2 (2000): 285–307.

[32] Zygmunt Bauman, 'Is There a Postmodern Sociology?', *Theory, Culture and Society*, 5/2-3 (1988): 217–237.

following Loic Wacquant, a 'deadly symbiosis' is linking the prison to the ghetto, thus entrapping the African-American poor.[33] In the same vein, the systematic exclusion of some categories of people (defined, as we will see, by their *dangerousness*), characterises the post-Fordist cities (in which the poor, the homeless and the new 'strangers' are kept away from many public and private spaces) as well as the post-disciplinary prisons. Finally, the selectivity of access finds its clearest concretization in the urban landscape, with the diffusion of 'no-go areas' and 'gated communities', but the same logic inspires some emerging policies for the control of information (and particularly electronic information), based on the imposition of limits to access. And the same holds true for the generalisation of surveillance.

All this being said, it is only for reasons of clarity that I will connect each technology to its 'most paradigmatic' field of deployment. Thus, I will start with the diffusion of strategies of 'mass surveillance' within the post-modern cities: here our attention will be attracted by the growing presence of CCTV systems, the self-constitution of 'gated communities' and the rhetoric of situational crime prevention. I will argue that all these policies and practices share a peculiar post-Fordist rationality of control: increasingly indifferent to the individual and oriented to whole categories of (potentially dangerous) 'others'. In the last section of this chapter I throw some light on the virtual world of the *net*: nothing more than a sketchy description of the diffusion of strategies of control and policies of privatisation whose aim is to prevent the post-Fordist labour force from horizontal access to (electronic) information and to (immaterial) resources.

In the next chapter, a critical analysis of 'mass confinement' will lead us to the changing role of imprisonment. Here my starting point will be the United States, whose experiment with mass incarceration is well known and has inspired a growing literature about its social causes and consequences.[34] However, the apparent exceptionalism of the American prison experiment should not prevent us from attempting to follow the diffusion of comparable policies in other places and different contexts. In fact, the renewed role of imprisonment – and other related practices, such as the detention of undocumented foreigners in immigration detention centres around the world – as an instrument for the control of the huge social contradictions implied by the transition to a neo-liberal order, can be observed also in many European countries whose 'variously' detained populations are growing steadily. However, more interesting than the commonalities in the diffusion of detention as a technology of control is the fact that these transcontinental experiments in 'warehousing' seem to follow the same criteria for the selection of their 'victims'. Therefore the main question will be: what makes some fractions of the post-Fordist labour force so suitable for mass confinement on both sides of the Atlantic Sea?

---

[33] Loic Wacquant, 'Deadly Symbiosis. When Ghetto and Prison Meet and Mesh', in David Garland (ed.), *Mass Imprisonment. Social Causes and Consequences* (London, 2001), pp. 82–120.

[34] See for example Nils Christie, *Crime Control as Industry: Toward Gulags Western Style* (London, 1994).

The Punitive Metropolis

In criminological literature, the city has been widely investigated both as a scenario for ambitious projects of inclusive and democratic social organisation, and as the site of emerging dystopias of total control and urban segregation.[35] In this context, the social geography of the city has been widely analysed as the site of disciplinary technologies: in *Discipline and Punish* Michel Foucault described the modern utopia of a 'carceral city' in which punitive practices, no longer confined within the walls of total institutions like the prison, would expand to the outside and shape the urban landscape by setting up an infinite theatre of micro-practices of punishment and correction. Thus, according to the French philosopher we would see:

> ... at the very centre of the carceral city, the formation of the insidious leniencies, unavowable petty cruelties, small acts of cunning, calculated methods, techniques, 'sciences' that permit the fabrication of the disciplinary individual.[36]

Two decades later we discover, with Mike Davis, that contemporary Los Angeles – probably the emblem of the post-Fordist city – is not a perfect mechanism of disciplinary techniques but a 'city of quartz', a post-modern prismatic fortress in which obsessions of social control are reflected and amplified, thus creating distorted images of seclusion that are very distant from the disciplinary dreams described by Foucault.[37] It would seem that the disciplinary practices have in fact abandoned the prison, but they are not expanding beyond its perimeter and inside the urban space – as Foucault had announced and others after him had observed:[38] instead, they seem to be abandoning the city as well.

No longer simply a 'theatre' of control, the metropolis itself becomes now a 'regime of practices' of control and surveillance: contemporary urban architecture – with its cleansed shopping malls and purified areas (what Marc Augè defines as 'non-places') – does not simply make surveillance possible or easier, as was the case with the Foucauldian carceral and panoptical city. In fact, architecture becomes itself a dispositive of surveillance, a mechanism of 'environmental control' once again not directed at individuals but at whole classes of subjects. The individual deviant is replaced here by a variety of 'criminogenic situations'[39] – including individuals and

---

[35] For an important example of the progressive attitude see Robert Park and Ernest Burgess, *The City* (Chicago, 1967). The catastrophic perspective is well exemplified by the writings of Mike Davis, who borrows some ideas from the 'Chicago School', but develops them in a very innovative direction. See Mike Davis, *Beyond Blade Runner: Urban Control. The Ecology of Fear* (Westfield, 1992).

[36] Michel Foucault, *Discipline and Punish* (London, 1991), p. 308.

[37] Mike Davis, *City of Quartz. Excavating the Future in Los Angeles* (New York, 1992).

[38] In the early 1980s, Stanley Cohen concentrated his attention on the city as a social laboratory in which some emerging features of contemporary control strategies could be observed, but he seemed to follow the disciplinary hypothesis – though with a particular attention to the processes of social exclusion already visible in the expanding 'zones of neglect': Stanley Cohen, *Visions of Social Control* (Cambridge, 1985), pp. 197–235.

[39] According to Ronald Clarke, situational crime prevention implies a 'paradigm shift involved in focusing on criminogenic situations rather than so exclusively on criminal actors': Ronald V. Clarke, 'Situational Crime Prevention', *Crime and Justice. A Review of Research*, 19 (1995): 92.

groups, human beings and physical objects, ecological issues and social problems. The common element is a perceived risk and the necessity to prevent it. Technologies of post-disciplinary urban control such as CPTED (*Crime Prevention Through Environmental Design*) and 'situational crime prevention' more generally, are so indifferent to the individuals and to their peculiar characteristics that they can even treat human behaviours like polluting agents, as one author explains:

> CPTED should be expanded to include both the external environment of the place and the internal environment of the offender ... This would entail testing for brain damage, nutritional defects, heavy metal contamination, neurological problems, and might lead to alteration of nutritional factors, environmental pollutants, drug treatment and so forth. The result would be crime prevention research and policy which would be interdisciplinary in nature and based on an organism-environment interaction model of behaviour.[40]

More importantly, social control in the post-Fordist cities does not seem to operate as a mechanism whose aim is to make individuals internalise disciplinary values, learn specific models of behaviour or follow predefined lifestyles. Everybody is free to choose their own lifestyle (assuming that they have the material resources to afford it), and those groups who remain outside because (according to the neo-liberal ideology) they lack 'agency' and 'responsibility' – be it the underclass in the US or the expanding population of the poor, illegal immigrants, the unemployed and drug addicts in Europe – will be managed like toxic wastes: through 'urban quarantine' areas, whose boundaries are defined by architectural design.[41]

Populated by a flexible and mobile multitude of producers composed to a large extent by immigrants, single women, young part-timers and 'mc-jobbers'; crossed by hidden economies and black labour markets in which a growing army of precarious workers struggles for subsistence; fractured along lines of race and class, the post-disciplinary metropolis (both in America and in Europe) tries to impose an 'order without a norm', as Zygmunt Bauman suggested some years ago.[42] And this has to do with the fact that the post-Fordist labour force escapes the disciplinary categories of normality and pathology, conformity and deviance, *labouriousness* and *dangerousness*: it entails all of them without being reducible to anyone in particular.

The new urban architecture and the various policies of 'situational' control based on it – be it 'zero tolerance', 'neighbourhood watch' or 'electronic surveillance' – define a social geography of risk-containment and danger-prevention that is relatively independent of individual behaviours (absence of a norm), and oriented to the segregation and containment of whole categories of subjects, according to their status (imposition of an order). Thus, the 'human ecology' of the Chicago School (which inspired potentially inclusive urban projects like the *Chicago Area Project*) is replaced

---

[40] Matthew B. Robinson, 'The Theoretical Development of CPTED: Twenty-five Years of Responses to C. Ray Jeffery', in William S. Laufer and Freda Adler (eds), *The Criminology of Criminal Law. Advances in Criminological Theory, vol. 8* (New Brunswick, 1999), p. 456.

[41] Probably the clearest example of this trend is offered by Oscar Newman's *Defensible Space: Crime Prevention through Urban Design* (New York, 1972).

[42] Bauman, *Work, Consumerism and the New Poor*, p. 85.

by an 'ecology of fear' whose visible signs are fortified areas, gated communities and automatic armed response systems.[43]

The 21,000 closed circuit TV cameras covering the urban territories of the UK; the directional towers in Los Angeles (equipped with automatic systems capable of tracking human movements); the technologies of biometric identification disseminated through the Western cities; the metal detectors performing 'immaterial searches' in shops, universities, banks and public libraries: taken together, all these dispositives of surveillance do not seem to configure a single and 'generalised' panopticon.[44] In fact, their objective is not so much to *control* individuals, as to *construct* them by assembling 'factual fragments' which, taken together, allow to assign the individuals to this or that risk category: the aim is not to catch any possible event, but to *prevent* actions and 'event*ualities*'.[45]

In turn, the classifications produced by these processes do not seem to function by selecting specific populations to be disciplined, regulated or 'normalised'; rather, they permit a differentiation in the possibilities of *access* to some areas of the city, based on the potential danger posed by these populations. In the words of an enthusiastic supporter of these strategies of control:

> Access control refers to measures intended to exclude potential offenders from places such as offices, factories, and apartment buildings. The portcullises, moats, and drawbridges of medieval castles suggest its preventive pedigree may be as lengthy as that of target hardening.[46]

In times of 'zero tolerance' (or, more euphemistically, 'quality of life policing') it is not too difficult to foresee what categories of people the label of 'potential offenders' will be applied to more easily, therefore banning them from growing (public and private) areas of the city.[47]

In other words, these technologies contribute to drawing the boundaries separating the chosen and un-chosen ghettoes which compose the post-Fordist city – the former being mainly shopping malls, theme-parks, airports and gated communities; the latter represented by the many neglected areas of the inner cities in the US and the decaying peripheries of Europe. Thus, they enforce those class- and race-based criteria on which the right to access (or to escape) is based. In this way they mark the many 'no-go-areas' disseminated through the contemporary metropolis, and

---

[43] Mike Davis, *Ecology of Fear* (New York, 1998).

[44] For a different perspective, see Leon Hempel and Eric Topfer, *On the Threshold to Urban Panopticon? Analysing the Employment of CCTV in European Cities and Assessing its Social and Political Impacts* (Berlin, 2002). On the rise of CCTV in Britain see also Clive Norris and Gary Armstrong, *The Maximum Surveillance Society. The Rise of CCTV* (Oxford, 1999). On the selectivity of apparently neutral technologies of surveillance like CCTV, see Katherine S. Williams and Craig Johnstone, 'The Politics of the Selective Gaze: Closed Circuit Television and the Policing of Public Space', *Crime, Law & Social Change*, 34 (2000): 183–210.

[45] David Lyon, *Surveillance Society. Monitoring Everyday Life* (Buckingham, 2001), p. 54.

[46] Clarke, 'Situational Crime Prevention', p. 110.

[47] On the exclusionary logic inspiring 'zero tolerance policing' and its dramatic consequences in New York, see Andrea McArdle and Tanya Erzen (eds), *Zero Tolerance. Quality of Life and the New Police Brutality in New York City* (New York, 2001).

remind everybody of the basic distinction between those social groups for which 'no go' is a matter of choice, and those for which 'no go' means the impossibility of escape.[48]

Thus, the post-Fordist metropolis seems to be defining new spaces of seclusion whose effect is to reproduce an artificial separation between the 'productive surplus' and the 'social surplus', the included and the excluded: the new labour force is thus segmented and divided through the management of space. And this fragmentation – whose consequence is a reduction in the degree of socialisation and political coalition among the various factions of the labour market – is grounded on a selective differentiation of the right to move and to interact with others: what emerges is thus the reproduction of a social hierarchy, measured by the unequal 'possibility of access to symbolically and/or economically valuable places'.[49] In this context, the city ceases to be a 'public space', to become a deleuzian 'apparatus of capture' through which the unobtrusive 'government at distance' of selected populations becomes possible. Control is embodied in architectural forms not to regulate encounters, but to prevent them from occurring in the first place; interaction is not so much governed, as blocked; 'disturbing' individuals are not disciplined, corrected or transformed, but removed. In other terms, symbolic and material barriers contribute to the reproduction of patterns of inclusion and exclusion within the urban space. As two scholars wrote commenting the diffusion of 'gated communities' in the American cities:

> Gated communities are part of the trend toward exercising physical and social means of territorial control. Some walls are meant to keep people in, some to keep people out. Some are meant to mark territory and identity, others to exclude.[50]

Challenged by the difficulty to govern, regulate and discipline individual behaviours, the urban dispositives of control seem to promote mass surveillance and selective containment, thus rebuilding inside the global cities those external frontiers of the nation-state that show increasing signs of crisis, due to the globalisation of the economy and to the pressures exercised by the immigrant labour force. It seems that the 'peripheries of the world', no longer contained by the militarised borders of the States, are now being transferred inside the Western cities, where new (architectural) frontiers separate the 'First' world from the 'Third'. Here we find also the new coordinates of the urban ghetto, which in a 'deadly symbiosis' with the prison enforces the fragmentation and hierarchisation of the labour force, thus preserving the social distance between 'insiders' and 'outsiders'.[51]

[48]   Zygmunt Bauman, *Postmodernity and its Discontents* (Oxford, 1997).

[49]   Olivier Razac, *Histoire politique du barbelé. La praire, la tranché, le camp* (Paris, 2000).

[50]   Edward J. Blakely and Mary Gail Snyder, *Fortress America. Gated Communities in the United States* (Washington DC, 1997), p. 30.

[51]   The hypothesis of a 'functional equivalence' between the ghetto and the prison is suggested by Loic Wacquant in his 'Deadly Symbiosis'. It should be recognised, however, that already in 1980 Dario Melossi foresaw some of these developments and announced the replacement of welfare-oriented policies of social control by strategies of urban containment and ghettoisation: see Dario Melossi, 'Oltre il Panopticon. Per uno studio delle strategie di controllo sociale nel capitalismo del ventesimo secolo', *La questione criminale*, 6/2-3 (1980): 277–361.

The restructuring of cities along lines of fortification and 'securisation' offers a plastic image of the artificial separation between the 'laborious' and the 'dangerous' classes. Organised in 'Neighbourhood Watch Schemes', 'vigilante groups' and 'quality of life collectives', the former struggle to preserve their conditions of privilege and (supposed) welfare against the latter, increasingly perceived as threatening others, dangerous strangers, unwelcome intruders. The segregation of immigrants in the European cities, the 'reclusion' of the African-American and Latino labour force in the American inner cities, and more generally the creation of urban areas with limited accessibility, enforce a regime of social distance and estrangement whose result is the destruction of social bonds, empathy and cooperation which – under the point of view of the neo-liberal order – represent a danger for the stability of the whole system. The consequence is a fragmentation of the multitude through the social reproduction of a 'fear' which in the urban areas is embodied by the stranger, the immigrant, the unemployed and the drug-addict. By representing some categories of subjects as 'dangerous classes' and threatening 'others' blamed for the growing insecurity and anxieties of contemporary urban life, this rationality of control prevents the formation of political alliances among the subordinates. Just to make one example, the mass-mediated representation of immigrants as 'dangerous others', 'welfare scroungers' or 'unfair competitors on the labour market' inculcates a resentment in the local labour force, whose result is to prevent the constitution of a common political conscience. Thus, social groups who share the same condition of existential insecurity, economic precariousness and social vulnerability, tend to perceive and to blame each other as the main source of these concerns.[52]

The urban confinement of the 'social surplus' – in prisons, ghettoes or immigration detention centres – contributes to its social construction as a dangerous class: here we see the sunset of a disciplinary power whose ambition was to produce useful and docile subjects to be included in the social pact, and the dawn of a power of control which supervises whole populations whose collective status justifies their *banishment*:

> As a result, deviance, seen in the context of public social interaction, is essentially projected, non materialised; feared, not deplored; avoided, not confronted; prevented, not suppressed.

---

[52] The political and civic implications of these developments are once again best exemplified by the diffusion of 'gated communities' in the American (but to some extent also European) cities: 'Gated communities go further in several respects than other means of exclusion. They create physical barriers to access. They also privatise community space, not merely individual space. Many gated areas also privatise civic responsibilities like police protection and communal services such as street maintenance, recreation and entertainment. The new developments can create a private world that need share little with its neighbours or with the larger political system': Blakely and Gail Snyder, *Fortress America*, p. 8. In this respect, McKenzie speaks of a 'secession of the successful' which increases their social distance from the 'losers'. See Evan McKenzie, *Privatopia. Homeowner Associations and the Rise of Residential Private Government* (New Haven, 1994). This process has involved also the 'dark ghetto', where an emerging black bourgeoisie has struggled to abandon the inner cities and to settle in the suburbs, thus breaking the 'politics of race' which dominated the urban ghetto in the 1960s and 1970s: see Loic Wacquant, 'Negative Social Capital: State Breakdown and Social Destitution in America's Urban Core', *The Netherlands Journal of the Built Environment*, 13/1 (1998): 1–36.

It is a completely renovated socio-cognitive realm arising from the clear-cut boundary between managed territories and dangerous others.[53]

The attribution of functions of control to space and architecture – dissociated as it is from the peculiar characteristics of subjects, independent of their specific forms of interaction, indifferent to the actual processes of socialisation, and grounded in the social construction of dangers whose real characteristics escape any precise comprehension – shows to what extent the logic of post-Fordist control is a result of a lack of knowledge about the 'social' and its complexity. Also, it shows how distant these technologies of control are from the modernist narrative of an inclusive citizenship.

Bridling the Net

It comes as no surprise that the Net-Economy reclaims new forms of social control adequate to the dramatic transformations which are taking place in the field of 'immaterial production'. A growing body of criminological literature is being devolved on the emerging 'immaterial' forms of crime, such as 'hackerism', 'electronic copyright violations', 'electronic sabotage', and so on.[54] In fact, *cyberspace* represents the field of maximum expansion of hi-tech production, the virtual place (or 'non-place') in which the productive cooperation of the post-Fordist multitude can materialise itself with increasing profits; but the Internet is also an emerging field of social conflict and struggle with unlimited potentials for expansion, and in which new forms of 'deviant' behaviours appear. I would suggest that a latent paradox can be detected in this new context: on the one hand the Internet – being one of the most important sites for the production and circulation of information – has to be left as unmanaged and free as possible, according to the laws of the market; on the other hand, however, some form of control over the access to immaterial resources is needed anyway, if capitalist profits (and private property in this new form) are to be preserved. In other words:

At its present very high level of techno-scientific development, corporate power finds itself dependent of levels of cooperative activity, unimpeded communications, and free circulation of knowledge that, far from being easily integrated into its hierarchies, exists in persistent tension with its command.[55]

Clear examples of this paradox are offered by mass-deviance phenomena like the practice of 'file sharing' (downloading copyrighted music, movies and software programs from the Internet) or the 'electronic strikes' (unauthorised mass-intrusions

---

[53] Michalis Lianos and Mary Douglas, 'Dangerization and the End of Deviance. The Institutional Environment', *The British Journal of Criminology*, 40/2 (2000): 74.

[54] For an overview see Douglas Thomas and Brian Loader (eds), *Cybercrime. Law Enforcement, Security and Surveillance in the Information Age* (London, 2000) and Paul Taylor, *Hackers. Crime in the Digital Sublime* (London, 1999).

[55] Nick D. Witheford, *Cyber-Marx. Cycles and Circuits of Struggle in High-Technology Capitalism* (Urbana, 1999), p. 237.

by internet users into politically targeted web sites) organised periodically by the 'anti-globalisation' movement against economic institutions, international agencies and governmental bodies.[56] What seems to be taking place here is a transposition of the industrial struggles and sabotages into a high-tech environment: once again, the labour force turns the power of enterprises and governments against themselves, thus exploiting the inevitable weaknesses and contradictions of the new organisational forms. In the same way as the industrial labour force was able to block whole productive systems by exploiting the rigidities of the disciplinary assembly line, so now the post-Fordist labour force can block vital flows of information and finance by exploiting the flexibility of the net.

Thus we can understand why social control in the 'age of information' must concentrate on the definition of 'how' and 'how much' access – to information, innovation and knowledge – can be authorised. In this context, given that any rigid 'disciplinary' regime must be avoided because it would be dysfunctional to the logic of the New Economy, control is oriented not so much to the actual use of immaterial resources – because once the effects of any misuse emerge it could already be too late – but, preventively, on *potential* uses. What has to be managed and restricted is *access* to some electronic resources, in order to prevent the *risk* of misuse:

> The new emergency is about monitoring, controlling and censoring electronic communication, and, more precisely, the behaviours of the new immaterial workers: they have access to know-how and innovations, thus obtaining an ever-growing autonomy from corporate organisation. Their use of computer and nets can become dysfunctional at any time, turning itself into sabotage, struggle and electronic civil disobedience.[57]

Here is one of the clearest examples of the deep vulnerability of the post-Fordist system of production and control: on the one hand, only universal access to (and unlimited sharing of) information, technology, electronic data and symbols allows the immaterial production to fully express itself; on the other hand, precisely this 'democratic' access to resources seems to represent one of the main threats to capitalist exploitation and to the private property of the new immaterial means of production.[58]

---

56 Today whole political movements organise themselves around media-activism and electronic strikes. Among the most targeted websites, we should mention the WTO, IMF, World Bank, Nestlé, McDonald's and Nike. For an overview, see Matteo Pasquinelli (ed.), *Media Activism. Strategie e pratiche della comunicazione indipendente* (Rome, 2002).

57 Luther Blissett Project, *Nemici dello Stato. Criminali, 'mostri' e leggi speciali nella società di controllo* (Rome, 2000), p. 15.

58 One should think here about the so called 'Internet Depression' which – against any financial prevision – is affecting the American net-economy since 2000: after a short period of miraculous growth, the Net Economy shows now some signs of recession. According to some commentators, an important factor in this respect has been the systematic violation of intellectual property rights by computer users: this would have reduced the margins of profit of many 'e-corporations'. See Michael J. Mandel, *The Internet Depression: the Boom, the Boost, and Beyond* (New York, 2001). In response to these mass-phenomena the US government has enacted very restrictive laws, like the *Digital Millennium Copyright Act*. Also the recent anti-terrorist legislation (*Patriot Act*, 2001) contains many provisions restricting the access to (and use of) electronic resources.

For this reason, according to economist Jeremy Rifkin, in the *age of access* it is access to intellectual resources that becomes the main target of the control strategies directed at high-tech workers.[59] Information-sharing by the immaterial labour force must be controlled, because to possess information means to have the power to endanger the whole economic system. Therefore, access to particular high technology services must be put under the condition of exhibiting a *password* which identifies who is allowed to log in: passwords assure that only some persons (better, some *categories* of persons), possess those requisites of trustworthiness which make their behaviour foreseeable. Inevitably, the mind goes back to Gilles Deleuze, who in a famous article argued that:

> The disciplinary societies have two poles: the signature that designates the individual, and the number of administrative numeration that indicates his or her position within a mass ... In the societies of control, on the one hand, what is important is no longer either a signature or a number, but a code: the code is a password, while on the other hand the disciplinary societies are regulated by watchwords. The numerical language of control is made of codes that mark access to information, or reject it.[60]

According to the French philosopher, these are signs of the transition from a disciplinary society – in which what mattered were the individuals, their behaviours and biographies – toward a 'society of control' – in which the individual no longer stands at the centre of control powers, being instead replaced by 'statistical groups' and 'databases'. In this new regime of control, what matters is the possibility to establish clear criteria under which the decision to allow or deny access can be taken safely.[61]

What I would like to stress, however, is that these strategies of preventive control cannot escape a structural contradiction, which grows to the point of becoming a true paradox: they pretend to establish a regime of preventability, anticipation and categorisation, but the post-Fordist productivity is based exactly on the opposite principles – flexibility, innovation, creativity and inventiveness. On the other hand, these technologies of control stand outside of the processes of communication and exchange driving immaterial production, and act only as external limits imposed to the free circulation of information and knowledge. Once again, however, these limits cannot become so rigid as to configure a new disciplinary logic, because this would endanger the very source of productivity of the net-economy. The horizontal sharing of information and the unlimited access to the virtual places where it is produced represent perhaps the most dangerous forms of assault on private property, and the new technologies of 'digital control' try to preserve this new, immaterial form of property.

---

[59] Jeremy Rifkin, *The Age of Access. The New Culture of Hypercapitalism where All of Life is a Paid-For Experience* (New York, 2000).

[60] Gilles Deleuze, 'Postscript on the Societies of Control', *October*, 59 (1992): 5.

[61] The same point is made by Richard Jones: 'Though based on various different technologies, such systems can be seen as conceptually similar approaches to the governing of access to places, whether these be real or 'virtual'. Each of the electronic access systems discussed relies on the existence of a secure perimeter, requiring potential users to obtain 'entry' via an automated gateway or checkpoint – each allows for a form of control-at-a-distance': Richard Jones, 'Digital Rule. Punishment, Control and Technology', *Punishment & Society*, 2/1 (2000): 14.

Interestingly, these processes take us back to the origins of the capitalist mode of production – in particular to eighteenth and nineteenth century Britain – where, according to Michel Foucault, it was the diffusion of manufactures, machineries and warehouses which needed protection against workers' robberies and assaults, that inspired the creation of the modern *police*:

> The point is that this wealth consisting of stocks of goods, raw materials, imported objects, machines, and workshops was vulnerable to theft ... Not surprisingly, then, the great problem of power in England during this period was to set up control mechanisms that would make it possible to protect this new material form of wealth. So we can understand why the creator of the police in England, Patrick Colquhoun, was someone who began as a merchant and was then commissioned by a shipping company to organise a system for overseeing goods stored in the London docks. The London police was born of the need to protect the docks, wharves, warehouses and stocks.[62]

If those necessities of control promoted the constitution of modern police forces as we know them, and helped to shape the disciplinary regime of work organisation within the emerging factories, then perhaps a further evolution is now taking place. New models of control might be emerging in light of new forms of wealth-production and new opportunities for 'virtual theft', if it is true, as Jeremy Rifkin argues, that whereas the industrial era was characterised by the control of material goods, the new era is characterised by the control of concepts and ideas.[63]

Thus, this model of post-disciplinary control tends to be *preventive*, because immaterial resources cannot be recovered once somebody has appropriated and made unauthorised use of them (as was instead the case with material goods); it tends to be *diffused*, because immaterial resources are not located in any specific place (as were industrial machineries and products), being instead embodied in fluxes, nets and virtual circuits; finally – as we will see in more detail in the next chapter – this model of control tends to be oriented to whole *categories* of individuals, because the flexible and mobile post-Fordist multitude cannot be reduced to the rigid forms of disciplinary individualisation – as was the case with the Fordist labour force, located in (and organised through) a defined space: that of the industrial factory.

---

[62] Foucault, 'Truth and Juridical Forms', p. 69.

[63] Rifkin, *The Age of Access*.

Chapter 4

Mass Confinement and Actuarial Penology

Mass Imprisonment: From the Welfare State to the Penal State?

It has almost become commonsensical to situate the crisis of Fordism in the first half of the 1970s – and more precisely in 1973, the year of the huge 'oil crisis'. Rigid periodisations like this are always questionable, because it is quite difficult to define precise historical moments in which dramatic transitions begin and paradigmatic shifts take place. However, if this criticism seems perfectly reasonable for economic facts, this does not seem to be case for the transformations which took place in the field of penal strategies in the last quarter of the twentieth century. In other words, in this case it seems possible to identify a clear watershed: and this can be found in the same years in which the crisis of Fordism has been located. There is also a geographical context where the rupture first emerged: the United States.

In the aftermath of the Second World War, the US prison population followed a constant downward trend, which intensified particularly in the 1960s due to a variety of factors. The 'tolerant' moral climate characterising the years of the civil rights revolution, the expansion of the *welfare state* and the increasing resort to alternatives to imprisonment: each of these elements played a peculiar role, whose aggregate effect was a gradual withering away of the prison as the main instrument of social control, both in the language of practitioners and in public opinion. According to David Garland, this was the period of 'penal welfarism' in which a set of ideas, practices and institutions oriented to the rehabilitation, reintegration, socialisation and treatment of offenders, became hegemonic:

> In the penal-welfare framework, the rehabilitative ideal was not just one element among others. Rather, it was the hegemonic, organising principle, the intellectual framework and value system that bound together the whole structure and made sense of it for its practitioners.[1]

This trend towards a reduction in the centrality of the prison was also experienced in other Western countries – for example in many European penal systems – where prison populations declined steadily, until they reached, in many cases, a historical minimum. It was the diffusion of this euphoria for 'rehabilitation', 'diversion', 'alternatives to imprisonment' and the re-emerging role of the 'community' – together with the mounting 'fiscal crisis of the State' – that led Andrew Scull to announce the

---

[1] David Garland, *The Culture of Control* (Oxford, 2001), p. 34.

age of *decarceration*.[2] Deviance was seen as the result of a multiplicity of social, economic, and cultural factors which had to be addressed by the penal-welfare complex in order to reduce crime. The main criminological ideas which contributed to legitimise and rationalise these welfarist strategies were the concepts of 'anomie' and 'relative deprivation': therefore, crime was seen as one among the many possible effects of individual and social deficits, whose deep economic causes had to be identified and removed through inclusive social policies and rehabilitative penal treatments.

Towards the end of the 1970s, however, the correctional model entered a crisis which produced a reversal in the official languages, practices and strategies about crime and crime control:

> In the course of a few years, the orthodoxies of rehabilitative faith collapsed in virtually all of the developed countries, as reformers and academics, politicians and policy-makers, and finally practitioners and institutional managers came to dissociate themselves from its tenets. With surprising speed, a liberal progressive ideal came to appear reactionary to the very groups that had previously championed it. And nowhere was this about-turn more spectacular than in the USA which, until then, had been the nation most fully committed to correctionalist policies and practice.[3]

This crisis did not affect only criminal policies. In fact, it was part of a larger shift in the political climate of the US. As many scholars have documented, it was not until the end of the 1970s (with the presidential election of Ronald Regan), that 'law and order' became a major issue in US politics – though it should be noted that in 1964 Barry Goldwater had already centred his electoral campaign around issues of crime control and law enforcement, but without much success. Richard Nixon followed the same path in the late 1960s, but in a different tone – by suggesting an explicit connection (with long-lasting consequences, as we will see) between welfare and crime. In other words, Nixon launched an offensive against what would later be called the 'culture of dependency' and its supposedly criminogenic effects:

> If it is entirely proper for the government to take away from some to give to others, then won't some be led to believe that they can rightfully take from anyone who has more than they? No wonder law and order has broken down, mob violence has engulfed great American cities, and our wives feel unsafe in the streets.[4]

---

[2]   Andrew Scull, *Decarceration* (New Brunswick, 1977). However, in the same years Stan Cohen identified some contradictions to this process, when he described the growth in 'community corrections' and 'alternatives to imprisonment' as a trend which would not reduce the total number of individuals under some form of institutional supervision. Cohen realised that these 'alternatives to imprisonment' were, in many cases, only 'alternatives to alternatives': measures that would be added to other – non custodial – measures. Therefore the prison population would not be reduced in the long term, more and more people being caught in the net of social control. This is why he spoke of 'net-widening' and 'mesh-thinning' processes. See Stanley Cohen, *Visions of Social Control* (Cambridge, 1985).

[3]   Garland, *The Culture of Control*, p. 54.

[4]   Quoted in Katherine Beckett, *Making Crime Pay: Law and Order in Contemporary American Politics* (New York, 1997), p. 28.

What seemed to emerge was an attitude of 'revenge' by the American establishment.[5] This revenge had to be waged against an intrusive welfare regime whose taxation system had taken too much from the white middle class to the benefit of the poor, now depicted as 'scroungers' and 'parasites'. But a revenge was also invoked against the black community, whose urban riots and civil rights mobilisations were perceived as unacceptable acts of ingratitude towards a generous welfare. However, it was only with Ronald Reagan's election that the 'race-welfare-crime' complex emerged as a new 'governmental rationality', and a new rhetoric of war ('war on crime' and 'war on drugs') started to dominate public discourse, leading to draconian legislations and overtly discriminatory penal policies: these were targeted mainly at the black community, blamed (or scapegoated) for the increasing rates of crime, the diffusion of lethal drugs and the fiscal crisis of the State.[6]

The new political mood also influenced practices and rationalities in the field of corrections: beginning in the late 1970s, a significant transformation emerged in the institutional definitions of success and failure of criminal policies. If until that time the main indicator of the effectiveness of crime (and drug) control strategies had been recidivism and rates of re-offending, some studies conducted in those years revealed that the correctional ideology had failed. Statistics showed an increase in street crimes, thus proclaiming the failure of those policies of treatment and rehabilitation whose aim was to reintegrate offenders by removing the social causes of deviance.[7] In effect, this increase was not as 'dramatic' as some governmental 'think thanks' proclaimed. But the consequence was that a public attitude of strong enthusiasm for individual treatment and correction – a sort of 'criminological progressivism' – gave way to sentiments of delusion, whose immediate translation was a kind of 'criminological scepticism'. In line with the new political climate, mainstream criminologists began to question some widely accepted assumptions about the origins of criminal behaviour, starting by refusing the idea that there was any causal relation between social marginality and crime. Deviance was seen instead as the result of a

---

5   As was said in chapter 1, according to Dario Melossi public attitudes toward social problems (and crime) are strongly affected by economic changes. The American reaction against crime, deviance and the 'liberal consensus' of the 1960s emerged in a context of recession and decreasing capitalist profits. It is in these situations of social and political uncertainty that ' … ideas expressed in a publicly available language about where the economy is going, what a social crisis is, what causes it and who is to blame for it etc., appear to change, in society, together and in a tight cultural exchange with publicly available ideas about crime, punishment, and responsibility': Dario Melossi, 'Changing Representations of the Criminal', *The British Journal of Criminology*, 40 (2000): 299.

6   For an overview of the 'anti-drug' and 'anti-crime' legislation enacted in the US under the umbrella of the 'Tough on Crime' movement, see Christian Parenti, *Lockdown America. Police and Prisons in the Age of Crisis* (London, 1999).

7   If it is undeniable that the 1960s witnessed an increase in crime, it should also be noted that already in 1973 this upward trend had ceased, giving way to a continuous decline in criminal activity. More precisely: 'From 1973 through 1994, the rates of violent crime victimisation had intervals of stability, increase and decrease, while the rates of property crime underwent a virtually uninterrupted decrease', Bureau of Justice Statistics, *Criminal Victimization, 1973–1995* (Washington DC, 1997), p. 1. This means that the 'get tough' policies emerged when crime rates were already declining. This paradox reappeared in the second half of the 1990s, when a dramatic reduction in criminal offences was accompanied by 'tough' laws like the 'Three strikes and you're out' legislations.

free choice: the criminal was first and foremost a rational subject, not a victim of hard social circumstances. This argument, together with the concomitant political assault on welfare and the mentioned 'culture of dependency', left the old 'modernist' strategies of penal-welfare without support: 'nothing works' became the official criminological slogan of the time.[8]

If one considers again the wider political climate in which these 'new' criminological perspectives emerged – the scene was indeed to be dominated by Reagan in the US and Thatcher in the UK – it is not difficult to realise how successfully these ideas could be translated into concrete crime policies:

> One reason for the success of this new criminology is that it was anchored in a larger political vision. It was much more than an intra-mural debate between criminologists and practitioners (though it was that) ... Rather, it was part of the neo-Conservative movement that emerged to assess the project of the Great Society ... and concluded that it had been a resounding failure. Their general policy prescription was that the government should concentrate on doing less better. The new criminology was simply a specific instance of this more general principle.[9]

'Doing less better' meant to 'understand less and punish more'. No longer should any importance be attached to the social conditions and contexts in which some deviant behaviours take place. Sociologically inspired theories of deviance, these criminologists argued, worked only to justify crime and to legitimise the leniency of criminal courts: the image of the deprived and under-socialised deviant was thus replaced by that of a depraved rational delinquent. This theoretical shift was then followed by a coherent change in the rationalities of correction: rehabilitation of offenders had to give way to deterrence and incapacitation.[10]

Sustained by a political rhetoric which – by emphasising the criminal dangers represented by the new 'rabble' (later the 'underclass') – inculcated fear and insecurity as a new commonsense, scepticism toward the 'correctional narrative' spread rapidly and found different translations depending on the various perspectives within conservative criminology. In any case, deterrence occupied the territory abandoned by the supposed failure of treatment. In the meantime, a renewed 'cost-benefits analysis' proposed new definitions of success and failure, leading to managerialism and to the adoption of a 'systemic rationality' in criminal justice.[11] The rational

---

[8]   Robert L. Martinson, 'What Works? – Questions and Answers About Prison Reform', *The Public Interest*, 35 (1974): 22–54.

[9]   Malcolm M. Feeley, 'Crime, Social Order and the Rise of neo-Conservative Politics', *Theoretical Criminology*, 7/1 (2003): 121. On the new conservative climate surrounding (and influencing) criminological thinking in that period, see also Anthony Platt and Paul Takagi, 'Intellectuals for Law and Order: A Critique of the New Realists', *Crime and Social Justice*, 8 (1977): 1–16.

[10] For eloquent examples of this trend within conservative criminology, see Ernest Van Den Haag, *Punishing Criminals* (New York, 1975) and James Q. Wilson, *Thinking About Crime* (New York, 1983).

[11] This point is emphasised by Theodore Caplow and Jonathan Simon. These authors argue that among the causes of 'mass imprisonment' in the United States, one should consider the increased 'reflexivity' of the penal system prompted by ' ... a series of reforms aimed at improving the fairness of the system'. This ' ... has operated to make the criminal justice system more efficient with the result that it can be far more responsive to pressures for growth than it might have been in the past':

choice of the deviant was assimilated to an economic behaviour: actual or potential criminals behave like market-actors who weigh the costs they are willing to sustain, against the expected benefits of a criminal act. In this respect, the deterrent effect of punishment has to be pursued through an increase in the expected costs: that is, through the imposition of harsher penalties.[12]

The concept of 'correction' was thus removed from the field of penality. The aim was no longer to adopt measures adequate to the social conditions of the individual deviant, but to apply those sanctions which, on average, would be harsh enough to deter people from committing crimes. Where this economic model could not work, the last resort would be the neutralisation of offenders: in this respect, 'selective incapacitation' represented an important step toward the new exclusionary rationality of punishment, whose effects are most visible in our times.[13]

In fact, 'selective incapacitation' means, on the one hand, to theorise explicitly the dismissal of any rehabilitative ideal and, on the other, to see punishment only as an instrument for the physical separation of the deviant from the wider social context. The project is to isolate, within the mass of actual or potential deviants, a restricted fraction of 'born criminals', 'incorrigible deviants' or 'chronic recidivists' who cannot be reintegrated into the community. What is of interest here is the logic behind this perspective: the idea that it is possible to select some categories of people who, all the rest being equal, should be punished more harshly than others because they display some indicators of a permanent crime-proneness.

However, an important point needs to be clarified here. Originally, the 'selective incapacitation' approach was presented by its advocates as a 'deflationary' measure: its (declared) aim was in fact to reduce prison population by limiting detention only to some restricted groups of 'incorrigible' offenders. So, where is the connection between 'selective incapacitation' and contemporary mass incarceration? What usually goes unnoticed is that the underlying logic of selective punishment could be extended discretionally, thus covering ever larger social groups defined as dangerous – by practitioners, probation officers, judges, and to a greater extent by the mass-media, public opinion or politicians. And this is exactly what seems to have happened in the US where, according to Richard Sparks:

> The most visible signal of new penological thinking is the trend towards selective (or, more accurately, categorial) incapacitation as a rationale for imprisonment. Here, 'incapacitation effects' are sought not on the traditional grounds of confining individuals who present a 'clear and present danger' of committing further grave (usually violent) offences but rather on the rationale that confining a sufficient number of 'high rate' offenders (principally burglars, drug dealers and robbers) for a long enough portion of the active phase of their

---

Theodore Caplow and Jonathan Simon, 'Understanding Prison Policy and Population Trends', in Michael Tonry and Joan Petersilia (eds), *Prisons. Crime and Justice. A Review of Research*, 26 (1999): 98. On the 'cost-benefit analysis' in particular, see Gary Becker, 'Crime and Punishment: An Economic Approach', *The Journal of Political Economy*, 76 (1968): 169–217 and Jan Palmer, 'Economic Analyses of the Deterrent Effect of Punishment: A Review', *Journal of Research in Crime and Delinquency*, 14/1 (1977): 4–21.

12 For a critique of this perspective, see David Greenberg, 'The Cost-Benefits Analysis of Imprisonment', *Social Justice*, 17/4 (1990): 49–75.

13 See Peter Greenwood, *Selective Incapacitation* (Santa Monica, 1982).

careers will produce appreciable decreases in the volume of crime. The logic of this position is to sentence on the basis of the offender's risk profile rather than on the gravity of his current offence. This is self-consciously an expansionist measure ... [14]

In fact, the short distance separating 'selective incapacitation' from 'mass-incapacitation' was covered quite rapidly. And this comes as no surprise, if one considers that the criteria on which criminals are judged as 'dangerous' depend on many factors, not just 'criminological', but also political and cultural ones. In other words, if the 'degree of tolerance' towards deviant behaviour is high, only a few people will be selected for incapacitation; but in times of 'law and order' and later 'zero tolerance policing', it is not difficult to foresee that the categories of people deemed to deserve imprisonment will become much larger. Even more so, if one considers that 'the factors identified by persistence studies are factors shared by many of the underprivileged: socio-economic deprivation; low family income and high family size; frequent unemployment; broken homes and early parental separation; criminal, anti-social and alcoholic parents'.[15] In other words, the target of 'selective incapacitation' became shortly the growing army of the American 'underclass'.

Suddenly, US prison and jail populations started to grow: from 400,000 people in prison in 1975 (a historical minimum), to 750,000 in 1985, to almost 2 million in 2000.[16] Direct public expenditure for justice and corrections grew exactly in the same period in which welfare, education and health spending suffered dramatic cuts.[17] Incarceration rates have thus reached levels never touched before in the history of the US, surpassing even those of South Africa at the time of *apartheid*: on average, the US today incarcerates five times more than European countries. If to the incarcerated population we add all those people who live under some form of penal supervision, the number reaches 6.5 million.[18]

However, it would be impossible to explain this trend by looking at criminal activity in the US. In fact, in the period we are considering here rates of crime remained more or less stable, if one excludes the rise in violent crimes that took place in the 1980s – due mainly to the diffusion of the market and culture of crack in the inner cities, particularly among the African American youth. And since the early 1990s these rates are declining steadily, for all the main categories of crime, while prison population continues to grow, though at a lower rate.[19] Another important

---

[14] Richard Sparks, 'Perspectives on Risk and Penal Politics', in Tim Hope and Richard Sparks (eds), *Crime, Risk and Insecurity* (London, 2000), pp. 131–132.

[15] Barbara Hudson, 'Punishment, Rights and Difference: Defending Justice in the Risk-Society', in Kevin Stenson and Robert Sullivan (eds), *Crime, Risk and Justice. The Politics of Crime Control in Liberal Democracies* (Devon, 2001), p. 155.

[16] Bureau of Justice Statistics, *Correctional Surveys* (Washington DC, 2000).

[17] According to the Bureau of Justice Statistics, *Expenditure and Employment Extracts* (Washington DC, 2002), in the years 1982–1999 expenditures for justice grew in the United States by 419 percent at Federal level, by 369 percent at State level and by 310 percent at County level.

[18] Bureau of Justice Statistics, *2002 At a Glance* (Washington DC, 2002).

[19] According to the Bureau of Justice Statistics, *National Crime Victimization Survey* (Washington DC, 2001), serious violent crimes remained stable between 1973 and 1983; they increased during the period 1985–1993, and finally declined sharply between 1993 and 2001. See also Michael Tonry, 'Why are US Incarceration Rates So High?', in Michael Tonry (ed.), *Penal Reform in Overcrowded*

element to be considered is that almost one million of US prisoners – that is, half the total – are behind bars for non-violent offences: crimes against property or public order, less serious drug offences and, in the case of immigrants, violations of the strict immigration laws.[20] The picture resulting from these data shows quite clearly that the new 'great confinement' experienced by the US is linked to a shift in crime control policies and more generally to a transformation in the politics of deviance, rather than to any significant change in the level of criminal activity.

The commonsensical explanation for the upsurge in US rates of incarceration holds that politicians – from Reagan to Clinton – only 'reacted' to a growing public demand for punishment, by introducing new punitive measures, promoting tough legislation and waging periodic wars on crime and drugs. In other words, the public – made insecure by a real increase in crime and by the crisis of traditional American values provoked by civil rights activists, feminist movements and anti-authoritarian ideologies – asked for harsher penalties, while the political system only satisfied this demand. And the results are before our eyes: 'truth in sentencing', 'three strikes and you're out', 'Megan's laws', 'mandatory minimum sentences', 'real offence sentencing schemes'.

However, Katherine Beckett has showed clearly that this hypothesis is questionable. It is true, she argues, that the American public opinion has become more punitive – as indeed many other Western public opinions – but this increased punitiveness did not shape political choices and discourses about crime: on the contrary, it was their product. In other words, the mass media and the political system pushed the American public opinion towards a more punitive attitude, by turning crime into a big issue.[21] Such a shift, synthesised by the transition from the 'war on poverty' to the 'war on crime', was more successful and easier in the United States than elsewhere.

In order to explain this apparent singularity of the American case I would follow Jonathan Simon, who argues that this paradigmatic shift was facilitated by the 'single-issue' orientation of American politics. Drawing on Mary Douglas' theory of risk and blame, Simon suggests that crime has become an opportunity for the development of a 'border' political discourse, in which 'sectarian' attitudes can emerge. The 'transversality' of crime makes it suitable for a rhetoric of 'good against evil', by which the State can represent itself as the defender of unspecified 'us' against suitable 'others'. In this way, Simon concludes, a new strategy of government has emerged in America, a strategy of 'governing through crime'. The mass-mediated discourse about crime as a major social problem affecting honest citizens, permits the social construction of some categories of people – the poor, the African-American youth, the 'underclass' – as a 'public enemy' against whom a real war must be declared. And

---

Times (Oxford, 2001), pp. 52–64. It must be said that the trend towards mass incarceration in the US seems to have slowed down since 2000. In 2001 the annual rate of growth of prisoners was 1.1 percent (the smallest increase since 1979). However, this was compensated by high rates of growth in the Federal prison population, and (following the events of 11 September 2001) by a dramatic increase in the population supervised by the INS (*Immigration and Nationalisation Service*).

20   John Irwin, Vincent Schiraldi and Jason Ziedenberg, 'America's One Million Non-violent Prisoners', *Social Justice*, 27/2 (2000): 135–147. According to these authors, between 1978 and 1996, 77 percent of prison population growth was accounted for by non-violent offenders.

21   Beckett, *Making Crime Pay*. See also Katherine Beckett and Theodore Sassoon, *The Politics of Injustice. Crime and Punishment in America* (Thousand Oaks, 2000).

this war – the war on crime – plays a fundamental role by legitimising, in the eyes of the public, a de-legitimated nation-state.[22]

In other words, the politicisation of crime succeeded in two peculiar ways: on the one hand it allowed the American establishment to reassert its own 'sovereign' power, thus constructing a new legitimisation of the State through a series of 'wars' against internal enemies (who replaced the crumbling Soviet Union, no longer fit to the role). On the other hand, by representing the poor and the 'outsiders' as the main threat to collective wellbeing, public opinion could be diverted from other sources of insecurity and fear – economic transformations, growing unemployment, increasing work insecurity etc. – thus confirming its attachment to the existing political system, given that 'scapegoating not only transposes the anxiety felt by many, but also offers to anchor the worth of objects according to the threat that is allegedly arrayed against them'.[23]

Indeed, if we look at the ethnic composition of American prisons, we realise that this strategy of selective exclusion has been very successful: African Americans represent, in fact, 12 percent of the American population, but they are the absolute majority of the US prison population. If in 1950 this was composed of 66 percent whites and 32 percent non-whites, today these proportions are reversed: whites constitute 30 percent, while African Americans are about 60 percent of the total. If one looks at incarceration rates, what emerges is that while whites are incarcerated at a rate of 919/100,000, blacks behind bars are almost 7000/100,000. This means that the probability for a black (male) to end up in prison during his lifetime is more than seven times higher than for whites:[24] one in three African Americans aged 18 to 35 is in prison or under some form of penal supervision.[25]

On the other hand, these data should always be read in conjunction with those concerning the class composition and the educational level of the imprisoned population.[26] As I mentioned before, the expansion of the penal system has coincided – almost in a perfect timing – with a substantial downsizing of the welfare state. The

---

[22] See Jonathan Simon, 'Fear and Loathing in Late Modernity. Reflections on the Cultural Sources of Mass Imprisonment in the United States', in David Garland (ed.), *Mass Imprisonment. Social Causes and Consequences* (London, 2001), pp. 15–27; Caplow and Simon, 'Understanding Prison Policy and Population Trends'.

[23] Barry Vaughan, 'The Punitive Consequences of Consumer Culture', *Punishment & Society*, 4/2 (2002): 207.

[24] Bureau of Justice Statistics, *Correctional Populations in the United States 1997* (Washington DC, 1998). In 2001, 10 percent of black males aged 25 to 29 were in prison (the percentage for whites was 1.2 percent): Bureau of Justice Statistics, *Prisoners in 2001* (Washington DC, 2002). On these trends see Loïc Wacquant, *Les Prisons de la misère* (Paris, 1999).

[25] Jerome Miller, *Search and Destroy. African American Males in the Criminal Justice System* (Cambridge, 1996).

[26] According to the Bureau of Justice Statistics, *Report on Education and Correctional Populations* (Washington DC, 2003), prisoners in Federal and State Prisons, as well as jailers and probationers are much less educated than the general population. In particular, 27 percent of Federal prisoners, 40 percent of State inmates, 47 percent of jailers and 31 percent of probationers have no high-school education, compared with 18 percent of the general population. The same *Report* shows that minorities are less educated than whites, and that in 1997 17 percent of inmates were unemployed at the time of admission.

vertical increase in incarceration has corresponded – in the same period and with the same intensity – to a dramatic reduction in public provisions for poor families, social assistance and aid to the unemployed. For instance, only in the years 1993–1998 has there been a 44 percent decrease in the number of American families receiving 'Aid For Families With Dependent Children' (AFDC: the main subsidy provided by the American welfare system). Furthermore, a recent study by Katherine Beckett and Bruce Western shows that the increase in penal severity (and therefore in prison population) has been more pronounced in those US states in which welfare provisions have been reduced more (Texas, California, Louisiana, Arizona).[27]

The exclusionary logic of the American 'penal state' is also confirmed by the effects of the so called 'invisible punishments', which join imprisonment as further instruments for banishing whole categories of people from civil, social and political life. One important example here is represented by the 'Felony Disenfranchisement Laws': in the United States, 46 States deprive convicted offenders of the right to vote while in prison; 32 States extend this ban to those on parole; 14 States disenfranchise also ex-offenders, and 10 States disenfranchise ex-felons for life, thus excluding them permanently from the political sphere As a result of these provisions, '… an estimated 3.9 million US citizens are disenfranchised, including over one million who have fully completed their sentence'.[28] However, the impact of these measures is not equally distributed among the American population: once again, black people are disproportionally represented:

> Thirteen percent of African-American men – 1.4 million – are disenfranchised, representing just over one third (36 percent) of the total disenfranchised population.[29]

But the logic of exclusion is not limited to political rights: it extends also to the denial of housing and welfare benefits to drug offenders,[30] as well as to the termination of parental rights and to occupational bars.[31] Taking these developments into account, it would be difficult to argue that the rehabilitation, reintegration and inclusion of deviants in the social pact are still among the aims of contemporary punishment.[32]

---

[27] Bruce Western and Katherine Beckett, 'Governing Social Marginality: Welfare, Incarceration, and the Transformation of State Policy', in Garland (ed.), *Mass Imprisonment*, pp. 35–50.

[28] Human Rights Watch/The Sentencing Project, *Losing the Vote. The Impact of Felony Disenfranchisement Laws in the United States* (Washington DC, 1998), p. 1.

[29] Ibid., p. 1.

[30] According to the 'Personal Responsibility and Work Opportunity Reconciliation Act' signed by President Clinton in 1996, which '… imposes a lifetime ban on eligibility for TANF (Temporary Assistance to Needy Families) to individuals with drug felony convictions': Gwen Rubinstein and Debbie Mukamal, 'Welfare and Housing – Denial of Benefits to Drug Offenders', in Marc Mauer and Meda Chesney-Lynd (eds), *Invisible Punishment. The Collateral Consequences of Mass Imprisonment* (New York, 2002), p. 41.

[31] See Jeremy Travis, 'Invisible Punishment: An Instrument of Social Exclusion', Mauer and Chesney-Lynd (eds), *Invisible Punishment*, pp. 15–36.

[32] As seems to be suggested, for example, by Dario Melossi when – following Thomas Dumm he argues that '… the penitentiary and the other "ancillary institutions" … can be conceived as machines to process those who were not "naturally" within the scope of the social contract, i.e. those who have been perceived historically as incarnations of "otherness" (criminals of course, but also proletarians and those socially constructed as too distant from the anthropological model in power –

What these punitive measures seem to pursue is the plain 'exclusion' of whole fractions of the population from society, by reproducing a cycle of deprivation and marginality that permits their representation as threats and public enemies.

Obviously, the fact that the absolute majority of the prison population is composed by poor people, the unemployed, precarious and unskilled workers is not new: in fact, it is a *leitmotiv* in the history of the institution itself. The prison was invented for the confinement of these categories of people, and continues to perform its task – though in a more exclusionary way:

> It is now, as it has always been, the case that the weight of penal discipline falls disproportionately on the poorest. Recalling the historical tenacity of the discourse of less eligibility reminds us that it is designed to do so.[33]

What seems quite new, however, is the relationship between penal and social policies in the management of poverty and the control of the labour force. The new 'problem population' – the 'surplus' labour force produced by the post-Fordist economy – is managed less through the instruments for the 'social' regulation of poverty, and more through penal technologies. The consequence is the transition from the 'social state' to the 'penal state', to which Loic Wacquant refers when he defines the 'irresistible growth of the American penal state' as a strategy for the 'criminalisation of poverty' – which is functional to the 'imposition of precarious and under-paid waged labour' – and this transition is prompted by the concomitant 'reformulation of social programmes toward a more punitive regime'.[34]

It would be difficult to suggest that the American experiment with mass imprisonment and social exclusion is being replicated in the same way in other areas of the world, and particularly in Europe. We know that the European context is quite different, and that, in particular, the persistence of a 'welfare-model' of social regulation has prevented (to some extent) the diffusion of a paradigm of 'government through crime'. If it is true, as Western and Beckett argue (and Wacquant agrees), that in the US the emergence of a neo-liberal model has given a substantial contribution to the expansion of the penal realm as an instrument for the control of social contradictions, then we might argue that the limited diffusion of this model in Europe has prevented a full

---

a model usually male and "white", whatever "white" means': Dario Melossi, 'Introduction', to *The Sociology of Punishment. Socio-Structural Perspectives* (Aldershot, 1998), p. XIX. More precisely, I agree entirely with Melossi when he refers this analysis to the 'birth' of the prison – and to its development until the crisis of the industrial society: as Melossi suggests, this is in fact an important aspect of the disciplinary project described by Michel Foucault. I would disagree from this perspective, however, if it is applied to contemporary punishment: my point of view is that mass incarceration and the connected 'invisible punishments' are exclusionary both in instrumental and symbolic terms. Instrumentally, by deepening the exclusion of growing segments of the post-Fordist labour force; symbolically, by reasserting hierarchies and divisions within the labour-force, thus preventing it from forming political coalitions which would question the legitimacy of the contemporary neo-liberal order.

[33]   Richard Sparks, 'Penal Austerity: the Doctrine of Less Eligibility Reborn ?', in Roger Matthews and Peter Francis (eds), *Prisons 2000. An International Perspective of the Current State and Future of Imprisonment* (London, 1996), p. 87.

[34]   Wacquant, *Les Prisons de la misère*.

development of the new penal strategies described so far: in other words, we can still refer to what is happening to the US in terms of 'American exceptionalism'.

However, Wacquant himself warns that the tendency toward the penalisation of poverty is not exclusive to the US, given that a 'neo-liberal penal commonsense' is also spreading across Europe. Indeed, we can identify some commonalities between the American and the European context. In the last decade, incarceration rates grew by 43 percent in England; 39 percent in France; 49 percent in Greece; 140 percent in Portugal (now the state with the highest rates in Europe); 192 percent in Spain and 240 percent in the Netherlands. The only countries witnessing a slight reduction in prison populations are Germany, Finland and Austria.[35] But more than these quantitative data – showing in any case that the trend toward mass incarceration is not unique to the US – what should attract our attention is the composition of the European prison population.

If the American prison is affected by a process of 'blackening' and 'impoverishment', the same pattern is also observable in European prisons. For example, immigrants are dramatically overrepresented in all European penal systems. In Italy, between 1990 and 2000, the percentage of foreigners on the total prison population has shifted from 15 percent to 30 percent: a shocking percentage if one considers that they represent just 4 percent of the general population.[36] In Greece 39 percent of prisoners are immigrants; 34 percent in Germany; 38 percent in Belgium and 32 percent in the Netherlands. But, as I will show in the next pages, the 'detention' of immigrants is not limited to prisons. In fact, prompted by the diffusion of anti-immigration policies – more and more restrictive since the early 1990s, both at the national and the European level – new institutions for the confinement of 'illegal aliens' are being built across the European territory. The external borders of the EU are now disseminated with 'Immigration Detention Centres' whose function is to 'detain' immigrants (in a prison-like environment) on the ground of their administrative position of 'irregularity' – something which happens also in the US, where thousands of immigrants are imprisoned in detention camps on the Mexican-American border. Finally, in Italy as in the rest of Europe, the hyper-incarceration of foreigners goes systematically hand in hand with the overrepresentation of drug addicts and poor people.[37]

These are the coordinates of the new Euro-American penal strategy characterising the transition from Fordism to post-Fordism and from the welfare state to the penal state. However, one might ask: to what extent are these strategies really different from the disciplinary ones we already know? After all, what is emerging is nothing other than a renewed centrality of the prison – the disciplinary institution *par excellence* – in the management of the new labour force and of marginal social groups, whose numbers are growing as a consequence of increasing unemployment,

[35] Pierre Tournier, *Statistiques pénales annuelles du Conseil de l'Europe. Enquete 1997* (Strasbourg, 1999). See also André Kuhn, 'Incarceration Rates Across the World', in Michael Tonry (ed.), *Penal Reform in Overcrowded Times*, pp. 101–115.

[36] See Salvatore Palidda, *Devianza e vittimizzazione tra i migranti* (Milan, 2001).

[37] According to Pierre Tournier, drug-related prison convictions represent 21 percent of total convictions in France, 32 percent in Spain, 36 percent in Portugal, 33 percent in Italy. See Tournier, *Statistiques pénales annuelles du Conseil de l'Europe.*

underemployment, precarisation of work and poverty. And the 'division of labour' between the criminal justice system and welfare institutions in the management of surplus populations is a well established feature of modern capitalism.[38] In other words, we could think that the contemporary experiments of 'great confinement' are not very distant from the one described by Michel Foucault, and that the disciplinary project has not vanished, because the aim of these institutions continues to be the disciplining of the unskilled work-force. Following this perspective, a second 'primitive accumulation' – the post-Fordist capitalist accumulation – would be on its way; and this process of accumulation – as was the case for the one described by Karl Marx in the first volume of *Capital* – would require the forging of a new labour force: through penal discipline, 'bloody legislations' and harsh penalties for those who refuse to work.[39] When this labour force is fully developed – economically, socially and politically – it will gain a renewed position of power, being thus in the condition to struggle for new welfare provisions, higher wages, better working conditions and so on. And this would also affect the penal sphere, where incarceration rates would start to decrease and rehabilitation could prevail again over neutralisation and less eligibility.

This perspective counts many adherents among critical criminologists. Indeed, it would be quite convincing, if we accept that the development of capitalism – and the history of its ancillary social practices and institutions, like punishment and welfare – follows a *cyclical* trend.[40]

However, I am trying to submit a different hypothesis. What I would argue is that contemporary institutions and practices of penal control follow a post-disciplinary logic which locates them beyond cyclical recurrences, and that what has changed – with the transition from the industrial working class to the post-Fordist multitude – is the very rationality of control. To this post-disciplinary rationality – as exemplified by the mass-confinement experiments described so far – I now turn again.

---

[38] 'One principle was simply to refuse aid to all who were deemed able-bodied and employable, no matter whether there was in fact available employment. Another was to make conditions for the receipt of aid so abhorrent and so shameful that even the harshest work was preferable': Francis F. Piven and Richard A. Cloward, *The New Class War. Reagan's Attack on the Welfare State and its Consequences* (New York, 1982), p. 61. See also Mark Colvin, 'Controlling the Surplus Populations: the Latent Functions of Imprisonment and Welfare in Late US Capitalism', Brian D. MacLean (ed.), *The Political Economy of Crime* (Ontario, 1986), pp. 154–165.

[39] See the first volume of Karl Marx's *Capital* (Chapter XXIV).

[40] On the theory of capitalist cycles in the economic literature, see the works by Kondratieff, Mandel and Schumpeter quoted in chapter 1. For an application of this perspective to the political economy of punishment see Raymond J. Michalowsky and Susan M. Carlson, 'Unemployment, Imprisonment, and Social Structures of Accumulation: Historical Contingency in the Rusche-Kirchheimer Hypothesis', *Criminology*, 37/2 (1999): 217–249; Dario Melossi, 'Punishment and Social Action: Changing Vocabularies of Punitive Motive within a Political Business Cycle', *Current Perspectives in Social Theory*, 6 (1985): 169–197; Dario Melossi, 'Discussione a mo' di prefazione: carcere, postfordismo e ciclo di produzione della "canaglia"' (Foreword to Alessandro De Giorgi, *Il governo dell'eccedenza. Postfordismo e controllo della moltutudine* (Verona, 2002), pp. 7–24).

Incarcerating Risk: The Actuarial Prison

I would agree here with those scholars who, beginning in the early 1990s, hypothesised that contemporary crime policies – and, in particular, the American experiment of mass incarceration – follow a new rationality which is configuring the realm of a 'new penology'.[41]

The leitmotiv of this new rationality is represented by the concept of risk. Increasingly, social control technologies – and the post-Fordist prison in particular – seem to perform the task of managing risks and incapacitating those social groups which are considered – by the mass media, politicians, public opinion, and the criminal justice system itself – as 'risk-producers'. No longer oriented to the neutralisation of individual risk-factors through the incapacitation of single dangerous offenders – as was indeed the case with 'selective incapacitation' – the system would thus concentrate on the categorial management of a burden of risk which cannot be reduced.

In this respect, the rationality of control I refer to is no longer disciplinary: in fact, it is *actuarial*. The term 'actuarial' defines the mathematical calculations adopted by insurance companies, and describes the complex of procedures, logic inferences, statistical methods through which insurances treat collective risks. As is well known, the object of these strategies is simply to perform a rational, efficient and economic management of irreducible risks. The actuarial technology is in fact a system for the monetisation and redistribution of 'unspecified' risk factors within 'specified' populations:

> In insurance the term (risk) designates neither an event nor a general kind of event occurring in reality (the unfortunate kind), but a specific mode of treatment of certain events capable of happening to a group of individuals – or, more exactly, to values or capitals possessed or represented by a collectivity of individuals; that is to say, a population.[42]

From the point of view of the insurance company, risk factors are randomly distributed within a community, and they can be referred to each individual only as far as they are part of a category defined by certain aggregate indicators. Therefore, the first requisite of the 'insurantial' strategy is a probabilistic evaluation of collective risks, so that individuals can be assigned to homogeneous groups. Then, depending on the risk-category to which an individual belongs, it becomes possible to monetise each subject's exposure to risk, and to manage this condition within a larger aggregate of people. Obviously, individual conditions of risk can change over time, depending on factors, events and circumstances often beyond the subject's own will or behaviour. But statistically defined variations in risk-exposure give place only to a re-classification of individuals: these are simply redistributed across different categories, to which

---

[41] See Malcolm M. Feeley and Jonathan Simon, 'The New Penology. Notes on the Emerging Strategies of Corrections and its Implications', *Criminology*, 30/4 (1992): 449–474, and 'Actuarial Justice: The Emerging New Criminal Law', in David Nelken (ed.), *The Futures of Criminology* (London, 1994), pp. 173–201; Pat O'Malley, 'Legal Networks and Domestic Security', *Studies in Law, Politics, and Society*, 11 (1991): 170–190, and 'Risk, Power, and Crime Prevention', *Economy and Society*, 31/3 (1992): 252–275.

[42] François Ewald, 'Insurance and Risk', in Graham Burchell, Colin Gordon and Peter Miller (eds), *The Foucault Effect. Studies in Governmentality* (Chicago, 1991), p. 199.

peculiar forms of monetisation will correspond again. In this way, risk is redistributed without ever being reduced. After all, it is not individual risks that are important according to the logic of insurance, but only the interaction between aggregate levels of risk and those criteria through which collective risks can be translated into monetary value.[43]

Now, my point here is not to argue that the European and American criminal justice systems are adopting such technical devices to manage their deviant populations. The term 'actuarialism' is in fact used here as a metaphor describing two recent trends in crime policies: first, the fact that crime tends to be considered – in the technical language of practitioners and experts – as a 'normal fact', as a social phenomena which cannot be eliminated (as instead was believed at the time of 'criminological progressivism'); second, the term refers to the fact that whole categories of people – defined by peculiar factors like poverty, social exclusion, welfare dependency, ethnic origins or nationality – become the privileged targets of contemporary punitive policies. The hypothesis is that these policies do not treat the members of these 'undeserving' categories as individuals – by deploying 'inclusionary' strategies of social control targeted at removing the 'social causes' of deviance – but as parts of wider 'classes' to be collectively neutralised, incapacitated and warehoused. In this respect, the recurrence of concepts like 'underclass' in political (and criminological) discourses has a peculiar meaning: according to Malcolm Feeley and Jonathan Simon:

> The underclass is a permanently dysfunctional population, without literacy, without skills and without hope; a self-perpetuating and pathological segment of society that is not integrable into the larger whole, and whose culture fosters violence. Actuarial justice invites it to be treated as a high-risk group that must be managed for the protection of the larger society.[44]

It is not difficult to find evidence of the shift toward a risk-based model of social control: one should consider how discriminatorily some Federal or State 'sentencing guidelines' are applied in the US;[45] how routinely some categories of people – stereotyped as dangerous in public discourse – get harsher penalties for the same crimes.[46] Another significant example is also offered by the evolution of drug-testing

---

[43]   'Risk only becomes something calculable when it is spread over a population ... Insurance can only cover groups: it works by socializing risks. It makes each person a part of the whole. Risk itself only exists as an entity, a certainty, in the whole, so that each person insured represents only a fraction of it': Ewald, 'Insurance and Risk', p. 203.

[44]   Feeley and Simon, 'Actuarial Justice', p. 192.

[45]   I think here in particular of the '1986 Anti-Drug Abuse Act', clearly an 'actuarial' legislation. This law punishes the possession of five or more grams of crack cocaine with 5 to 20 years in prison. To get the same sentence for possession of powder cocaine, one has to be found with 500 grams. How can such a disproportion be justified? Only if one considers who is the average possessor of each variety of the same drug: crack is the poor, 'black' version of cocaine, while powder will be found more often in the pockets of the white middle- and upper-class. Clearly, African American youths are considered a dangerous category, and following an actuarial rationality they must be punished more harshly than their white, less dangerous, counterparts. See Beckett and Sassoon, *The Politics of Injustice*, pp. 94–97.

[46]   A clear example is represented by the treatment of immigrants in Italy. In this country – as in many others in Europe – the refusal to exhibit an Identity Document if requested to do so by a police

policies in the US. Until recently, using drugs would expose an individual to rehabilitative treatment, and therefore the priority of drug-control agencies was to identify users in order to plan for the most suitable programme, today the situation looks quite different. Individual drug-treatments have been replaced by random drug-testing: as a consequence, the aim is no longer to deliver suitable programmes to rehabilitate individuals, but to identify and isolate whole categories of drug-takers within the population. Random drug tests help to define a whole class of subjects and to prevent the risks they are deemed to pose to the community – by excluding them from the workplace, the neighbourhood, the gym:

> To use drugs would no longer be to challenge the moral sanction of the State and expose oneself to punishment, but instead to risk being denied access to the system. Rather than being defined as a 'deviant malefactor', the drug user becomes the self-selected occupant of a high-risk category that is channelled away from employment and the greater access it brings.[47]

Also some recent developments in the field of 'alternatives to imprisonment' – in particular, parole in the US – seem to be leading towards an actuarial model. No longer do rehabilitation, support, counselling and the reduction of recidivism represent the main objectives of the parole service: these ideals survive as rhetorical tools in the minds of some well-intentioned practitioners, but the concrete operational model has shifted towards a different framework. The main task of the parole officer is now to identify those categories of people who, given their actuarial 'status', are most suitable for parole revocation: so much so that 'parole and probation as sources of prison admissions have become almost as important as the court system itself'.[48] The indicators of success and failure of parole schemes have thus been reversed: no longer is success measured by the amount of people who do not re-offend, but (quite paradoxically) by the number of individuals who are channelled to prison, because this confirms the correctness of the risk-predictions made on them. In this sense, parole operates as a 'waste management' system, and the 'toxic waste' is represented by the 'underclass' communities.[49]

The same can be argued also about other segments of the criminal justice system. For instance, in probation the 'clinical model' for the prediction of dangerousness – based on the study of individual cases, the analysis of subjective variables and the

---

officer is a crime. However, if this crime is committed by an immigrant, both the fine and the prison term imposed by the law are *twice* the ones provided for an Italian citizen. This provision was introduced by the Italian '1998 Immigration Law' as an amendment to the *Penal Code*.

[47] Jonathan Simon, 'The Emergence of a Risk Society: Insurance, Law, and the State', *Socialist Review*, 95 (1987): 85. On the issue of drug control, see also Pat O'Malley and Stephen Mugford, 'Moral Technology: the Political Agenda of Random Drug Testing', *Social Justice*, 18/4 (1991): 122–146.

[48] Caplow and Simon, 'Understanding Prison Policy and Population Trends', p. 102. On this aspect, see also Joan Petersilia, 'Parole and Prisoner Reentry in the United States', Tonry and Petersilia (eds), *Prisons. Crime and Justice. A Review of Research*, 26 (1999): 479–529.

[49] Jonathan Simon, *Poor Discipline: Parole and the Social Control of the Underclass, 1890–1990* (Chicago, 1993). For a critique of this position, based on an ethnographic research conducted in California, see Mona Lynch, 'Waste Managers: The New Penology, Crime Fighting, and Parole Agent Identity', *Law & Society Review*, 32/4 (1998): 839–871.

reconstruction of single 'biographies' – is being put increasingly under question by the diffusion of 'actuarial models' for the assessment of categorial risk 'based upon the statistical analysis of data derived from sample groups of the population'.[50]

Finally, signs of a risk-oriented rationality of control can be detected also in the US Juvenile Justice System: here, according to Kempf-Leonard and Peterson, three different models for the treatment of juveniles have been hegemonic in the course of twentieth century: an early model – developed around 1900 – emphasised individual reform and correction, thus overlooking the principles of justice and equality; a second model – which gained its momentum around 1960 – privileged due process and treatment, in coherence with the correctional project prevailing in the criminal justice system; finally, the last decade of the century has witnessed the emergence of managerialism and 'tough justice', and here 'actuarial' technologies find their way into juvenile justice.[51]

However, it is not just in the universe of penality that actuarial rationalities appear to prevail over individual-oriented technologies: for example, important signs also come from the field of psychiatry, where according to Robert Castel:

> The essential component of intervention no longer takes the form of the direct face-to-face relationship between the carer and the cared, the helper and the helped, the professional and the client. It comes instead to reside in the establishing of flows of population based on the collation of a range of abstract factors deemed liable to produce risk in general.[52]

Now, let us turn back to the prison again. Here actuarialism means that the selection of the prison population takes place through the identification (better, the 'artificial construction') of whole categories of people as 'risk producers'.[53] It is not so much the individual characteristics of subjects that are the object of penal control, as instead those social factors which permit to assign some individuals to a peculiar risk-class. In other words, whole categories of people virtually cease to *commit crimes*, in order to *become crimes* themselves.[54]

---

[50] Hazel Kemshall, *Reviewing Risk. A Review of Research on the Assessment and Management of Risk and Dangerousness: Implications for Policy and Practice in the Probation Service* (London, 1996), p. VI. This author suggests that the 'actuarial model' and the 'clinical model' can be used jointly by probation officers. However, actuarial predictions should always precede individual assessments: 'Staff will need to learn and apply the appropriate baseline actuarial knowledge prior to carrying out in-depth interviews aimed at clinically assessing patterns of behaviour and motivations': Ibid., p. 31. In other words, an individual would be given the right to see their own biography taken into consideration only after they have been actuarially classified.

[51] Kimberly Kempf-Leonard and Elicka Peterson, 'Expanding Realms of the New Penology. The Advent of Actuarial Justice for Juveniles', *Punishment and Society*, 2/1 (2000): 66–97.

[52] Robert Castel, 'From Dangerousness to Risk', in Burchell, Gordon and Miller (eds), *The Foucault Effect*, p. 281.

[53] It is important to note that very often an important contribution to the 'construction' of this population is offered by the functioning of the other systems analysed earlier. The psychiatric system, parole and probation services and drug-enforcement agencies: all these practices and institutions of social control cooperate to the selection of populations suitable for mass-incarceration. One should look at the proportion of American inmates who are mentally-ill, drug addicts, ex-probationers and ex-parolees!

[54] On this 'ontological' aspect of deviance, see Lydia Morris, *Dangerous Class. The Underclass and Social Citizenship* (London, 1999).

By presenting these examples of new practices of penal control, what I am suggesting is that concrete individuals and the social interaction in which they are involved tend to be replaced by the production of classes and categories that are 'simulacra' of the real. 'Illegal immigrants', 'African Americans from the inner city', 'drug addicts', 'the unemployed': it is toward these artificial categories that post-disciplinary control – in its various reclusive forms – is exercised. Whereas disciplinary technologies defined a complex of 'human laboratories' in which the development of control strategies permitted the constitution of new knowledge about the subject – which would in turn be applied reflexively to the same subjects in order to increase their productivity – actuarial mass incarceration (and the other risk-based technologies described so far) seem to break this circle.

Actuarial control declares the irrelevance of any knowledge about individuals and replaces it with the construction of arbitrary categories and forms of individuation, based on the ephemeral concept of dangerousness, and oriented to the confinement of socially constructed 'dangerous others'. The peculiarities of the subject, which disciplinary technologies aimed to know, to subjugate and to forge, leave way to social aggregates on which the agencies of crime control base their new guidelines for selecting the population to be confined.

Thus, the diffusion of a risk-based rationality gives birth to a complex of practices whose aim is to de-structure individuals; in other words, actuarial technologies do not simply 'represent' individuals according to some risk-assessment procedures: in fact they 'produce' individuals. Following Jonathan Simon: 'These practices do not merely represent us. To represent us in a certain way is also to shape how we actually are, if our society makes vital choices based upon such representations.'[55]

In the field of criminal justice, the emergence of an actuarial logic goes hand in hand with the diffusion of a managerial rationality: a 'systemic' rationality based on the principles of economisation of resources, monetisation of risks, and cost-effectiveness.[56] It should be noted however, that *this is a fully post-Fordist managerial rationality*: external to the complexity of the social world and incapable of producing a real knowledge about its own fields of application, it replaces the disciplinary regulation of social forces with an attempt at managing potentialities it can no longer control. I would argue that it is exactly the increasing difficulty of separating the deviant from the precarious worker, the criminal subject from the 'illegal' immigrant, the hidden worker from the informal one, which prompts the grouping of human 'diversities' into dangerous classes. In other words, it is as if the difficulty to redraw the traditional distinction between 'dangerous' and 'laborious' classes as they can be inferred from the characteristics of individuals, compelled post-disciplinary institutions of control to perform this task by resorting to categorial risk.

Nonetheless, it should be remembered that the presence of an actuarial logic within institutions and practices of social regulation does not represent a complete novelty in the history of Western societies: in fact, the welfare state itself can be described as a model of government which connected disciplinary practices for the control of individuals, to actuarial systems for the socialisation of the risks affecting the

---

[55] Simon, 'The Emergence of a Risk Society', p. 65.
[56] On these aspects of actuarialism see in particular Ian Taylor, *Crime in Context. A Critical Criminology of Market Societies* (Cambridge, 1999).

population as a whole. In that context, actuarial technologies worked as instruments for the social redistribution of risks produced by industrialisation, the labour market, dangerous productions, polluting factors and so on: it was a socialised mechanism for relieving individuals from the risks emerging in industrial society. In this sense, this 'social version' of the actuarial technology was part of what Michel Foucault defined as a *bio-political* model of government: a 'power over life' whose visible embodiments were the national health systems, social insurances, labour legislations, unemployment benefit systems, etc. In all these cases, actuarial rationality informed the bio-political dispositives for the regulation of populations.[57]

What seems to be changing, however, is the way in which risk technologies are connected to the new strategies of social control. Whereas in the welfarist version, the actuarial rationality produced mechanisms of regulation based on the socialisation of collective risks, thus enhancing social interactions inspired by cooperation, empathy and solidarity, contemporary technologies of control lead to the opposite direction: they limit, neutralise and de-structure those forms of social interaction now deemed to be dangerous. In systematic connection with a political rhetoric which promotes the social perception of fear, insecurity, risk and criminal dangers as always posed by 'strangers', these technologies perform both the instrumental role of selecting a surplus population suitable for mass confinement, and the symbolic role of de-structuring the social bonds within the post-Fordist labour force.[58] Mass incarceration, sustained by a political rhetoric of war, invasion and siege, contributes to the public representation of the 'social surplus' as a new dangerous class, and thus de-socialises the post-Fordist multitude by preventing the formation of stable relationships of cooperation within it. Thus, empathy is replaced by what Pat O'Malley defines 'new prudentialism': a regime of universal diffidence opposed to any reciprocal recognition among individuals, as parts of the same labour-force. To make just one example, by representing immigrants as a dangerous class and as public enemies, the dominant class prevents the lowest strata of the national labour force from recognising in their foreign fellows suitable allies in the struggles over work conditions, welfare benefits, etc: in this way, the 'immigrant' becomes either a competitor in the labour market – as a worker – or a scapegoat for all social insecurities – as a criminal.

Thus, the process of constructing diversity – of places, situations, individuals and whole social groups – as dangerous, defines new hierarchies and imposes new social distances: 'communities of fear' replace other forms of communal self-identification,

---

[57] It is the French philosopher Ewald who first studied the relationship between actuarial rationality and the birth of the welfare state: see François Ewald, *L'Etat-Providence* (Paris, 1986), 'Norms, Discipline and the Law', *Representations*, 30 (1990): 136–161 and 'Insurance and Risk'.

[58] '[The past decade] has witnessed the partial transformation of socialised actuarialism into privatised actuarialism (or prudentialism) as an effect of political interventions promoting the increased play of market forces. More specifically this has involved three integrally related changes: the retraction of socialised risk-based techniques (public benefit) from managing the risks confronting the poor; their progressive replacement by disciplinary or sovereign remedies; and the privatisation of public benefits as an aspect of the extension of privatised risk-based technique': Pat O'Malley, 'Risk, Power and Crime Prevention', p. 257, but see also his 'Risk, Crime and Prudentialism Revisited', in Stenson and Sullivan (eds), *Crime, Risk and Justice*, pp. 89–103.

and prevent a common sense of belonging from emerging within the post-Fordist experience of work:

> Threats and dangers, and fears about them, are dealt with by the construction of suitable enemies, and attendant negative labelling, denial, avoidance and exclusion. Solidarity is based on a commonality of fear. In some cases, such as the war on drugs, insecurities are cultivated and focused on unfortunate people to gain political purchase and to offset the endemic insecurity experienced more generally in everyday life.[59]

As a result, the multiplicity of differences, the mixture of languages, the irreducibility of experiences – in short, all those aspects which suggest to define the contemporary labour-force as a multitude – are successfully depicted by the dominant public discourse as sources of insecurity, panic, and fear of 'strangers'.[60]

In conclusion, the preservation of contemporary social order seems to invoke the deployment of strategies of control capable of disarticulating those very forms of socialisation and social cooperation which the Fordist system had to enhance because they represented the source of its productivity: in fact, they appear now as dangerous interactions to be prevented.[61] As we will see in the following chapter, this rationality of 'preventive repression' is expanding well beyond the field of crime control, to cover other fields of social life. In this respect, one of the most paradigmatic examples is offered by the recent developments in the penal government of immigration, on both sides of the Atlantic Ocean.

---

[59] Richard V. Ericson and Kevin Carriere, 'The Fragmentation of Criminology', in Nelken, *The Futures of Criminology*, pp. 102–103. Gregg Barak puts it another way: 'In television, for example ... the working class has all but disappeared. As a result, there are basically three kinds of classes constructed by the mass media: the rich classes, the middle classes, and the criminal classes': Gregg Barak, 'Between Waves: Mass-mediated Themes of Crime and Justice', *Social Justice*, 3 (1994): 134. However, the meaning does not change: work and exploitment as grounds for the construction of a shared sense of belonging are replaced by fear and insecurity. This analysis is not very distant from the one proposed by David Garland, who suggests that – in our contemporary 'culture of control' – the symbolic role traditionally played by the 'oppressed' in modern society has been taken by the universal 'victim'. In other terms, 'victimhood', more than 'oppression', has become a common base for mutual identification and solidarity: sentiments that find their most coherent expression in the emerging punitive attitudes: Garland, *The Culture of Control*, pp. 200–201.

[60] For a description of the process of construction of 'strangers', and for an analysis of its role in the reproduction of an 'existential insecurity' which legitimises contemporary forms of power, see Zygmunt Bauman, *Liquid Modernity* (Cambridge, 2000).

[61] In this context one can make sense of the process of 'normalisation of emergencies' we witness in Western societies. I am referring here to the systematic reproduction – by the mass media and by the political system – of 'criminal emergencies' which, on the one hand, allow to construct new 'dangerous classes' (and to attach them a clear identity: paedophiles, Satanists, Islamic fundamentalists, hackers, Albanians, nomads, etc.); on the other, to produce a social consensus around new repressive measures. We can speak of 'normalisation' in two senses: first, because these emergencies are more and more frequent; second, because once they have ceased to exist (and thus disappear from the scene of the mass-media, their only level of existence), the punitive measures adopted to deal with them remain in place, thus normalising the authoritarian effects of their application and implementation. A good example is offered here by the various 'anti-terrorism' legislations enacted around the Western world in the aftermath of the terrorist attacks of 11 September 2001.

Chapter 5

The Criminalisation of International Migrations: Towards an Actuarial Model of Control?

Introduction: Migrations in a Global Economy

Labour migrations represent a constant feature in the history of the capitalist system of production: according to the French sociologist and historian Yann Moulier Boutang, the genealogy of Western capitalism is deeply inscribed in the conflict between workers – struggling for the freedom to move – and the capitalist classes – whose interest has always been to reach a complete control over the mobility of labour.[1] This perspective has been very helpful for the emergence of non-orthodox reconstructions of the historical relations between capital and labour, but it shows an even greater utility if it is applied to the current phenomenon of international migrations and their regulation.[2] In fact, in the global economy of our times this historical conflict reappears in what Malcolm Anderson defines as the contemporary 'regime of frontier' – the body of practices, laws and institutions regulating the political, administrative, economic and social meaning of national and continental borders.[3]

Many observers of the present condition argue that the globalisation of the economy has produced a crisis of the nation states, due to a growing difficulty to exercise a political control over economic phenomena: financial capital, global transactions, and more generally the 'new economy' seem in fact to escape any attempt at regulation by the states. It has become virtually impossible for national governments to prevent flows of capital, information or money from crossing their borders. A new commonsense has thus emerged, which sees the contemporary world as a 'borderless'

---

[1] Yann M. Boutang, *De l'esclavage au salariat. Economie historique du salariat bridé* (Paris, 1998). In this sense I agree with Dario Melossi when he argues that: 'Processes of globalisation, migration and "modernization" go back at least to the Middle Ages. Migration constituted in a sense the womb within which all kinds of working class have originated … ': Dario Melossi, '"In a Peaceful Life"'. Migration and the Crime of Modernity in Europe/Italy, *Punishment and Society*, 5/4 (2003): 371.

[2] For an analysis of the recent history of migrations, see Saskia Sassen, *The Mobility of Labor and Capital. A Study in International Investment and Labor Flow* (New York, 1988); Stephen Castles and Mark Miller, *The Age of Migration: International Population Movements in the Modern World* (New York, 1998).

[3] Malcolm Anderson, 'The Transformation of Border Controls: A European Precedent?', in Peter Andreas and Timothy Snyder (eds), *The Wall around the West. State Borders and Immigration Controls in North America and Europe* (Lahnam, 2000), pp. 15–29.

entity: a feature alternatively execrated by the nostalgic of the national sovereignty and celebrated by the apologues of neo-liberalism.[4]

My point of view is that this version is at least partial and incomplete. In fact, I would agree that the borders of the nation states are becoming weak barriers to the circulation of capital, investments and commodities; they might also be losing their meaning as symbolic frontiers to the circulation of cultural and consumerist models – be it 'Third World music', 'ethnic restaurants' or 'non-Western cinema'. In this respect, it is reasonable to conclude that globalisation implies a rewriting of the economic, cultural and social geographies of the world, in which the concepts of 'movement' and 'mobility' become the main coordinates of a new hegemonic philosophy. But the 'de-bordering' of the Western world on the financial, economic and cultural level, has been accompanied by a simultaneous process of 're-bordering':

> The celebrated debordering of the state is far more selective than the inflated rhetoric of globalization would suggest. Debordering is being accompanied in many places by a partial rebordering in the form of enhanced policing. Even as many borders have been demilitarized in the traditional realm of national security, as well as economically liberalized to facilitate commercial exchange, they are also now more criminalized to deter those who are perceived as trespassers.[5]

In other words, the borders seem to maintain all their symbolic meaning and material impact concerning the circulation of *people* – particularly asylum seekers and migrant workers. However, also these restrictions are not 'democratically' distributed: it is not all non-US or non-Europeans that are prevented from crossing the external borders of Europe or the American frontier with Mexico. In fact, only some categories of people suffer a process of criminalisation for their international mobility: in particular, those coming from the *poor countries*, from the Southern or Eastern world. As a matter of fact, a non-EU citizen can be American or Swiss as well as Nigerian or Palestinian: in a strict legal sense, there is no difference between them. But as a matter of fact, there are many differences concerning formal and informal practices – visas, passports, civil rights and judicial or extra-judicial treatment.

In other words, we see here a first important divide between the 'regime of frontiers' concerning capital and people, and a second divide between 'First-World' and 'Third-World' citizens. Mobility and freedom of circulation are among the most important resources for economic success in a competitive and individualistic society, but they are not equally distributed. Thus, capital (in any form: money, ideas, signs, commodities) and a 'privileged' minority of people can circulate almost without control, whereas the circulation of those individuals whose work guarantees the reproduction of capital and the high standards of living of First-World citizens – is constrained by strict immigration laws. In this sense, what we witness is not so much the disappearance of borders, as their fragmentation and flexibility: borders no longer exist as unitary entities, as clear boundaries separating one territory from the other.

---

[4]   See Kenichi Ohmae, *The Borderless World: Power and Strategy in the Interlinked Economy* (New York, 1990).

[5]   Peter Andreas, 'Introduction: The Wall after the Wall', in Andreas and Snyder (eds), *The Wall around the West*, p. 2.

Instead, they represent flexible instruments for the reproduction of a hierarchical division between 'deserving' and 'undeserving' populations, 'wanted' and 'unwanted' others.

Therefore, the meaning of contemporary borders has less to do with the geographic delimitation of sovereign powers, and much more with the capacity to keep at distance some categories of people: those people whose visible presence endangers the legitimacy of the neo-liberal order. Borders become themselves mobile, and can be shifted in order to track the actual or potential movements of those people who must be prevented from leaving their countries of origin. As a consequence, institutional and economic actors such as consulates, private actors, 'third countries', internal and external police forces play now the role of 'flexible border enforcers'.

The de-bordering of the world for capital and its flexible re-bordering for human beings are strictly connected phenomena. In other words, the reappearance of borders against labour migrations does not represent 'the most compelling exception to liberalism in the operation of the world economy', as one commentator suggests.[6] Instead, I would argue that the criminalisation of migrations is in effect 'the other side' of the liberalisation of capital and investments.[7] In fact, how would Western multinationals gain their profits from the Third-World's deregulated labour markets if workers were free to leave those countries? The result is not too far from a condition of 'global apartheid' in which:

> ... the most economically developed and affluent countries are banding together to protect their privileged position in much the same way that Afrikaners and others of European descent sought to maintain their dominance in South Africa.[8]

Again, the attempt to regulate, contain and prevent the movements of workers is not a novelty in the history of Western capital: to some extent, the 'colonial experiences' of many Western countries can be understood as attempts by the dominant nations to exert a direct control over the labour force of the 'underdeveloped' areas of the world. And in this sense '... the immigration of manual workers to Western Europe [resembles] colonization in reverse'.[9] However, what deserves our attention is the visible contradiction already mentioned: the paradox for which our societies, dominated by the philosophy of flexibility, mobility, freedom, economic initiative and other imperatives of the neo-liberal ideology, deploy all technologies of control, segregation and neutralisation whenever 'other' people – often coming from the former colonies of the Western world – try to adapt themselves to this ideology, thus leaving their own territories in search of a better life.

---

6 Jagdish N. Bhagwati, 'Incentives and Disincentives: International Migration', *Weltwirtschaftliches Archiv*, 120/4 (1994): 680.

7 Thus we can understand why, for example, labour was excluded from the *North American Free Trade Agreement* (NAFTA), despite Mexico's pressures. On this aspect, see Peter Andreas, *Border Games: Policing the US-Mexico Divide* (Ithaca, 2000). See also Wayne Cornelius, *et al.* (eds), *Controlling Immigration: A Global Perspective* (Stanford, 1994).

8 Anthony Richmond, *Global Apartheid: Refugees, Racism and the New World Order* (New York, 1994), p. 216.

9 Stephen Castles and Godula Kosack, *Immigrant Workers and Class Structure in Western Europe* (London, 1973), p. 481.

A plausible explanation for this paradox is offered by the growing inequalities between the 'developed' and 'underdeveloped' areas of the world: something I cannot analyse in depth here. However, as a quick incursion in this very complex field, I would argue that the contemporary policies of immigration control perform at least two important tasks: first, by making it almost impossible for the 'wretched of the Earth'[10] to leave their countries – through a rigid control of the borders and the provision of strict 'quotas' of immigrant workers – Western capital reproduces a large army of cheap labour which can be exploited for the most dangerous and polluting productions dislocated in the poorest areas of the world; in this respect, immigration controls play a crucial role in the global division of labour. Second, by systematically denying a condition of full citizenship to those people who finally cross the borders, Western economic systems reproduce a population of localised workers who will accept any condition of work, as this will be preferable to being deported to their countries of origin.[11] This vicious circle configures a regime of 'global less eligibility', in which Western immigration policies and criminal justice systems seem to be almost replacing international relations as instruments for the regulation of the global labour force.[12]

The recent history of immigration in advanced economies shows a generalised tendency toward stricter controls, and more generally a 'negative' public attitude toward the international mobility of people: something which can be observed both in the US and in Europe. In the next pages, I will concentrate particularly on the European case, which in my view is paradigmatic of the more general tendency mentioned above: in fact, the making of the EU has marked important shifts in the regulation of international migrations, thus defining a new framework to which European countries must adapt. Later, this framework will help us to understand also some developments of US immigration policies.

More generally, however, some important changes took place in the same years in which I located both the transition from Fordism to post-Fordism and the emergence of a new punitive philosophy exemplified by actuarial mass incarceration: in fact, the 'get tough' policies on immigration and the process of 're-bordering' now affecting all industrialised countries started around 1973, both in Europe and in the US.[13] Until that period, Central and Northern European countries – particularly Germany, France, Britain, Belgium and the Netherlands – adopted a 'tolerant' approach to foreign workers coming both from Southern Europe – Italy, Turkey, Greece and Spain – and from the former Western colonies – India, Pakistan, and some African countries. Though with some differences and peculiarities connected to the particular history of

---

[10] Frantz Fanon, *The Wretched of the Earth* (New York, 1963).

[11] As suggested for example by Kitty Calavita, 'A "Reserve Army of Delinquents". The Criminalization and Economic Punishment of Immigrants in Spain', *Punishment and Society*, 5/4 (2003): 399–413.

[12] This 'radical' perspective on immigration regimes is suggested by, among others, Michael Burawoy, 'The Functions and Reproduction of Migrant Labor: Comparative Materials from Southern Africa and the United States', *American Journal of Sociology*, 81 (1976): 1050–1087.

[13] This periodisation is largely accepted in the international literature on migrations. For a review, see Saskia Sassen, *Migranten, Siedler, Fluechtinge. Von der Massenauswanderung zur Festung Europa* (Frankfurt am Main, 1996) and Costis Hadjimichalis and David Sadler (eds), *Europe at the Margins: New Mosaics of Inequality* (New York, 1995).

each country, European nations accepted, and to some extent even promoted, immigration during the Fordist period (1945–1975) for economic reasons: the expansion of mass-industrial production needed workers to be employed in 'heavy productions', and the scarcity of 'natives' who would accept over-exploitative conditions of work suggested that a certain amount of labour force had to be 'imported' from abroad. In other words, as far as these countries needed a surplus of labour force, their immigration policies were substantially tolerant and the international mobility of labour was perceived as necessary for capitalist development.

In this context – and considering that this was also the period of expansion of the welfare state – migrants were recognised some citizenship rights which contributed to their integration in the countries of destination.[14] As far as social rights were recognised on a 'semi-universal' basis, public resources were abundant and employment was guaranteed, immigrant workers (and their families) experienced a condition of relative social inclusion – though in a subordinated status and often suffering discrimination and racism, especially those coming from non-European countries.[15]

This situation changed suddenly in the early 1970s. In these years many European countries started to close their borders and to impose a moratorium on immigration: in 1972 France and Germany started to block immigration and developed programs for the repatriation of foreign workers; Austria followed in 1974; in 1973 the United Kingdom promoted a restrictive reform of immigration laws which would culminate in 1981 with a complete reform of the rules of citizenship.

It would be difficult here to offer a full description of the reasons for the transformation of immigration policies which took place in these years. Instead, I would try to list some of the more debated and accepted ones: the international oil crisis and its consequences for Western economies; the fiscal crisis of the welfare states; the capitalist restructuring which opened the way to the new economy; the dismissal of mass-industrial production.[16] Growing unemployment, labour flexibility, the crisis of the Fordist factory: all these factors instilled growing feelings of insecurity and vulnerability in Western citizens. These sentiments were easily exploited by the mass media and by politicians in search of legitimacy, thus leading public opinions to think that foreign workers were subtracting workplaces from the local economies, 'scrounging' welfare benefits, collapsing the national health and public housing

---

14 However, it should be noted that there were significant differences in the 'immigration regimes' of the European countries: it is possible to identify some peculiar models concerning the legal and social status of foreigners, which often depended on the 'colonial past' of these countries. For example, Germany adopted a non-assimilation policy, for which immigrants were considered as 'temporary hosts' (*Gastarbeiters*) who would leave the country after short periods of residence, whereas France adopted a policy of 'naturalization' – foreigners had to be absorbed within the French citizenship as soon as possible. Britain seemed to adopt a mixed policy: assimilation for those coming from the former colonies, and temporary residence for the others.

15 See Robin Cohen (ed.), *The Cambridge Survey of World Migration* (Cambridge, 1995).

16 According to Nigel Harris, the closing of borders took place in Europe and the US almost in the same years. What differentiates these two continents is that the crisis of Fordism produced different consequences in the two contexts: in Europe it was characterised by an increase in unemployment, whereas in the US the main effect was the diffusion of precarious and insecure work, with growing economic inequalities. See Nigel Harris, *The New Untouchables. Immigration and the New World Worker* (Harmondsworth, 1996).

systems. Last but not least came the process of European unification with the related issues of 'border control' and 'internal security': as we will see, the abolition of intra-European frontiers went hand in hand with a renewed emphasis on the need to reinforce the external borders.

Though we should not overlook the important (legal, political and social) differences characterising the European nations in this shift toward stricter immigration policies, some common traits are nonetheless observable (as they are also between Europe and the US). First, though the policy of 'borders closure' did not simultaneously affect all states, it is now shared by everyone: those countries who had experienced consistent flows of immigration since the Second World War closed their borders in the early 1970s, whereas other countries like Spain and Italy – which are experiencing immigration only since the late 1980s – would develop anti-immigration laws later but with the same intensity.[17] Second, the 'get tough' policies emerged in a context of growing moral panic about the 'problem' of immigration: the equation between immigration and crime became quickly a *leitmotif* in mass-mediated representations of this issue, as well as the assumption that more immigrants meant less work, social guarantees, public housing, medical care, pensions, and so on.[18]

The third commonality, which actually appears to be a consequence of the former two, is that anti-immigration policies are not limited to a stricter control of the borders (in order to prevent undesired entries): this is just one side of a much wider political strategy whose strongest impact is felt at the level of citizenship rights. Recent policies on immigration are in fact two-sided: on the one hand their aim is to make it almost impossible for immigrants to gain access to the European territory – but the same can be said about the militarization of the Mexican border with the US. On the other hand, they negatively affect the legal status and social conditions of those who cross the borders: here a systematic denial of civil, political and social rights configures a new regime of non-citizenship or 'semi-citizenship' for large numbers of people, which relegates them to a condition of permanent exclusion.[19] Even a cursory glance at the European legislations regulating the civil status of immigrants – particularly of 'illegal' immigrants, a category whose growth is a direct consequence of the closing of borders – reveals that it is appropriate to define them as *non-persons*. In the words of the Italian sociologist Alessandro Dal Lago:

---

[17]   Until the end of the 1970s Italy, Spain, Greece and Portugal were 'exporters' of migrants. Thousands of workers left these countries in search of a better life in the northern regions of Europe (Germany, France, Belgium, Great Britain). Since the early 1990s however, these nations ceased to be countries of 'emigration' and started to be 'immigration' countries, thus sharing the same 'problems' experienced earlier by the strongest European economies. It should be noted that the 'memory' of 'emigration' did not mitigate the negative attitudes of Southern Europeans toward the new immigrants. Quite to the contrary, the commonsensical perception is that 'we' were good immigrants in search of work and life opportunities, whereas 'they' (immigrants coming now from Eastern Europe, Northern Africa and Asia) are dangerous 'others' and potential criminals.

[18]   Sara Diamond, 'Right-Wing Politics and the Anti-Immigration Cause', *Social Justice*, 23/3 (1996): 154–168.

[19]   See for example Lydia Morris, 'Britain's Asylum and Immigration Regime: the Shifting Contours of Rights', *Journal of Ethnic and Migration Studies*, 28/3 (2002): 409–425.

To begin with, one should think about the limits which language imposes to the definition of these categories of human beings. As we can see from the image of migrants in the press and more generally in the mass-media, a foreigner will be alternatively an 'extra-European', an 'immigrant', a 'clandestine', an 'illegal' – categories which do not refer to some peculiar characteristic of his/her being, but to what s/he is not, compared to our categories: non-European, non-native, non-citizen, non-regular, not one of us. Starting from this linguistic opacity, to which a total social invisibility corresponds, we pose the conditions for these people not to be persons, and to be literally neutralised.[20]

We will see in the next pages how this condition of social, juridical and economic inferiority of immigrants is being promoted in the European and Northern American context. The chapter ends with a critical review of the various regimes of detention which are imposed to migrants on both sides of the Atlantic Ocean (in conditions often resembling those of 'concentration camps'). In this respect, the regulation of immigrants offers itself as a paradigmatic case-study of the emerging strategies of social control described in the earlier chapters: penal and extra-penal policies play, in fact, a crucial role in the management of immigrant populations, and concepts like the transition from the welfare state to the penal state or the diffusion of risk-based technologies of detention become much clearer here. My hypothesis is that the field of contemporary immigration policies should be seen as a 'laboratory' in which new strategies, practices and institutions for the authoritarian control of the post-Fordist 'advanced marginality' are experimented.[21] Therefore, in the actual condition of immigrants in Europe and the US, I would identify one of the clearest examples of what Charles Murray refers to, when he celebrates the idea of a 'custodial democracy' which '... takes as its premise that a substantial portion of the population cannot be expected to function as citizens'.[22]

In the next few pages I concentrate on the process of European unification (particularly in the fields of penal policies and immigration control), taken as a paradigmatic example of the process of 'bifurcation of citizenship'. We will see to what extent the construction of a 'European entity' is based on the imposition of a 'custodial democracy' to some categories of people: the same categories usually targeted for mass incarceration and other forms of administrative detention.

European Immigration Control: Towards a 'Penal State'?

As was suggested earlier, the process of European unification represents one of the clearest examples of the mentioned process of 'de-bordering' and 're-bordering' which is characterising the evolution of the nation-state. In fact, the construction of the European Union has proceeded along two parallel and complementary paths: internally, the national borders have been gradually abolished, thus opening the way toward the creation of a unified monetary, economic and (to some extent) political

---

[20] Alessandro Dal Lago, *Non Persone. L'esclusione dei migranti in una società globale* (Milan, 1999).

[21] See Loïc Wacquant, 'The Rise of Advanced Marginality', *Acta Sociologica*, 39/2 (1996): 121–139.

[22] Charles Murray, 'The Underclass Revisited', quoted in John Lea, *Crime and Modernity* (London, 2002), p. 116.

space. Externally, however, the borders regain their importance as barriers to the free circulation of non-European citizens. Not only have these two processes proceeded simultaneously, but to some extent the former caused the latter: as far as the circulation of capital, services, money and European citizens became almost free within the territory of Europe, it became more and more necessary to exert a stricter control over the access of 'foreigners' into that territory.

The European entity does not materialise itself in an empty space. Its construction is not disconnected from the political and economic transformations affecting the Western world since the last quarter of the twentieth century. My mind goes here to the gradual restriction of social citizenship, which has accompanied the restructuring of the Fordist economy and of the social institutions based on that model of development; to the drastic 'reforms' of welfare systems which started in the early 1970s and the consequent reduction of social rights; to the 'crisis of legitimacy' affecting the nation-states in the context of a global economy. But another important aspect is the 'reaction' of Western states to this erosion of their sovereign prerogatives. A reaction which sees the governmental powers of the state – public intervention in the economy, individual and social welfare, protection of citizens from the 'global risks' – being reduced to one dimension: the monopoly over the use of force.[23] Thus, we see this force materialising itself – both in Europe and in the US – in the systematic criminalisation of the new 'others' and the new excluded: immigrants, poor, single mothers, drug-addicts and more generally the new 'dangerous classes'.

In the wake of the crisis of public institutions (whose causes are to be found in the gradual substitution of the 'public sphere' by a totalising 'economic reason'), it becomes possible and 'necessary' to represent the 'collateral effects' of neo-liberalism (the poor, displaced people, immigrants) as 'enemies' and as the real causes of insecurity and fear. In this context, the unquestioned hegemony of the market is accompanied by the exhibition of a penal power against the new enemies of the existing order.[24] Dangers come from abroad and risks are always 'external': by blaming 'others' for the diffusion of feelings of insecurity and vulnerability, the deep contradictions of contemporary societies are obscured and the legitimacy of the whole system is guaranteed. In this process, the symbolic meaning of the borders becomes crucial, as Kai Erikson already suggested 40 years ago, when he wrote that:

> The deviant is a person whose activities have moved outside the margins of the group, and when the community calls him to account for that vagrancy it is making a statement about the nature and placement of its boundaries. It is declaring how much variability and diversity can be tolerated within the group before it begins to lose its distinctive shape, its unique identity.[25]

---

[23] For a description of the transformations of sovereignty, in which 'security' remains the only field the state can reclaim as its exclusive competence, see Ole Waever, 'European Security Identities', *Journal of Common Market Studies*, 34/1 (1996): 103–132.

[24] In this direction see Loic Wacquant, 'The Penalization of Poverty and the Rise of Neo-Liberalism', *European Journal on Criminal Policy and Research*, 9 (2001): 401–412.

[25] Kai T. Erikson, *Wayward Puritans. A Study in the Sociology of Deviance* (New York, 1966), p. 11. Erikson's work was significantly inspired by Emile Durkheim's *The Division of Labour in Society* (Glencoe, 1960).

With these words, the American sociologist attempted to define the role played by the stigmatisation of difference and the criminalisation of deviance, both in the definition of the moral boundaries of a community, and in the consolidation of a shared social, cultural and political identity within those boundaries. In other words, there is a structural nexus between the definition of what/who is beyond the borders, and the reproduction of a social identity: we exist – as communities, nations, societies – as far as it is possible for us to state what we are not, and to draw the line that keeps the 'other' at a convenient distance.

This issue leads to the concept of 'public enemy': the dangerous other who reappears periodically in different guises, often invoked by a political discourse which exploits the feeling of uneasiness, insecurity and vulnerability affecting the contemporary 'global citizen'. The invention of the enemy – be it the heretical or the witch in the historical period covered by Erikson's study, or the illegal immigrant of our times – plays two important and complementary tasks. On the one hand, it permits the channelling of fears, anxieties and insecurities towards a visible target, a perceptible scapegoat. On the other hand, the enemy legitimates a sovereign power which through periodic 'wars' can testify its own meaning: being a punitive entity, capable of providing security and 'defending society' from its external threats. At the same time, however, the enemy consolidates peculiar forms of social interaction: it defines particular criteria of belonging and exclusion, and establishes the prevalence of one model of citizenship on the others. In this sense, we could argue that the representation of the enemy offers a reversed image of the community which tries to ban them from its territory.[26] Accordingly, in his critical analysis of the current policies of security in the EU, Jef Huysmans writes that:

> Security policy is a specific policy of mediating belonging. It conserves or transforms political integration and criteria of membership through the identification of existential threats. In security practices the political and social identification of a community and its way of life develop in response to an existential threat. The community defines what it considers to be good life through the reification of figures of societal danger such as the criminal, the mentally abnormal and the invading enemy.[27]

If we look for a moment at the experience of Western modernity, and in particular at the process of formation of the political entities which characterised its recent history – the nation-states – we discover that the definition of a border capable of discriminating between the insider and the outsider, or between the social body and its pathologies, is a structural feature of the so called 'unfinished citizenship' of the Modern Age: a

---

[26] In this sense, I agree with Dario Melossi that the debate around the issue of migrations and crime is in fact a debate on the European identity prompted by the lack of a European public sphere. See Dario Melossi, 'Remarks on Social Control, State Sovereignty and Citizenship in the New Europe', in Vincenzo Ruggiero, Nigel South and Ian Taylor (eds), *The New European Criminology. Crime and Social Order in Europe* (London, 1998), pp. 52–63.

[27] Jef Huysmans, 'The European Union and the Securization of Migration', *Journal of Common Market Studies*, 38/5 (2000): 757. On the complex relationship between identity and security in the context of European unification, see also the important contribution by Ole Waever, 'Identity, Integration and Security. Solving the Sovereignty Puzzle', *Journal of International Affairs*, 48/2 (1995): 389–431.

peculiar mixture of universal principles and material exclusion, formal equality and material despotism, abstract freedom and concrete authority which defined the historical trajectory of Western liberalism.[28] My point of view is that – notwithstanding the universalistic rhetoric surrounding it – the process of European unification is in fact following a similar path: even a cursory glance at the European policies on security and immigration reveals in fact that these are oriented almost exclusively at preserving the external borders from the risk of an 'invasion' by outsiders. In other words, the concept of 'security' tends to be articulated in terms of 'security from' or 'against' an external enemy: against the threat posed by unwanted people who try to violate the borders.[29]

The aim of the new European 'politics of the border' (which started in 1985 with the Schengen Agreements) seems to be not so much to stop the circulation of labour and to 'block' migratory flows, as instead to impose to the immigrant labour force a legal status that is different from that recognised to European citizens. Under the constant threat of expulsion and administrative detention, this status is marked by a systematic reduction of citizenship rights, with the result of widening the margins of economic exploitability of foreign workers.

Here we see the coordinates of the new 'European racism' described by Etienne Balibar: a model of discrimination of the 'other' based not so much on a hypothetical hierarchy among 'races' or 'ethnicities', as on the functioning of legislative, judicial and police practices of spatial segregation.[30] The assimilation of immigrants to potential criminals makes it possible to justify any discrimination against whole groups of people in terms of 'security' and 'social defence'. In the same way, by defining the incarceration of asylum seekers in detention camps as an 'administrative measure', it becomes possible to deny allegations of inhuman treatment, arbitrary punishment, and violation of human rights.

The consequence of these processes is that the European space is defined mainly through the identification of those categories of people who are excluded from full citizenship:[31] in this respect, the hegemonic European model for the management of migrations is not so much one of plain 'exclusion' as instead one of 'subordinate inclusion'.[32] In fact, by enlarging the area of irregularity and precariousness, immigration laws reproduce a workforce that is deprived of social rights and legal guarantees: according to the principle of 'less eligibility', this labour force is forced

---

[28] On this 'paradoxical' feature of modern citizenship, see Mariana Valverde, 'Despotism and Ethical Liberal Governance', *Economy and Society*, 25/3 (1996): 352–372.

[29] For an analysis of how in the last thirty years the concepts of 'security' and 'freedom' in Western societies have shifted toward a purely 'negative' meaning, see Paolo Ceri, *La società vulnerabile. Quale sicurezza, quale libertà* (Rome and Bari, 2003). See also Theodora Kostakopoulou, 'Is There and Alternative to "Schengenland"'?, *Political Studies*, 46 (1998): 886–902.

[30] Etienne Balibar, 'Is There a "Neo-Racism"?', in Etienne Balibar and Immanuel Wallerstein, *Race, Nation, Class* (London, 1991), pp. 17–28.

[31] See Verena Stolcke, 'Le nuove frontiere e le nuove retoriche culturali dell'esclusione in Europa', in Sandro Mezzadra and Agostino Petrillo (eds), *I confini della globalizzazione. Lavoro, Culture, Cittadinanza* (Rome, 2000), pp. 157–182.

[32] According to the formula suggested by Vittorio Cotesta in *La cittadella assediata. Immigrazione e conflitti etnici in Italia* (Rome, 1992).

to accept any condition of work as this is preferable to being deported, and exercises a strong pressure also on the 'local' labour force.[33]

Started silently with the constitution of *ad hoc* groups, the organisation of semi-clandestine meetings between state officials and police officers, and the definition of secret inter-governmental agreements, the construction of a European system of penal policy and immigration control has been consolidated particularly in the last two decades. The initial technocratic secrecy has thus been replaced by an unprecedented activism by the governmental actors of the EU, with the creation of new institutions (*Europol, Eurojust, Police Chiefs Operational Task Force, European College, Eurobord*, the *European Public Prosecutor*); the definition of new political objectives (a common policy on immigration and asylum and the creation of a *Space of Freedom, Security and Justice*); the identification of a new model of action and decision in the fields of security and penal control (the communitarisation of the so called *Third Pillar*).[34]

Many critical observers of the process of 'securisation of Europe' have insisted on the fact that these developments took place in a condition of absolute 'democratic deficit'. Important innovations in the fields of security, police cooperation, immigration control and freedom of circulation were in fact introduced without any democratic control by the European Parliament, national assemblies and civil society, whereas the European public opinion was denied the possibility to know what was being decided by its representatives. I think here of the Schengen Agreements, which revolutionised the regime of circulation with the result of generalising a condition of 'irregularity' for non-European citizens; or the institution of Europol, whose powers – initially limited to some restricted fields of intervention – are now being expanded more and more, whereas the Court of Justice has no control on the activities of this new European police force.[35]

It seems clear that the main targets of these new restrictive policies are migrants and asylum seekers, and that the main objective is the reinforcing of the external borders of the EU. In other words, the birth of a European system of penal control and policing is not something that will have a real impact on the everyday life of European citizens, being instead oriented to 'strangers'. This aspect could explain how it was possible to subtract these processes from public discussion and democratic

---

[33] On this aspect see the special issue of the *International Journal of Urban and Regional Research*, 23/2 (1999) on 'Immigrants and the Informal Economy in European Cities'.

[34] We can identify three main phases in the development of a European model of security and penal control, each with its own peculiarities. The first phase (1985–1991), under the umbrella of the Schengen Agreements, is characterised by informal cooperation, secret negotiations and the proliferation of *ad hoc* groups on the issues of security and immigration control. The second phase started with the Treaty of Maastricht (1992), to end in 1999 with the Treaty of Amsterdam: cooperation is here still based on negotiations among the states. The third phase starts with the approval of the Treaty of Amsterdam, which subtracts the issues of security from the competence of the states, and puts them under the communitarian framework. For a detailed reconstruction of this evolution, see Theodora Kostakopoulou, 'The "Protective Union": Change and Continuity in Migration Law and Policy in Post-Amsterdam Europe', *Journal of Common Market Studies*, 38/3 (2000): 497–518.

[35] See Hartmut Aden, 'Convergence of Policing Policies and Trans-national Policing in Europe', *European Journal of Crime, Criminal Law and Criminal Justice*, 9/2 (2001): 99–112.

procedures: what is taking place is not simply an 'immunisation' of these policies from democratic control, but more precisely a replacement of democratic legitimacy with a dangerous form of 'social' legitimacy. Following Ian Loader:

> ... 'legitimacy' all too easily becomes self-confirming – amounting to not much more than law enforcement agencies responding to popular anxieties that are in part the consequence of in/securisation projects championed by political elites, the media or police institutions themselves.[36]

By using the term 'social legitimacy', I refer to the 'tacit consent' expressed by a large part of the European public opinion to repressive measures oriented exclusively against an *external* enemy: against *those who are behind the borders and try to enter illegitimately*.[37] Popular legitimation is thus replaced by populist consent. The success of this new European punitive populism seems to be the product of two converging circumstances: on the one hand, the quasi-secrecy of the processes of decision through which the new scenario has been defined – the absence of information, the scarce accessibility of documents, the intentional exclusion of groups, associations and organisations for the promotion of civil rights – favoured the diffusion of an abstract perception of what was being decided. On the other hand, the targets of this new punitive climate – principally immigrants and asylum seekers, easily assimilated to potential terrorists especially after the events of 11 September 2001 – become the objects of a mass-mediated representation which describes them as public enemies who endanger the European entity. If to all this we add the rhetoric of emergency affecting Europe in the last years – a language of 'war on crime' quickly translated into a 'war on illegal immigration' – the circle is closed.

In this context I would also note the ambiguity of a process like the communitarisation of the so called Third Pillar, promoted by the Treaty of Amsterdam in 1999: a process welcomed also by some critics of the European policies of security, as a first step toward a democratisation of the field. In my view, the fact that police cooperation becomes a communitarian issue – no longer in the hands of the state – does not imply a democratisation, nor an automatic expansion in the legal guarantees and judicial rights of those categories of people who are more exposed to police abuses and miscarriages of justice. Quite to the contrary, it seems more reasonable to conclude that this process will situate penal policies and immigration control directly at the core of the European project, thus turning security into a *leitmotif* of the new European citizenship. The securisation of Europe would then be transferred from the borders to the centre, becoming in effect a basic principle inspiring the constitution of Europe as a unified political entity.[38]

---

[36] Ian Loader, 'Policing, Securization and Democratization in Europe', *Criminal Justice*, 2/2 (2002): 140.

[37] Again, Ian Loader raises this point very clearly: 'In the field of European policing, however, these benefits and burdens have been almost de-coupled – the policing of trans-national crime being an activity directed largely *at Others* (migrants, organized criminals, drug-traffickers, etc.) on *behalf of us* (Europe's citizens). These various categories of Other are, moreover, both routinely represented as alien, marginal and dangerous, and generally lacking in cultural or political capital': Ibid., p. 143.

[38] In the words of Theodora Kostakopoulou: 'Communitarization has thus not only left the conceptual parameters of the security paradigm which characterised the Third Pillar intact, but the latter have

On the other hand, in the European policies of immigration control we see a clear example of the contradiction – illustrated in the earlier chapters – between a model of social citizenship based on 'Fordist labour', and a material structure of Western societies characterised by the gradual disappearance of this model of work as a universal gateway to economic inclusion and social integration. If one excludes the case of asylum seekers – which is of limited extension, in part as a consequence of the intense diplomatic activities to restrict the international definition of 'refugee' – both at the national and communitarian level the shared principle inspiring the regulation of migrations is that 'foreigners' can legally enter the European territory only if they can prove that there is a regular work contract awaiting them. In other words, the 'tolerability' of immigration is strictly connected to the labour market, and the legal status of immigrants depends directly on their working-position. This means that immigrants can stay as long as they are regularly employed, but today this condition is harder and harder to reach even for the local labour force. The consequence is a widening of the condition of potential 'irregularity' for some categories of people, with the effect of reproducing a large basin of precarious and insecure workers to be exploited in the underground economy. Through the threat of criminalisation, administrative detention and expulsion for all those who do not satisfy the strict conditions for regularity, Western economic elites guarantee the reproduction of this circle, inspired again by the principle of less eligibility.

Perhaps one of the clearest example of this tendency is offered by the recent Italian legislation on immigration, the so called 'Bossi-Fini' law – after the names of the two proponents: the vice-prime minister Gianfranco Fini, secretary of the neo-fascist party *Alleanza Nazionale*, and the minister Umberto Bossi, secretary of the 'secessionist' party *Northern League*. There are many important innovations in this law (passed in 2002), which could be listed under two main headings: the first is 'precarisation', and the second is 'criminalisation' of immigrants. The Bossi-Fini law precarises the condition of migrants in many ways. For example, the Italian government will define each year the 'quotas' of foreign workers to be regularly admitted, but it can also close the borders indefinitely; the possibility of family reunification is reduced; immigrant workers can apply to public job centres, but the local labour force must have precedence in the lists.

Moreover, the law establishes a direct connection between the right to stay and the existence of a work contract: the old 'residence permit' is replaced by a 'contract of residence' privately stipulated by the immigrant worker and their employer, and the duration of residence depends on the duration of the work contract. This means that if the worker is dismissed (or decides to search for a better work) they must find another job within the next six months, after which they become 'irregular' and can be detained in an 'immigration detention centre', to be later deported. Here it is not difficult to see how a public prerogative – defining the legal status of a citizen – is assigned to a private actor – the employer – because the citizenship rights of an employee are 'written' in a work-contract: a condition not distant from slavery.

---

now come to define the terms of the free movement of persons in Community law. The Community has welcomed the Schengen project of creating a unified European migration area surrounded by a uniformly controlled border': Kostakopoulou, 'The "Protective Union"', p. 508.

Coming to the side of 'criminalisation' – which is complementary and functional to the developments described above – the law treats immigrants as potential delinquents and provides a variety of measures aimed at containing this supposed dangerousness: the immigrant is fingerprinted each time they ask for a renewal of the 'contract of residence';[39] the maximum duration of administrative detention is prolonged and new immigration detention centres will be built in the next few years; finally, judicial guarantees are drastically limited, given that an appeal eventually presented by the immigrant does not suspend deportation.[40]

In short, for the immigrant the possibility to avoid criminalisation and physical segregation depends on their acceptance of any opportunity available in the labour market, at any given condition. This situates European (and Italian) immigration policies within the wider process of 'criminalisation of poverty' described by Loic Wacquant in his analysis of the transition from the 'social state' to the 'penal state': a process in which, as we have seen, 'mass incarceration' plays a crucial role. However, what makes the criminalisation of migrations paradigmatic is that the *actuarial logic* outlined earlier as one feature of contemporary 'mass confinement', in the case of immigrants seems to become the *organising principle*. This argument will become clearer in the next pages, where our attention will be captured by the various extra-penal measures targeted at criminalising 'illegal immigrants'.

Immigration as an 'Ontological Crime'

The development of restrictive policies on immigration – both in Europe and in the US – has been presented systematically in terms of 'security', 'crime prevention' and public order: the public discourse on immigration control has been, in fact, dominated by an implicit equation between 'immigration' and 'crime'. The diffusion of this perception of immigration as a 'crime-related issue' has contributed to the legitimation of restrictive measures aimed at limiting the freedom of circulation for some categories of foreigners. Constantly supported by the mass media and by politicians in search of popularity, Western public opinions are led to believe that immigrants – particularly if 'illegal' – commit more crimes than locals: something which has turned immigrants and asylum seekers into suitable scapegoats for public anxieties and fears. In this sense I would argue that immigration policies – and particularly the public discourse surrounding them – are a significant part of the wider paradigm of 'governing through crime', described by Jonathan Simon.[41]

---

[39] The debate which arose in Italy around the issue of 'fingerprints' reveals how stereotyped our perception of who is a non-European can be. Legally speaking, non-Europeans are Swiss and Northern Americans, as well as Moroccans, Albanians or Kurds. Now, one of the points made by the critics of the 'Bossi-Fini' law, was that it would also impose fingerprinting to Americans, Swiss, Canadians, Australians, etc. and this would turn out to be, at least, 'embarrassing' for the Italian authorities. This argument shows to what extent public debate is affected by a neo-colonial attitude towards immigrants.

[40] And in the case of asylum seekers, this is a blatant violation of international conventions on refugees, as has been denounced by *Amnesty International* on many occasions.

[41] Jonathan Simon, 'Governing Through Crime', in Lawrence Friedman and George Fischer (eds), *The Crime Conundrum: Essays on Criminal Justice* (Boulder, 1997), pp. 171–189.

However, it should be noted that the social construction of immigration in terms of criminal danger is not new. It characterised the US in the first quarter of the twentieth century, when the criminal threat was represented in particular by the German, Italian, Polish and Irish immigrants.[42] It affected Northern European public opinions in the 1960s and 1970s, when Germany, France, Belgium, etc. hosted thousands of workers from Spain, Italy, Greece and Turkey.[43] And the same stereotype is now attached, particularly, to Northern African and Eastern European immigrants in Europe, and to Latin American immigrants in the US.[44]

It is not my aim here to show that these fears are unjustified and to argue that a less prejudiced analysis would reveal that 'immigrants' are in fact equally or less 'deviant' than nationals. There is already enough criminological evidence to show that the equation between migration and crime is false, and that more critical attention should be given to factors like judicial discrimination and 'institutional racism'. Thus, I will not repeat here that all official Commissions of Inquiry instituted in the US between 1880 and 1930 showed no significant differences between the rates of crime of immigrants and US citizens, and that the same results were found both in Australia in the 1960s and 1970s and in Europe more recently.[45] Also, I will not insist on the fact that the crimes usually committed by immigrants – crimes against property and drug-related crimes – should be seen as an implicit consequence of the condition of potential irregularity (and economic vulnerability) produced by the hegemonic 'prohibitionist' regimes of immigration control. Not to mention the fact that some crimes can be committed only by immigrants, like those concerning immigration laws, the falsification of documents, the violation of expulsion orders, etc.[46] In the same way, it is not necessary to stress again that, at least in Europe, the probability for an immigrant to end up in prison is much higher than for nationals, and that this is not necessarily a consequence of the seriousness of the crimes committed. In fact, other circumstances like the systematic application of pre-trial detention, the lack of adequate defence and the systematic denial of alternatives to prison seem to explain the overrepresentation of immigrants in European prisons more than rates of crime.[47]

---

[42] See for example William I. Thomas and Florian Znaniecki, *The Polish Peasant in Europe and America* (Chicago, 1918).

[43] See Castles and Kosack, *Immigrant Workers and Class Structure in Western Europe*; Franco Ferracuti, 'European Migration and Crime', in Marvin E. Wolfgang (ed.), *Crime and Culture: Essays in Honour of Thorsten Sellin* (New York, 1968), pp. 189–219.

[44] See Ineke H. Marshall (ed.), *Minorities, Migrants and Crime. Diversity and Similarity across Europe and the United States* (London, 1997).

[45] See for example Ronald D. Francis, *Migrant Crime in Australia* (St. Lucia, 1981) and Martin Killias, 'Criminality among Second-generation Immigrants in Western Europe: A Review of the Evidence', *Criminal Justice Review*, 14/1 (1989): 13–42.

[46] The so called 'crimes of immigration' (behaviours whose illegality derives entirely from immigration laws) form a considerable fraction of the crimes committed by immigrants in Europe and in Italy. Another peculiar phenomenon is that some deviant behaviours which are usually tolerated tend to be criminalised if the authors are identified as 'immigrants' – the clearest example here being street prostitution. See Salvatore Palidda, *Devianza e vittimizzazione tra i migranti* (Milan, 2001).

[47] For Italy see Alessandra Naldi, 'Mondi a parte: stranieri in carcere', in Stefano Anastasia and Patrizio Gonnella (eds), *Inchiesta sulle carceri italiane* (Rome, 2002), pp. 33–52.

Instead, what I would like to outline here is that in the case of immigrants the processes of criminalisation are relatively independent from any deviant behaviour, being in fact connected almost exclusively to their 'status'. Immigration tends to be criminalised in itself, as a 'human condition' which is socially perceived and institutionally treated as a risk, and the penalisation of immigrants is not enforced primarily through penal laws and criminal justice policies.[48] As we will see, the European and US restrictive rules about immigration define a whole new category of subjects, whose legal status of quasi-citizens makes them suitable for penal and *extra-penal* processes of criminalisation, in which the rights and guarantees usually embodied in the 'rule of law' are dismissed.

These developments deserve our attention for two main reasons. The first is that in the field of immigration control new strategies of punishment and confinement are experimented, in which the actuarial logic described earlier about mass-imprisonment is much visible: an aspect which turns immigration control into a paradigmatic case-study for my hypotheses on the transformations of social control. The second reason is that these developments take place in strict connection with the role of the immigrant labour force in contemporary Western economies. In this respect, the penalisation of immigrants illustrates clearly the connection between the social and institutional criminalisation of the new 'dangerous classes', and the development of a post-Fordist economy.

The War on Immigrants across Europe and the United States

In these pages I will thus analyse some features of Western migratory policies which seem to exemplify better the emergence of an actuarial logic of selective control. As was said earlier, these policies – especially since the early 1990s – are more and more characterised as techniques for the criminalisation of immigration itself, independent of individual behaviours: this is the reason for which I spoke of immigration as an 'ontological crime', as a subjective condition exposing whole categories of people to the repressive action of the State. What inspires the 'penal' treatment of migrations is thus not so much the supposed 'criminality' of immigrants – though this represents the main form of legitimation of these policies in public discourse – as instead the social and political construction of immigration as a deviant phenomenon in itself. As the Algerian sociologist Abdelmalek Sayad has shown with extraordinary clarity, the migrant is already guilty from the beginning, due to their condition of being foreign/immigrant. The consequence is that any criminal behaviour by a 'stranger' requires a 'double punishment':

> The fact of being an immigrant is a latent and camouflaged crime in which the individual has no direct responsibility; one which the crime ... investigated by the criminal justice system brings again into light. Any trial against a delinquent immigrant is also a trial

---

[48]   This is not to say that these are of secondary importance: the vertical growth in the number of foreigners in Western prison populations is in fact a clear indicator of this importance. In Italy, between 1990 and 2000, the percentage of foreigners on the total prison population has shifted from 15 percent to 30 percent. In Greece 39 percent of prisoners are immigrants; 34 percent in Germany; 38 percent in Belgium and 32 percent in the Netherlands. See Pierre Tournier, *Statistiques pénales annuelles du Conseil de l'Europe* (Strasbourg, 1999).

against immigration, conceived primarily as an act of delinquency in itself, and secondarily as a cause of delinquency. Thus, well before we can speak of racism and xenophobia, the notion of double punishment is embodied in all the judgements formulated about the immigrant.[49]

Privileging a materialist interpretation of these processes, I would say that the 'double deviance' to which this 'double punishment' is attached, bears also a 'political' meaning: contemporary migrations seem in fact to represent a form of 'practical critique' of the international division of labour. They denounce the unsustainable inequalities between the 'First World' and the 'Third World'; implicitly they contest the ambiguous nature of borders – abolished for the circulation of goods and financial capital, militarised against the circulation of some categories of people; they reclaim a right to 'access' for the most marginalised fractions of the global labour force; they synthesise the whole colonial experience of the Western world, by questioning a paradigm of citizenship still tailored to the image of a white, male, working citizen.[50]

Here, my analysis concentrates in particular on two political and geographical areas – the US and Europe – though I am aware that this choice raises some problems in terms of comparative analysis. In fact, between the two continents there are profound social, economic and political differences (concerning both history and the present) which inevitably reflect themselves on contemporary migratory policies. For example, in the US the new migrations are situated in a social context already fractured along ethno-racial lines, in which the penal apparatus exercises a fundamental role of 'differentiation' between labouring classes and dangerous classes.[51] This aspect characterises Europe only marginally: here the new migrations are inserted into a much more homogeneous social context, whose cleavages can be observed mainly in the economic sphere – employment, income, working conditions and social rights.

However, I think that these differences make the attempt to compare the two universes even more stimulating. In fact, under the point of view of the consolidation of socially disadvantaged 'ethnic minorities', the US seems to offer an anticipation of the European future: the production of a racially and economically defined underclass – to which, in the US, concurred discriminatory penal policies, punitive welfare reforms, processes of racial stigmatisation, and forms of urban segregation of poverty – represents also the foreseeable result of contemporary European policies on immigration, if they proceed in the current direction.[52] In other words, the constant marginalisation of immigrants – especially through the normative reproduction of the status of 'irregularity' – might consolidate a condition of permanent social vulnerability, comparable to that of African-Americans in the US. I refer here to the systematic limitation of civil, social and political rights which affects immigrants, to

---

[49] Abdelmalek Sayad, *La doppia assenza. Dalle illusioni dell'emigrato alle sofferenze dell'immigrato* (Milan, 2002), p. 372.

[50] On these aspects, see Rainer Baubock and John Rundell (eds), *Blurred Boundaries: Migration, Ethnicity, Citizenship* (Aldershot, 1998).

[51] See Loic Wacquant, 'Deadly Symbiosis: When Ghetto and Prison Meet and Mesh', in David Garland (ed.), *Mass Imprisonment. Social Causes and Consequences* (London, 2001), pp. 82–120.

[52] See Douglas Massey and Nancy Denton, *American Apartheid: Segregation and the Making of the Underclass* (Cambridge MA, 1993).

their dramatic overrepresentation in prison populations and to the re-emergence of racist attitudes in countries like Austria, Italy, Germany, England and France. Besides the differentiating factors, however, there are also many features which justify a common analysis of transatlantic migratory policies, so much so that I would speak of a 'Euro-American framework'.

The first commonality is represented by the strong politicisation of the issue of migration. The need to protect the borders against a supposed foreign invasion, the urgency to protect internal security, the association of immigration with international terrorism in mass-mediated discourses, the apparent polarisation of public debate between economic actors – supporting a reopening of the borders which would guarantee a flow of unskilled labour force, possibly without rights – and political representatives – eager to present themselves as the defenders of law and order: these are the essential coordinates of the political debate around immigration on both sides of the Atlantic Ocean. And in both cases, this debate has been characterised by populist tones resulting in recurrent moral panics about immigrants. Following Goode and Ben-Yehuda:

> Members of this category are collectively designated as the enemy, or an enemy, of respectable society; their behaviour is seen as harmful, or threatening to the values, interests, possibly the very existence, of the society, or at least a sizeable segment of that society.[53]

This climate has certainly contributed to legitimating the adoption of discriminatory measures against immigrants. We touch here on the second commonality between Europe and the US: the penalisation of immigrants is not only a kind of 'ontological' criminalisation – that is, attached to the very status of 'immigrant' – but it is also 'preventive' – that is, based on a social and institutional perception of immigrants as a 'collective danger'. The aim of these policies seems thus to be that of preventively neutralising the cultural, political and social risks posed by strangers, independent of their individual characteristics and actual behaviours.

Furthermore, by observing the (penal and extra-penal) treatment of immigrants, we discover that these policies of control articulate themselves mainly on two levels: the first concerns the protection of borders, and sees the deployment of policies, technologies and police practices aiming to limit the possibility of access to Western territories by immigrants. Once beyond the 'wall around the West', a second level of control emerges, concerning directly the legal and social condition of immigrants: both in Europe and in the US, this condition is characterised by the development of selective policies, driven by a logic of 'categorial suspicion'. As we will see, 'extra-penal detention' and 'expulsion' are the main instruments of these policies, which

---

[53] Erich Goode and Nachman Ben-Yehuda, *Moral Panics: the Social Construction of Deviance* (Cambridge MA, 1994), p. 33. This panic has grown even more after the terrorist attacks of 11 September 2001 and the consequent war on terrorism launched by Bush and his European allies. In effect, as many critical observer have argued, the war on terrorism has soon revealed its 'other side': a preventive war on immigrants and asylum seekers. On this aspect, see Tony Bunyan, 'The "War on Freedom and Democracy". An Analysis of the Effects on Civil Liberties and Democratic Culture in the EU', *Statewatch Analysis*, 13 (2002).

impose on immigrants a harsh reality of permanent insecurity, which in my perspective is functional to their exploitation in the post-Fordist economy.[54]

Detention and Expulsion as Actuarial Technologies

As I suggested earlier, the external borders of Europe are being turned into a mobile and flexible frontier, whose defence sees the involvement of a multiplicity of public and private actors: national police forces and the European police (*Europol*); air companies – who are now responsible for the condition of regularity or irregularity of their passengers, with the duty to return them to their countries of origin or to a *safe third country* if they travel without documents;[55] the countries seeking admission into the EU – who are requested to play the role of 'filters' against irregular immigration.[56] Here two apparent contradictory (but in fact complementary) aspects emerge: on the one hand, the borders become flexible, mobile and to some extent even 'immaterial' – one example being the Schengen Information System.[57] On the other hand, the borders are more and more militarised and the practice of contrasting illegal immigration through military means is spreading across Europe[58] – though the same can also be said about the US-Mexico border:

> This thin 2,000-mile-long police state is still the ultimate testing ground for law enforcement power and technology. The geographic frontier is also the political frontier where systems of militarised social control undergo constant refinement and expansion ... Here on the

---

[54] In this respect, Kanstroom speaks of the condition of immigrants in the US in terms of 'eternal probation': Daniel Kanstroom, 'Deportation, Social Control, and Punishment: Some Thoughts About Why Hard Laws Make Bad Cases', *Harvard Law Review*, 113 (2000): 1907.

[55] As regards the involvement of the 'carriers' in the control of immigration, two commentators argue that 'These methods also permit states to circumvent constraints imposed by judicial and civil rights groups, which may be present at the national or international level. In this vein, airline cooperation on matters of same-day removals of inadmissible foreigners on the "carrier's next regularly scheduled departure" is critical. It allows the state to avoid the costs of detention, which also include the prevention of access to lawyers': Gallya Lahav and Virginie Guiraudon, 'Comparative Perspectives on Border Control: Away From the Border and Outside the State', in Andreas and Snyder (eds), *The Wall Around the West*, p. 64. We see here a critique that has also been raised against private prisons.

[56] On this aspect, see Milada A. Vachudová, 'Eastern Europe as Gatekeeper: The Immigration and Asylum Policies of an Enlarging European Union', in Andreas and Snyder (eds), *The Wall around the West*, pp. 153–171.

[57] The Schengen Information System is an electronic database, in which all data concerning goods or people who cross – or try to cross – the European borders converge. The system can be checked in real time both by the national police forces of the European countries and by Europol, thus permitting the refusal of entry to all those people who are considered 'unwanted'. A similar system, called MAL (Movement Alert List) has been recently introduced in Australia. According to the Australian government: 'Its effectiveness hinges on its ability to deter people of concern while simultaneously ensuring that genuine travellers are processed quickly': Australian Immigration Fact Sheet, *Border Control* (www.immi.gov.au/facts/70border.htm).

[58] For example, the mentioned Italian law on immigration (the so called 'Bossi-Fini') provides explicitly the deployment of the Italian navy for contrasting illegal immigration: 'The Italian boat which, during a police service, encounters in the territorial sea or in a nearby area a boat about

US-Mexico border law enforcement sees through military eyes. Since the early 1980s the massive paramilitary build up here has involved new equipment, expanded police powers, and unprecedented inter-agency cooperation. Urban sectors of the border now seethe with guard towers, motion sensors, night scopes, impassable 18-foot-high concrete 'bollard fencing', and swarms of Border Patrol agents – 7,000 of them to be exact.[59]

Also in this case, the 'defence' of the border is not an exclusive task of the border police, as it witnesses the fundamental role of private actors – driven by what appears to be a real 'business of war against immigrants', similar to the prison-industrial complex. If in Europe international airports are often furnished with 'waiting areas' in which immigrants are detained for the time necessary to check their identities and eventually to evaluate their requests for asylum, in the US air companies are requested to act directly as police forces, and even to detain illegal immigrants: in fact some hotels near international airports have been equipped with holding rooms, in which passengers without documents are detained, often for long periods of time. These 'hotels' are managed by the multinationals of private security and private incarceration – like Wackenhut and Group 4 – and the conditions of detention are described by some critics as 'Kafkian'.[60]

The border is not a 'democratic' institution: it is not an undifferentiated limit to the circulation of 'non-nationals': to the contrary, the border selects, distinguishes and discriminates between 'desirable' and 'undesirable' or 'deserving' and 'undeserving' foreigners. According to a logic of exclusion which resembles the one governing the American and European 'gated communities' – fortified islands of wellbeing, security and social homogeneity in a context of growing inequalities – in this case too, being 'undeserving' means to be 'the wrong person in the wrong place': that is, to be poor,

---

which there are reasonable grounds to believe that it is carrying illegal immigrants, shall stop it, inspect it and bring it to the nearest port within the Italian territory', L. 189/2002, art. 11. In effect, this practice was already common even before the law authorised it formally, often with dramatic consequences. The thousands of immigrants who died while attempting to reach the Italian coast allow us to speak of a 'state-massacre'. To offer just one example, on 28 March 1997, during a police operation the Italian corvette 'Sibilla' rammed a boat of immigrants coming from Albania, causing the death of 300 people. Since the early 1990s, in the Italian southern regions the army has been involved in anti-immigration operations. It should be noted that earlier it had been employed only in Sicily and Calabria, for 'anti-Mafia' operations.

59   Christian Parenti, *Lockdown America. Police and Prisons in the Age of Crisis* (London, 2000), pp. 154–155. Specific initiatives aimed at reinforcing the borders were promoted by the *Immigration and Naturalization Service* (INS) in the early 1990s: 'Operation Held the Line' was launched in 1995 to strengthen a 20 mile barrier around El Paso, Texas. The following year the INS started 'Operation Gatekeeper' in the region of San Diego, by installing new fencing and high intensity lights. The same trend is also observable on the coasts of Australia: here, the *Department of Immigration and Multicultural and Indigenous Affairs* has launched a 'war on immigrants' which sees the Australian Navy engaged in daily confrontations with dilapidated boats carrying hundreds of 'illegal' immigrants.

60   According to Michael Welch, who collected testimonies from many immigrants detained in these hotels: 'In several incidents, detainees have been held in a motel room for months, where they are deprived of fresh air and telephones, and in some cases they are shackled and sexually abused by the security staff': Michael Welch, *Detained. Immigration Laws and the Expanding INS Jail Complex* (Philadelphia, 2002), p. 109.

to come from 'underdeveloped' countries, and to reclaim access to the territories of consumption, welfare and 'freedom'. The 're-bordering' of the Western world against immigrants seems thus to give birth to a regime of 'global zero tolerance' in which, once again, the equation between poverty and dangerousness, marginality and risk, legitimates the adoption of preventively repressive technologies of control. But I would also subscribe to Zygmunt Bauman's hypothesis, and argue that this 're-bordering' is part of a wider 'emic' strategy which contemporary societies set in motion in order to keep at distance any threatening form of 'otherness':

> The extreme variants of the 'emic' strategy are now, as always, incarceration, deportation and murder. The upgraded, 'refined' (modernized) forms of the 'emic' strategy are spatial separation, urban ghettos, selective access to spaces and selective barring from using them.[61]

From what I said until now, one could get the impression that the result of these policies is to impose a real 'block' to the flows of immigrants into Western territories: in effect, as we saw earlier, the actual outcome seems to be quite different. Taking into account also the mentioned polarisation between economic and political actors, the aim of migratory policies seems to be to 'limit' immigration, to make it more difficult and to restrict legal access. The philosophy seems to be to construct artificially some groups of population to be included in a subordinate condition. The militarisation of the border is thus one of the various instruments through which Western governments can refurnish the post-Fordist economic system with an insecure, blackmailed and precarious labour force, and themselves with 'suitable enemies' through which they can legitimate their role in the eyes of the public. The more presided and defended are the borders, the more it is possible to represent those who violate them as invaders, as uncontrollable desperate and 'dangerous classes' threatening our security – in a sort of 'self-fulfilling prophecy' for which the more we defend ourselves against an enemy, the more it appears menacing.

However, it is particularly inside the borders that the treatment of immigrants as a 'dangerous class' produces its results. The logic of categorial and preventive criminalisation visible here is emerging also within the 'ordinary' penal systems (i.e. oriented to the 'citizens'), and the mass incarceration described in Chapter 4 is a clear example of these processes. But the important difference is that in the case of immigrants this logic is absolutely prevalent, to the point of defining the main coordinates of their legal and social condition. And this happens for two reasons: first, because the penal system and its agents are the main public institutions in charge of migrants' biographies – because immigrants are deemed to bear an 'implicit blame' which exposes them to the eye of formal social control. Second, because both in Europe and in the US a tendency is emerging toward the construction of a 'special' legal regime – characterised almost exclusively in repressive terms – which finds application only to immigrants. The proliferation of extra-penal forms of detention and the systematic resort to expulsion (also as an alternative to imprisonment), represent the clearest examples of these tendencies, which in my view are actuarial.

---

[61] Zygmunt Bauman, *Liquid Modernity* (Cambridge, 2000), p. 101.

At this point it would be necessary to take two legal distinctions into consideration, which in theory should prevent us from speaking of an undifferentiated 'criminalisation of immigrants'. First, the basic distinction between 'immigrants' and 'asylum-seekers': two distinct categories of people for which the international law establishes different rules. In my view, however, in light of the recent punitive developments of Western legislations, this distinction has become almost exclusively theoretical. The recognition of someone as a 'refugee' (and thus as a person who has the right to obtain asylum) is more and more referred to the arbitrary evaluation of the countries of destination.[62] Quite often, these are the same Western governments whose 'international police operations' or 'humanitarian wars' (Iraq, former-Yugoslavia, Kossovo, Somalia) aggravated the conditions of humanitarian emergency asylum seekers escape from.[63]

Not to mention the fact that European countries sign international agreements with dictatorships and anti-democratic governments – that is, governments responsible for systematic violations of human rights – so that these will make any effort to 'contrast' emigration from their territories. As a matter of fact, this is a way to 'abolish' political asylum, not by confronting the circumstances originating 'fleeing', but by forbidding it.[64]

Finally, especially in Europe, the condition of 'asylum seeker' does not imply more 'tolerance' or more respect for immigrants' rights: as it happens for all immigrants, asylum seekers can be detained and expelled, and their rights are limited in significant ways. Ironically, they are object of even more discriminatory forms of 'categorial suspicion', so much so that it seems that there is a 'presumption of falsity' toward their claims.

The second legal distinction intersects the one between 'immigrants' and 'asylum seekers', and has to do with the different conditions of 'regular' and 'irregular' immigrants. In almost all Western countries, an immigrant's legal condition of regularity is linked to two requisites. At the time of entry into the national territory, the immigrant must possess a document justifying access – a visa or a passport. As regards to residence, the condition of regularity depends on the recognition of a

---

[62] And we should note that this decision is often influenced by electoral, political and economic contingencies, to which humanitarian reasons can be easily subordinated. One example is offered by the UK after 11 September 2001, where the war on terrorism has legitimated a true war on asylum seekers. On the recent developments of UK immigration policies, see Jock Young, 'To These Wet and Windy Shores. Recent Immigration Policy in the UK', *Punishment and Society*, 5/4 (2003): 449–462.

[63] A clear example of this dynamic is offered by the behaviour of the Italian government towards Kosovo refugees. During the Kosovo war, the Italian government recognised the status of 'refugees' to all those coming from that region, thus granting them 'temporary protection'. However, as soon as military operations ceased (and in the same days in which the humanitarian emergency was exploding), the Italian government suddenly modified the former provision, thus turning thousands of people fleeing from Kosovo to Italy into illegal immigrants. More recently, during the second 'Gulf War', the Italian government (among the more enthusiastic supporters of US military intervention) declared that it would not accept war refugees from Iraq.

[64] A good example is offered by the many 'readmission agreements' signed by the Italian government with countries like Tunisia, Libya, Morocco, Algeria and Albania, whose democratic deficits are well known.

legitimate reason to stay – and usually this is the existence of a work-contract. Particularly in light of this circumstance, what I would argue is that between the two legal conditions there is no definite distinction: in fact, they do not represent two separate and distinct universes, but are subjective conditions situated along a continuum of insecurity and precariousness. The main consequence of the restrictive policies on immigrants' residence is this: illegality represents a constant threat infringing on the biographies of immigrants. In other words, the condition of regularity is reversible at any time, and the shift to irregularity is a very frequent circumstance. In European countries, for example, in order to become irregular it is sufficient to lose the work-place which justified the residence – nothing easier in a flexible economy; moreover, the documents legitimising residence for reasons of work are temporary, and their expiration causes an automatic condition of illegality.

Irregularity – and the subsequent 'illegal' condition – is the consequence of a legislative definition which imposes to the migrant the mark of undesirability and un-deservingness. In this sense, irregularity is in fact an actuarial dispositive, because it is a label which identifies whole categories of subjects, exposing them to penalising and criminalising treatments – detention, expulsion, deportation – only on the grounds of their status (work/income/home/documents), and independent of their behaviour or from the reasons which led to this condition. This aspect turns the threat of irregularity into the most effective instrument of restrictive immigration laws.

The legal management of irregularity shows also to what extent the criminalisation of immigrants takes place outside the penal field, through administrative procedures. In many European countries (Italy, Sweden, Austria, the Netherlands, Spain, Denmark and Portugal), to be an 'illegal' does not represent a crime in itself: an illegal immigrant is not a 'criminal' to whom penal law applies. But the consequences of this 'formally administrative' condition are 'concretely penal' – I think in particular of detention, which usually takes place in appositely instituted detention centres, but in some cases even in ordinary prisons. It is perhaps exactly the partial subtraction of immigration from the sphere of penal law that allows the suspension of the traditional guarantees of criminal justice: the fact that the detention, expulsion and deportation of immigrants are not considered as real 'punishments', permits a *de facto* criminalisation which leaves aside the principles of the rule of law. And this ambiguous treatment – 'formally administrative' and 'concretely penal' – concerns potentially all immigrants, regular and irregular.

The field in which this 'shift' in the boundaries of penality appears more evident – in the US as in Europe – is clearly that of 'administrative detention'. In all European countries, immigrants can be detained in semi-carceral conditions while the identification procedures necessary for their expulsion or deportation are performed; in the same way refugees can be detained for the time necessary to evaluate their requests for asylum. Therefore, administrative detention concerns individuals whose legal conditions are quite different: it can affect persons to be expelled because they committed a crime, but also peoples who suddenly became irregular because they lost the work-place which justified their residence, or persons fleeing persecutions, wars, poverty, and thus deserving protection according to the international law. In any case, individual behaviours and personal motivations lose any importance, because the single relevant factor – which legitimates the grouping of these people in a homogeneous class to be preventively controlled through punitive strategies – is the fact that they are all undocumented immigrants.

In European countries detention can last for long periods of time: up to eight months in Belgium; six months in Austria and Germany; two months in Italy and Portugal; one month in Spain, France and Finland. In other cases – Ireland, Great Britain, Denmark and Greece – detention is indeterminate, as it can last for the time necessary to take a decision on expulsion or asylum.[65] As I said, in the majority of cases detention takes place in appositely instituted detention centres, but in some countries – like the UK – ordinary prisons are used for this purpose.[66] In any case, this practice represents a clear violation of the right to personal freedom, imposed without any respect for the rights and guarantees normally recognised to 'citizens'.

Also in the case of administrative detention – as was noted about the restrictive discipline of borders – we see the emergence of a 'flexible' system of control: another aspect of the actuarial logic inspiring these policies. First, detention is also privatised: in the UK, for example, many detention centres are managed by private entrepreneurs of security, who make growing profits on the war against immigration. In Italy, detention centres are run by non-profit associations and by the Red Cross. Quite often the contracts through which the management of these centres is leased to these groups are inaccessible to the public, and it is not difficult to foresee that soon these non-profit organisations will be replaced by 'for profit' private enterprises.

At the same time detention tends to be de-territorialised: in fact, a recent proposal by the UK government prospects the possibility to build detention centres outside the European territory, in countries like Albania and Croatia. The new *Transit Processing Centres* (TPC) would detain not only asylum seekers travelling to Europe, but also illegal migrants 'intercepted' at the border while trying to enter Europe illegally. The

---

[65] For a wide review of the different detention/expulsion regimes in European countries, see Bruno Nascimbene (ed.), *Expulsion and Detention of Aliens in the European Union Countries* (Milan, 2001).

[66] In the UK there are nine immigration detention centres: Campsfield (184 places), Harmondsworth (550 places), Harmondsworth II (550), Oakington (400), Tinsley (150), Yarl's Wood (900), Queen's Building (Heathrow, 15 places), Manchester (Airport, 16 places), Longport (Eurotunnel Dover, 8 places). Four more detention centres are located in former prisons: Dover (400 places), Dungavel (150), Haslar (150) and Lindholme (110). These have been renamed 'removal centres', but are in fact prisons holding mostly asylum seekers whose claims are being processed and therefore cannot be deported. Four 'accommodation centres' (open door but with a curfew) are due to open in isolated areas in 2003/2004, each to hold 750 asylum seekers. Finally, many other 'ordinary' prisons hold immigration detainees, despite the July 2001 statement of the Home Secretary David Blunkett, who said that this 'scandal' would end.

In Italy there are 16 immigration detention centres, whose official name is *Centri di permanenza temporanea e assistenza* (Centers for Temporary Permanence and Assistance). They were instituted in 1998 by a centre-left government, and the former law established that the maximum period of detention would be 30 days. Under the centre-right government a new immigration law was passed, which provides that immigrants can be detained in these centres for a maximum of 60 days. According to the explanatory documents of the law, the existing centres can hold a maximum of 1,400 people, but this number is expected to grow up to 36,000 people, as a consequence of increased efforts to fight illegal immigration. For this reason, the law establishes that 10 new centres shall be built in the next few years.

true innovation, however, would be the possibility to return asylum seekers back to these *Transit Processing Centres* for the time necessary to evaluate their claims, even after they have reached British soil.[67]

Living conditions inside European detention centres are comparable to those in prisons – limited freedom of movement, impossibility to communicate with the exterior except at certain hours of the day, continuous surveillance, a heavy presence of police forces – but some critics argue that these conditions are in fact even worse than in prisons. The fact that immigrants are not 'formally' prisoners – again, because these centres are not ordinary prisons – legitimates further violations of their individual rights: in Italian detention centres, for example, it is almost impossible for detainees to have access to their lawyers and to receive visitors. Furthermore, access to the centres by journalists, members of Parliament and civil associations is denied systematically by national and local authorities, thus making the reality of immigration detention centres invisible to the Italian and European public opinion. Therefore, it is not difficult to understand why police brutality, attempts to escape, self-mutilations and attempted suicides are so common inside these centres, both in Italy and in Europe.[68]

However, the situation is not much different in the US. Here too – besides the militarisation of the border with Mexico – detention (without trial) represents the main instrument for the control of migrants. And also in this context, the circumstances legitimating this semi-penal treatment are not necessarily connected to any criminal behaviour, being instead attached to the collective status of immigrants. Detention is the responsibility of the *Immigration and Naturalization Service* (INS), and takes place both in special centres very similar to the European ones, and in state prisons or county jails.[69] More precisely, the INS owns ten detention centres which it manages directly, whereas six other facilities are contracted out to private corporations like Corrections Corporation of America, Correctional Service Corporation and Wackenhut Corrections. To these one should add 'a haphazard network of 900 private state prisons and county jails, including 250 facilities where it rents beds regularly'.[70]

---

[67] For a critique of this proposal, which configures a clear violation of the Geneva Convention for the protection of refugees, see Teresa Hayter, 'Open Borders: the Case Against Immigration Controls', *Capital & Class*, 75 (2001): 149–156.

[68] Just a few names: Yarls Wood (United Kingdom), Serraino Vulpitta (Italy), Sangatte (France), Malaga (Spain). Hundreds of immigrants detained in these Immigration Detention Centres died by suicide, police brutality, or while attempting to escape.

[69] According to the *American Civil Liberties Union* 'No other law enforcement agency has as many armed officers with arrest powers than does the INS, and no other law enforcement agency arrests as many people': American Civil Liberties Union, *ACLU Joins Fix '96 Campaign For Justice For Immigrants* (Washington DC, 1996).

[70] Welch, *Detained*, p. 108. In another article, this author argues: 'Clearly, INS is responding to ideological and market forces in American society that rest on the uncritically accepted notion that more enforcement activities and less service provision is rational and legitimate, as well as lucrative … In concert with other components of the criminal justice system, the INS responds to the market imperatives of the prison-industrial complex, an enterprise whereby lawbreakers and undocumented immigrants are commodified as raw materials for private profit': Michael Welch, 'The Role of the Immigration and Naturalization Service in the Prison-Industrial Complex', *Social Justice*, 27/3 (2000): 73. On the privatization of immigration-detention in the US, see also Michael Welch,

Official data on the detention of undocumented immigrants in the US shows that between 1996 and 2002 the incarcerated population has quadrupled: from 6,000 detainees in 1996, to 16,000 in 1998, to 24,000 in 2002.[71]

According to some critical observers – supported by human and civil rights associations, such as the American Civil Liberties Union and Amnesty International – living conditions of immigrants detained in INS facilities are much worse than those of 'ordinary' prisoners: here, too, it seems that the subtraction of detention to penal law and to its guarantees legitimates discriminatory and punitive treatments, like frequent transfers, lack of legal representation, harsh conditions of confinement, inadequate medical care and mental health services, and in many cases even brutality against detainees.[72]

All American critics agree that a fundamental contribution to the expanding detention of undocumented immigrants was given by two important laws passed by the US Congress in 1996: the *Anti-Terrorism and Effective Death Penalty Act* and the *Illegal Immigration Reform and Immigrant Responsibility Act.* Resulting from a true moral panic about immigration and international terrorism,[73] these laws have indeed consolidated the process of 'ontological' and 'extra-penal' criminalisation of immigrants, legitimating the suspension of the principles of the rule of law:

> The new statutes gutted due process, issuing the INS unparalleled powers and limiting judicial review of deportation and detention decisions made by immigration judges. Those laws authorized the INS to use secret evidence to detain and deport suspected terrorists and

---

'Detention in INS Jails: Bureaucracy, Brutality and a Booming Business', in Rosemary Gido and Ted Alleman (eds), *Turnstile Justice: Issues in American Corrections* (Englewood Cliffs, 2000), pp. 202–214. A similar trend is also observable in Australia. Here there are seven detention centres (Villawood, Maribyrnong, Perth, Port Hedland, Baxter, Woomera and Christmas Island), and these facilities are run by the private operator Australasian Correctional Services Pty Ltd through its operational company Australasian Correctional Management. However, the Australian government is going to revise this agreement, and to contract the management of these centres with Group 4 Falck Global Solutions Pty Ltd. More than 8,000 immigrants are currently detained in Australia.

[71] Data from the INS web site: http://www.ins.usdoj.gov/graphics/aboutins/thisisins/overview.htm.

[72] See for example Amnesty International, *Treated as Criminal: Asylum Seekers in the USA* (New York, 1998) and *Asylum-Seekers Detained in the USA: A Disproportionate and Harsh Measure* (New York, 1999). See also American Civil Liberties Union, *Justice Detained: Conditions at the Varick Street Immigration Detention Center. A Report by the ACLU Immigrants' Rights Project* (Washington DC, 1993) and *Indefinite Detention* (Washington DC, 2000).

[73] In this respect, Welch argues that ' … The problem of illegal immigration – embodied in the threat of terrorism – emerged as a national issue in 1993, when an explosion ripped through the World Trade Centre in New York City. Two years later, when the Murrah Federal Building in Oklahoma City was bombed, the immediate reaction of law enforcement officials and many citizens was to assume that it, too, was the act of foreign terrorists. Although investigations led to US born Timothy McVeigh, and not foreign terrorists, public hostility against immigrants remained': Michael Welch, 'Ironies of Social Control and the Criminalization of Immigrants', *Crime, Law & Social Change*, 39 (2003): 319. A similar framework can be observed in the reactions against the terrorist attacks of 11 September 2001: here too, a simple equation between illegal immigration and international terrorism has been made by Western governments, producing a further criminalisation of immigrants in Europe and in the US.

expanded the scope of crimes considered aggravated felonies that are grounds for deportation. Compounding matters, that provision was made retroactive, meaning that any person convicted of a crime now reclassified as an aggravated felony could be deported, regardless how old the conviction.[74]

In the same year (and parliamentary session) in which the Congress toughened up the treatment of immigrants with these laws, another important (and complementary) law was passed – the *Personal Responsibility and Work Opportunity Reconciliation Act* – which '... denied Supplemental Security, food Stamps and Aid to Families with Dependent children to legal immigrants during their first five years of US residency'.[75] How can we not see here a full coherence with the principle of 'less eligibility' inspiring Euro-American migratory policies as a whole?

In short, these laws seem to establish that the legal status of immigrants is not the same as that of 'normal' citizens: to be legal residents of a country, to contribute to its wellbeing through honest work, and to abide by its laws does not guarantee to migrants any protection against penal and extra-penal institutions. In fact, detention and deportation take place independent of individual behaviours, to be grounded instead on the collective status of 'foreigners', 'immigrants', 'non-nationals'. A clear evidence of this is offered by the fact the 'aggravated felonies' which (according to these laws) are grounds for 'mandatory detention' and 'mandatory deportation' include such crimes as shoplifting, petty theft, drunk driving and low level drug violations: crimes which do not seem to endanger the internal security of a State, though they did destroy families and personal biographies – the families and lives of those people who were detained and then deported for having committed a crime even 30 years earlier – given that the 1996 laws were retroactive.

I would insist, however, that all this becomes possible – both in Europe and in the US – mainly because of the stigmatisation of immigrants at the social, economic and political level (connected to their public perception as 'dangerous classes' and 'undeserving poor'), permits to conceive punitive measures like detention and deportation not as 'punishments', but only as administrative provisions, to be

---

[74] Ibid., p. 320. In the summer of 2001, the High Court ruled that deportation and detention cannot automatically operate retroactively. But the *USA Patriot Act* of 2001 has again aggravated the status of immigrants, introducing racial profiling, mass detention and secret information as ordinary measures to be employed in the 'war on terrorism'.

[75] Welch, *Detained*, p. 50. According to Teresa Miller, the mentioned restrictive welfare reform should not be dissociated from the wider 'moral crusade' surrounding the Californian anti-immigration law called *Proposition 187*: 'Welfare reform peaked at the same time consensus emerged on the need to reform illegal immigration. Proposition 187 galvanized welfare reform with popular notions of illegal immigrants draining California's resources. Similar to the Bush-era stereotype of urban, black welfare mothers and "welfare queens" defrauding honest taxpayers of hard-earned dollars, so too were poor, Mexican immigrant women stereotyped as illegally entering the country, having their babies in US hospitals, sending children without English proficiency to public schools, and leaving taxpayers to pick up the tab': Teresa Miller, 'The Impact of Mass Incarceration on Immigration Policy', in Marc Mauer and Meda Chesney-Lind (eds), *Invisible Punishment. The Collateral Consequences of Mass Imprisonment* (New York, 2002), p. 224.

evaluated under the point of view of their 'effectiveness'.[76] What emerges here is a punitive strategy based on the social and institutional construction of immigrants as a homogeneous category, as an undifferentiated threat to the law and (b)order of Western societies, which must be neutralised preventively.[77] More importantly, however, this is a strategy which guarantees the reproduction of a labour force that is subordinated, flexible and without rights, available for any kind of integration into the labour market, as this will be in any case preferable to the risk of detention and expulsion. In the case of immigrants less eligibility – which for the post-Fordist labour force in general is a 'principle' governing penal institutions – becomes a 'reality' of everyday life.

I think it would be impossible not to see, in the ontological criminalisation of immigrants, the guidelines of a logic oriented to the punitive management of whole populations, characterised by the fact that they cannot fully satisfy the conditions of contemporary citizenship. We see this logic in action at the borders of the Western world, where limitations on the freedom of movement concern people more than capital, and some categories of people more than others. We see it in action whenever private actors – be it employers whose work-contracts regulate the legal residence of thousands of immigrants, or entrepreneurs of security who make profits on the human tragedies of refugees – are given the power to define the citizenship-status of whole factions of our society, thus reproducing a condition of post-Fordist slavery. We see it in the construction of hundreds of 'concentration camps' in which – in Europe as well as in the US – men and women who did not commit any crime can be detained for months, without a trial and without judicial rights. Finally, we see it in the enduring threat of expulsion, which Western governments impose to all migrants – regular and irregular, workers and asylum seekers – as if with them it were possible to neutralise the growing contradictions of global capitalism.

---

[76] 'This principle reduces to the basic idea that non-citizens have no substantive claim to remain in the US and are therefore subject to whatever rules the Congress chooses to make, even if they are retroactive. They are not being punished; they are simply being regulated': Kanstroom, 'Deportation, Social Control, and Punishment', p. 1895.

[77] Michael Welch makes this point about the US: 'Instead of reviewing individualized cases of asylum and applications for citizenship, the INS tends to resort to the processing of large aggregates – groups of specific nationalities, namely Cubans, Central Americans, and Nigerians': Michael Welch, 'The Immigration Crisis: Detention as an Emerging Mechanism of Social Control', *Social Justice*, 23/3 (1996): 180.

Conclusion

The issue of this research – the transformations of social control in post-Fordist society – seems to be open to unpredictable outcomes. Rather than offering a comprehensive description of the emerging policies of control in Western societies – perhaps an impossible challenge, considering the complex and often contradictory features of contemporary social control strategies both at the global and local level – in this work I attempted to identify some emerging tendencies, with the expectation that these could suggest some new research agendas within the political economy of punishment.

Starting from what appeared as the 'limits' of the 'orthodox' Marxist approach in criminology – a kind of 'obsession' with quantitative analysis, and a scarce attention to the qualitative transformations taking place in the field of production and work organisation – I tried to argue that the emergence of a new post-Fordist labour force – precarious, flexible and mobile – invites to a rethinking of the main coordinates of materialist criminology.

If the principle of less eligibility – formulated by Georg Rusche and later adopted by many other materialist criminologists in their attempts to produce a radical critique of contemporary penal systems grounded on the political economy of capitalist societies – seems to retain its full analytical worth today, nonetheless it needs to be enriched with new elements. In particular, I would suggest that the contemporary declinations of this principle cannot be based only on the transformations of the labour market (as was the case in Rusche's original formulation): the transformations of work in a post-industrial economy, the declining significance of 'rates of unemployment' as an indicator of the economic situation, the restructuring of the welfare state and the new features of the post-Fordist labour force described in this work suggest that any formulation of the principle of less eligibility in purely quantitative terms appears to be inadequate. Therefore, my first suggestion is that a post-Fordist political economy of punishment should concentrate more on the transformations of work (both at a global and local level) than on variations in the labour market.

Another important aspect of this analysis – exemplified in particular by the current reality of global migrations and their punitive regulation by Western governments – is that less eligibility should no longer be considered only as a state-based strategy for the control of the labour force through punitive institutions. In a global economy it would seem in fact that this principle (in order to be effective) must operate at least at two different levels – global and local. Globally, the neo-liberal policies of international organisations like the WTO, FMI and WB help to reproduce those conditions of relative and absolute deprivation and economic frustration which prompt large factions of the labour force to migrate from impoverished countries to the Western world in search of better life chances. Once there, punitive immigration laws work to guarantee that immigrant workers will accept any condition of work, as this will be preferable to being treated as illegal aliens – and thus to be detained indefinitely in immigration detention centres and later deported to the countries of origin.

On the other hand, however, I suggested also that the principle of less eligibility tends now to be increasingly dissociated from the disciplinary technologies, practices and institutions which guaranteed its functioning in the Fordist age. The main hypothesis here is that the contemporary labour force – which, following Michael Hardt and Antonio Negri, I defined a 'post-Fordist' multitude – is constitutively irreducible to the disciplinary strategies described by Michel Foucault, and that the very capitalist restructuring which started in the early 1970s, renders those strategies inadequate to the reproduction of the labour force. This restructuring – promoted in part as a reaction to the 'anti-disciplinary' struggles of the 1960s – has in fact contributed to the fragmentation of the spaces and times of the disciplinary society (exemplified by the Fordist factory), thus imposing on the labour force new forms of subjectivity which seem incompatible with the disciplinary logic. At the same time, however, the growing contradictions produced by the neo-liberal model of development require the development of technologies of social control adequate to the present condition, and still coherent with the principle of less eligibility. I would locate here the transition from the welfare state to the penal state described by Loic Wacquant and other criminologists as the new paradigm for the regulation of the contemporary labour force. However, I disagree with these authors when they suggest that the punitive logic inspiring the penal treatment of contemporary 'advanced marginality' is still disciplinary.

In fact, I argued that the model of control emerging from this new condition can be defined as a 'bio-politics without discipline': a government of surplus populations no longer based on the discipline of individuals, but on the penal management of whole categories of people, inspired by a logic of preventive risk neutralisation. I also suggested that the growing difficulty to produce an individualised (in this sense, disciplinary) knowledge about the subjects prompts their regrouping into 'risk categories', whose physiognomy depends on the changing political definitions of risk: thus, new 'dangerous classes' emerge as the privileged targets of the new strategies of social control: *mass surveillance* (in the form of situational crime prevention schemes, the diffusion of CCTV systems, crime prevention through environmental design, urban zoning, community-gating, and so on); *limited access* to the material and symbolic spaces of contemporary life (for example, by reinforcing the boundaries of the nation-states and making them almost inaccessible to the immigrant labour force, or by exerting a strict control over the access to communication and immaterial resources); *mass confinement* (including not only the experiments with mass-imprisonment conducted in the US and – to a lesser extent – in many European countries, but also the creation of new peculiar places of confinement, such as the Immigration Detention Centres).

My point of view is that these strategies operate at two levels: an instrumental level which has to do with the management of the contradictions of the post-Fordist economy, and concerns the role punitive policies play in the global and local division of labour: the principle of less eligibility is crucial here. But also a symbolic level, which has to do with the political declinations of social control: the public representation (and institutional treatment) of some categories of people as new dangerous classes and public enemies, against whom periodic wars must be waged, seems in fact to prevent the consolidation of political alliances inside the post-Fordist labour force. In other words, the technologies of social control described in this work seem to disarticulate the constitution of a collective consciousness by the globalised labour force: what could become anti-systemic struggles is thus preventively translated into a war among the poor, in which the responsibility for the growing insecurity, precariousness and social vulnerability is constantly blamed on those who are 'one step below' – immigrants, the unemployed, drug addicts, street criminals, single mothers, etc.

Here, I am not in the condition to decide whether these processes represent a paradigmatic shift in the recent history of punitive systems and of their ancillary role in the development of Western capitalism, or if instead we witness a cyclical trend which preludes to a new phase, in which the post-Fordist labour force will regain a consciousness of its own condition, and therefore will start a cycle of struggles for new rights and a different model of citizenship. In this work I opt for the first scenario; but this does not mean that I read the present condition as a linear process, unaffected by social change and untouched by practices of resistance and struggle. In this respect, in an interview released more than 20 years ago Michel Foucault said:

> You see, if there was no resistance, there would be no power relations. Because it would simply be a matter of obedience. You have to use power relations to refer to the situation where you're not doing what you want. So resistance comes first, and resistance remains superior to the forces of the process; power relations are obliged to change with the resistance. So I think that resistance is the main word, the key word of this dynamic.[1]

Many forms of resistance against the 'penal government' of the post-Fordist surplus are in fact emerging: even though we are not always able to recognise and nominate them, these resistances erupt periodically, often in the form of *molecular* struggles against the new social inequalities prompted by the neo-liberal ideology. These resistances are diffused and often invisible, perhaps because with the crisis of the Fordist factory and the implosion of the disciplinary technologies, we lose sight of those disciplinary places within which we were accustomed to locate resistance – the factory, the prison, the psychiatric hospital, the school, etc. Indeed, outside these closed institutions, the conflicts emerging around the new strategies of control are characterised by a multiplicity of practices and by the absence of any hegemonic subject.

As Michel Foucault suggested, each *dispositif* of control is constituted by a complex of practices, strategies and discourses defining its internal economies and peculiar rationalities of power: resistances are grounded on those economies and rationalities, and work to sabotage and make them ineffective. This assumption represents an axiom of the Foucauldian genealogy of the relation between power and resistance, though this is not to suggest that there is always a dialectic relation between powers and resistances, as if to each regime of power specular forms of rebellion corresponded. What I would suggest, however, is that the new strategies of social control prompt new practices of self-subtraction, refusal and struggle against the places, times and social structures in which individuals are organised by the technologies of power.

---

[1] Michel Foucault, 'Sex, Power, and the Politics of Identity', in Paul Rabinow (ed.), *Essential Works of Foucault 1954–1984, vol. I. Ethics, Subjectivity and Truth* (New York, 1997), p. 167.

Let us return for a moment to the disciplinary model. Disciplinary technologies – operating as mechanisms for the production of a docile subjectivity within the factory, the prison, the psychiatric hospital, the school, and so on – defined some peculiar spaces and times of individualised control, which at the same time became also important fields of resistance.

In that context, resistance could express itself as an 'exit' from the places of control – escape from the prison, the factory, the asylum; or as their 'destructuring' from inside – industrial sabotage, atypical forms of strike; or finally as a re-appropriation of those places, in order to make alternative uses of them – anti-psychiatric practices, occupation of factories, women's communities against violence.

Thus, for example, the same mechanisms of disciplinary organisation which permitted the productivity of the Taylorist factory, in the 1960s became weapons in the hands of the industrial working class, which started to turn them against the capitalist organisation of work. Thus, the whole system of control of the labour force revolted against the very capitalist elite which had projected it: the same rigidities, machineries, assembly lines and hierarchical structures which exasperated alienation, exploitation and subordination, now allowed the Fordist labour force to exercise an effective counter-power against the production system. In other words, resistances ground themselves on the same fields on which powers are grounded, and are fed by the same features which render those powers effective.

Now, the technologies of control I have described in these pages would seem to reduce the margins of resistance, because – as I tried to show in earlier chapters – they tend to replace 'real' individuals and concrete social interactions with simulacra, fluxes of data and numbers, statistics and actuarial populations: something against which any form of resistance seems difficult to imagine. The statistical table, the zoning and mapping of risky urban areas, the differentiation of prison regimes according to the ethnic composition of the population, the resort to biometric technologies, passwords and electronic gates, as well as the preventive detention of immigrants on the basis of their condition of non-citizens, are some examples of actuarial technologies which make resistance seem unthinkable, because they appear to neutralise its subjective dimension: they de-structure the individuals and the forms of interaction which disciplinary technologies pretended to transform and to regulate. Following Jonathan Simon:

> Actuarial classification, with its decentred subject, seems to eliminate, in advance, the possibility of identity, of critical self-consciousness and of inter-subjectivity. Rather than making people up, actuarial practices unmake them.[2]

But perhaps we can read developments differently, and suppose that actuarialism in the form of mass surveillance, mass confinement and limited access are not strategies which neutralise resistances, but rather attempts to ignore them by situating the practices of control on a different level, in which instead of real subjects we find deformed representations of social interactions.

---

[2]   Jonathan Simon, 'The Ideological Effects of Actuarial Practices', *Law and Society Review*, 2/4 (1988): 795.

In suggesting that post-Fordist control – being oriented to the social representation and punitive treatment of artificial categories of individuals – tends to assume the form of 'simulacra', it is not my intention to dematerialise it, nor to overlook the violence which inspires it. In fact, the current conditions of urban segregation, destruction of public space, mass confinement and 'global apartheid' are indeed real phenomena with real consequences. They produce suffering, isolation, desperation, and in many cases the 'biographic death' mentioned in the Introduction. Indeed, here I would identify the transition towards a model of control which *no longer produces subjectivities, but simply destroys them*. Through generalised surveillance, mass-detention, the war on immigration, humanitarian wars, etc. this system of power attempts to confine the post-Fordist labour force within defined categories, and to situate it along hierarchical lines. No longer able to capture individuals in their concrete interactions, the government of surplus crystallises them in predefined identities, necessary for the functioning of a regime of generalised surveillance: immigrants, the unemployed, criminals, the underclass, etc. The various classes of individuals thus produced are then distributed across the many 'non-places' of post-disciplinary control: immigrants in the 'waiting areas' of the Empire, the unemployed in urban 'hyper-ghettoes', deviants in warehousing prisons, immaterial workers in the privatised net, human diversity at the margins.

But if we look at the forms of resistance which have emerged in the last years on many fronts – from sexual identities to work, from immigration to citizenship rights – we discover that they are emerging as practices which oppose those very mechanisms which compel individuals to accept pre-constituted categorial identities and to behave coherently. I am not thinking so much about forms of resistance which came to recognise themselves as such, and reached some degree of political organisation (like the new global movements which made their appearance in Seattle, Geneva, Porto Alegre, and so on); rather, I refer to those molecular resistances that emerge silently from the everyday lives and conditions of the contemporary labour force.

A paradigmatic case in question is again represented by the subjective dimension of contemporary migrations. In the post-Fordist metropolis migrants are deprived of their voice, their language and the possibility to share their existential condition with other factions of the labour force: indeed, they are reduced to aphasia. Here we can see the rationality of post-Fordist control in its clearest form: at the same time 'laborious' and 'dangerous' class, immigrants must be deprived of those communicative and affective faculties which make them part of the contemporary labour force. The aim is in fact to prevent the formation of a self-consciousness of being part of the same global labour force and thus to prevent the consolidation of social and political ties with other sections of it. In this sense, immigrants offer a paradigmatic image of the post-Fordist multitude, and their condition inside the 'wall around the West' clearly exemplifies the contradictions of post-disciplinary control.

The challenge here, as I suggested earlier, is to see migrations not only as the consequence of 'objective' global issues – wars, poverty, famine, persecutions and so on – but also as the result of 'subjective' choices. In other words, I suggest that contemporary migrations should be seen not as the mechanical consequence of 'push' and 'pull' factors, or as global phenomena corresponding to variations in the global labour markets, but instead as collective life-trajectories inspired by individual choices, changing life expectations and new desires. In this respect, migrations could be read as 'social movements', because they represent an attempt to cross the geographical and symbolic borders which condemn growing factions of the global labour force to conditions of marginality and frustration: acts of resistance against the new international division of labour, against the destructive economic policies implemented by the IMF and the World Bank and against the regime of 'global apartheid' enforced by the Western world – not least through the strategies of post-Fordist social control described in this book.

Bibliography

Adamson, C., 'Toward a Marxian Penology: Captive Criminal Populations as Economic Threats and Resources', *Social Problems*, 31/4 (1984): 435–458.

Aden, H., 'Convergence of Policing Policies and Trans-national Policing in Europe', *European Journal of Crime, Criminal Law and Criminal Justice*, 9/2 (2001): 99–112.

Aglietta, M., *A Theory of Capitalist Regulation*, London: New Left Books, 1979.

Alquati, R., *Lavoro e attività. Per un'analisi della schiavitù neomoderna*, Rome: Manifestolibri, 1997.

Althusser, L., 'Ideology and Ideological State Apparatuses', in *Lenin and Philosophy and Other Essays*, London: New Left Books, 1971, pp. 85–126.

American Civil Liberties Union, *ACLU Joins Fix '96 Campaign For Justice For Immigrants*, Washington DC, 1996.

American Civil Liberties Union, *Indefinite Detention*, Washington DC, 2000.

American Civil Liberties Union, *Justice Detained: Conditions at the Varick Street Immigration Detention Center. A Report by the ACLU Immigrants' Rights Project*, Washington DC, 1993.

Amin, A. (ed.), *Post-Fordism. A Reader*, Oxford: Blackwell, 1994.

Amin, S., *Accumulation on a World Scale: A Critique of the Theory of Underdevelopment*, New York: Monthly Review Press, 1974.

Amnesty International, *Asylum-Seekers Detained in the USA: A Disproportionate and Harsh Measure*, New York, 1999.

Amnesty International, *Treated as Criminal: Asylum Seekers in the USA*, New York, 1998.

Anastasia, S. and Gonnella, P. (eds) *Inchiesta sulle carceri italiane*, Rome: Carocci, 2002.

Anderson, M., 'The Transformation of Border Controls: A European Precedent?', in Andreas, P. and Snyder, T. (eds), *The Wall around the West. State Borders and Immigration Controls in North America and Europe*, Lahnam: Rowman & Littlefield Publishers, 2000, pp. 15–29.

Andreas, P., *Border Games: Policing the US-Mexico Divide*, Ithaca: Cornell University Press, 2000.

Andreas, P., 'Introduction: The Wall after the Wall', in Andreas, P. and Snyder, T. (eds), *The Wall around the West*, Lahnam: Rowman & Littlefield Publishers, 2000, pp. 1–14.

Andreas, P. and Snyder, T. (eds), *The Wall around the West. State Borders and Immigration Controls in North America and Europe*, Lahnam: Rowman & Littlefield Publishers, 2000.

Arendt, H., *Labor, Work, Action*, Trustee: Mary McCarthy West, 1987.

Arendt, H., *The Human Condition*, Chicago: The University of Chicago Press, 1958.

Aronowitz, S. and Di Fazio, W., *The Jobless Future*, Minneapolis: University of Minnesota Press, 1994.

Augè, M., *Non-Places. Introduction to an Anthropology of Supermodernity*, London: Verso, 1995.

Balibar, E., 'Is There a "Neo-Racism"?', in Balibar, E. and Wallerstein, I., *Race, Nation, Class*, London: Verso, 1991, pp. 17–27.

Balibar, E. and Wallerstein, I., *Race, Nation, Class*, London: Verso, 1991.

Barak, G., 'Between Waves: Mass-mediated Themes of Crime and Justice', *Social Justice*, 21/3 (1994): 133–148.

Barlow, D.E. and Hickman-Barlow, M., 'Federal Criminal Justice Legislation and the Post-World War II Social Structure of Accumulation in the United States', *Crime, Law and Social Change*, 22 (1995): 239–267.

Barlow, D.E., Hickman-Barlow, M. and Chiricos, T.G., 'Long Economic Cycles and the Criminal Justice System in the US', *Crime, Law and Social Change*, 19 (1993): 143–169.

Baubock, R. and Rundell, J. (eds), *Blurred Boundaries: Migration, Ethnicity, Citizenship*, Aldershot: Ashgate, 1998.

Baudrillard, J., *In the Shadow of the Silent Majorities or 'the Death of the Social'*, New York: Semiotexte, 1983.

Bauman, Z., *Globalisation. The Human Consequences*, Cambridge: Polity Press, 1998.

Bauman, Z., 'Is There a Postmodern Sociology?', *Theory, Culture and Society*, 5/2-3 (1988): 217–237.

Bauman, Z., *Liquid Modernity*, Cambridge: Polity Press, 2000.

Bauman, Z., *Postmodernity and its Discontents*, Oxford: Blackwell, 1997.

Bauman, Z., *Work, Consumerism and the New Poor*, Milton Keynes: Open University Press, 1998.

Beck, U., *Schoene Arbeitswelt. Vision: Weltburgergesellschaft*, Frankfurt am Main: Campus Verlag, 1999.

Becker, G., 'Crime and Punishment: An Economic Approach', *The Journal of Political Economy*, 76 (1968): 169–217.

Beckett, K., *Making Crime Pay*, New York: Oxford University Press, 1997.

Beckett, K. and Sassoon, T., *The Politics of Injustice. Crime and Punishment in America*, Thousand Oaks: The Pine Forge Press, 2000.

Berk, R., Messinger, S., Rauma, D. and Berecochea, J., 'Prisons as Self-Regulating Systems', *Law and Society Review*, 17 (1983): 547–586.

Bhagwati, J.N., 'Incentives and Disincentives: International Migration', *Weltwirtschaftliches Archiv*, 120/4 (1994): 678–701.

Blakely, E.J. and Gail Snyder, M., *Fortress America. Gated Communities in the United States*, Washington DC: Brookings Institution Press, 1997.

Blumstein, A., Cohen, J. and Nagin, D., 'The Dynamics of Homeostatic Punishment Process', *Journal of Criminal Law and Criminology*, 67 (1976): 317–334.

Bonefeld, W. and Holloway, J. (eds), *Post-Fordism and Social Form. A Marxist Debate on the Post-Fordist State*, London: Macmillan, 1991.

Bonefeld, W., Gunn, R. and Psychopedis, K. (eds), *Open Marxism, Vol II: Theory and Practice*, London: Pluto Press, 1992.

Bonger, W., *Criminality and Economic Conditions*, Boston: Little, Brown & Co., 1916.

Bottomore, T.B. and Rubel, M. (eds), *Karl Marx. Selected Writings in Sociology and Social Philosophy*, Harmondsworth: Penguin, 1969.

Boutang, Y.M., *De l'esclavage au salariat. Economie historique du salariat bridé*, Paris: Puf, 1998.

Box, S., *Recession, Crime and Punishment*, London: Rowman & Littlefield, 1987.

Box, S. and Hale, C., 'Economic Crisis and the Rising Prisoner Population in England and Wales', *Crime and Social Justice*, 17 (1982): 20–35.

Box, S. and Hale, C., 'Unemployment, Crime and Imprisonment, and the Enduring Problem of Prison Overcrowding', in Matthews, R. and Young, J. (eds), *Confronting Crime*, London: Sage, 1986, pp. 72–99.

Box, S. and Hale, C., 'Unemployment, Imprisonment and Prison Overcrowding', *Contemporary Crises*, 9 (1985): 209–228.

Boyne, R., 'Post-Panopticism', *Economy and Society*, 29/2 (2000): 285–307.

Braidotti, R., *Metamorphoses. Towards a Materialist Theory of Becoming*, Cambridge: Polity Press, 2002.

Braithwaite, J., 'The Political Economy of Punishment', in Weelwright, E. and Buckley, K.D. (eds), *Essays in the Political Economy of Australian Capitalism*, Sydney: Australian and New Zealand Book Company, 1980, pp. 192–208.

Bratton, W., 'Crime is Down in New York City: Blame the Police', in Dennis, N. (ed.), *Zero Tolerance. Policing a Free Society*, London: IEA, 1997, pp. 33–34.

Brenner, R. and Glick, M., 'The Regulation Approach: Theory and History', *New Left Review*, 188 (1991): 45–119.

Bridges, G.S., Crutchfield, R.D. and Simpson, E.E., 'Crime, Social Structure and Criminal Punishment: White and Non-white Rates of Imprisonment, *Social Problems*, 34/4 (1987): 345–361.

Bunyan, T., 'The "War on Freedom and Democracy". An Analysis of the Effects on Civil Liberties and Democratic Culture in the EU', *Statewatch Analysis*, 13 (2002).

Burawoy, M., 'The Functions and Reproduction of Migrant Labor: Comparative Materials from Southern Africa and the United States', *American Journal of Sociology*, 81 (1976): 1050–1087.

Burchell, G., Gordon, C. and Miller, P. (eds), *The Foucault Effect*, Chicago: The University of Chicago Press, 1991.

Burchell, G., 'Governmental Rationality', in Burchell, G., Gordon, C. and Miller, P. (eds), *The Foucault Effect*, Chicago: The University of Chicago Press, 1991.

Bureau of Justice Statistics, *Expenditure and Employment Extracts*, Washington DC, 2002.

Bureau of Justice Statistics, *2002 At a Glance*, Washington DC, 2002.

Bureau of Justice Statistics, *National Crime Victimization Survey*, Washington DC, 2001.

Bureau of Justice Statistics, *Correctional Populations in the United States, 1997*, Washington DC, 1998.

Bureau of Justice Statistics, *Correctional Surveys*, Washington DC, 2000.

Bureau of Justice Statistics, *Criminal Victimization, 1973–1995*, Washington DC, 1997.

Bureau of Justice Statistics, *Prisoners in 2001*, Washington DC, 2002.

Bureau of Justice Statistics, *Report on Education and Correctional Populations*, Washington DC, 2003.

Burrows, R. and Loader, B. (eds), *Toward a Post-Fordist Welfare State?*, London: Routledge, 1994.

Calavita, K., 'A "Reserve Army of Delinquents". The Criminalization and Economic Punishment of Immigrants in Spain', *Punishment and Society*, 5/4 (2003): 399–413.

Caplow, T. and Simon, J., 'Understanding Prison Policy and Population Trends', in Tonry, M. and Petersilia, J. (eds), *Prisons. Crime and Justice. A Review of Research*, 26 (1999): 63–120.

Castel, R., 'From Dangerousness to Risk', in Burchell, C., Gordon, C. and Miller, P. (eds), *The Foucault Effect*, Chicago: The University of Chicago Press, 1991, pp. 281–298.

Castells, M., *The Rise of the Network Society*, Oxford: Blackwell, 2000.

Castles, S. and Kosack, G., *Immigrant Workers and Class Structure in Western Europe*, London: Oxford University Press, 1973.

Castles, S. and Miller, M., *The Age of Migration: International Population Movements in the Modern World*, New York: Guilford, 1998.

Ceri, P., *La società vulnerabile. Quale sicurezza, quale libertà*, Rome and Bari: Laterza, 2003.

Chiricos, G.T. and Bales, W.D., 'Unemployment and Punishment: An Empirical Assessment', *Criminology*, 29/4 (1991): 701–724.

Chiricos, T. and Delone, M., 'Labour Surplus and Imprisonment: A Review and Assessment of Theory and Evidence', *Social Problems*, 39/4 (1992): 421–446.

Christie, N., *Crime Control as Industry: Toward Gulags Western Style*, London: Routledge, 1994.

Clarke, R.V., 'Situational Crime Prevention', *Crime and Justice. A Review of Research*, 19 (1995): 91–150.

Cleaver, H., *Reading Capital Politically*, Brighton: Harvester, 1979.

Cohen, R. (ed.), *The Cambridge Survey of World Migration*, Cambridge: Cambridge University Press, 1995.

Cohen, S., *Visions of Social Control*, Cambridge: Polity Press, 1985.

Cohen, S. and Scull, A. (eds), *Social Control and the State*, Oxford: Martin Robertson, 1983.

Colvin, M., 'Controlling the Surplus Population: the Latent Functions of Imprisonment and Welfare in Late US Capitalism', in MacLean, B.D. (ed.), *The Political Economy of Crime*, Ontario: Prentice Hall, 1986, pp. 154–165.

Coriat, B., *Penser à l'envers. Travail et organisation dans l'enterprise japonaise*, Paris: Christian Bourgois, 1991.

Cornelius, W., *et al.* (eds), *Controlling Immigration: A Global Perspective*, Stanford: Stanford University Press, 1994.

Cotesta, V., *La cittadella assediata. Immigrazione e conflitti etnici in Italia*, Rome: Editori Riuniti, 1992.

Dal Lago, A., *Non Persone. L'esclusione dei migranti in una società globale*, Milan: Feltrinelli, 1999.

Davis, M., *City of Quartz. Excavating the Future in Los Angeles*, New York: Vintage Books, 1992.

Davis, M., *Ecology of Fear*, New York: Metropolitan Books, 1998.

Davis, M., *Beyond Blade Runner: Urban Control. The Ecology of Fear*, Westfield: Open Magazine Pamphlet Series, 1992.

De Haan, W., *The Politics of Redress. Crime, Punishment and Penal Abolition*, London: Unwin Hyman, 1990.

Dean, M., *Governmentality. Power and Rule in Modern Society*, London: Sage, 1999.

Deetz, S., 'Discursive Formations, Strategized Subordination and Self-surveillance', in McKinlay, A. and Starkey, K. (eds), *Foucault, Management and Organisation Theory. From Panopticon to Technologies of Self*, London: Sage, 1998, pp. 151–172.

Deleuze, G., 'Postscript on the Societies of Control', *October*, 59 (1992): 3–7.

Deleuze, G. and Guattari, F., *A Thousand Plateaus. Capitalism and Schizophrenia*, Minneapolis: University of Minnesota Press, 1987.

Diamond, S., 'Right-Wing Politics and the Anti-Immigration Cause', *Social Justice*, 23/3 (1996): 154–168.

Dobbins, D.A. and Bass, B.M., 'Effects of Unemployment on White and Negro Prison Admissions in Louisiana', *Journal of Criminal Law, Criminology and Police Science*, 48 (1958): 522–525.

Doob, A. and Greenspan, E. (eds), *Perspectives in Criminal Law*, Ontario: Canada Law Book Inc., 1985.

Durkheim, E., *The Division of Labour in Society*, Glencoe: The Free Press, 1960.

Ehrenreich, B., *Nickel and Dimed. On (Not) Getting by in America*, New York: Metropolitan Books, 2001.

Eisner, M., 'Cycles of Political Control: The Case of Canton Zurich, 1880–1983', *European Journal of Political Research*, 15 (1987): 167–184.

Ericson, R.V. and Carriere, K., 'The Fragmentation of Criminology', in Nelken, D. (ed.), *The Futures of Criminology*, London: Sage, 1994, pp. 89–109.

Erikson, K.T., *Wayward Puritans. A Study in the Sociology of Deviance*, New York: Wiley & Sons, 1966.

Esping-Andersen, G., *Social Foundations of Postindustrial Economies*, Oxford: Oxford University Press, 1999.

Ewald, F., 'Insurance and Risk', in Burchell, G., Gordon, C. and Miller, P. (eds), *The Foucault Effect*, Chicago: The University of Chicago Press, 1991, pp. 197–210.

Ewald, F., *L'Etat-Providence*, Paris: Grasset, 1986.

Ewald, F., 'Norms, Discipline and the Law', *Representations*, 30 (1990): 136–161.

Fanon, F., *The Wretched of the Earth*, New York: Grove Press, 1963.

Federici, S., *Wages Against Housework*, London: Power of Women Collective and Falling Wall Press, 1975.

Feeley, M., 'Crime, Social Order and the Rise of neo-Conservative Politics', *Theoretical Criminology*, 7/1 (2003): 111–130.

Feeley, M. and Simon, J., 'Actuarial Justice: The Emerging New Criminal Law', in Nelken, D. (ed.), *The Futures of Criminology*, London: Sage, 1994, pp. 173–201.

Feeley, M. and Simon, J., 'The New Penology. Notes on the Emerging Strategies of Corrections and its Implications', *Criminology*, 30/4 (1992): 449–474.

Ferracuti, F., 'European Migration and Crime', in Wolfgang, M.E. (ed.), *Crime and Culture: Essays in Honour of Thorsten Sellin*, New York: Wiley & Sons, 1968, pp. 189–219.

Ferrari Bravo, L., 'Sovranità', in Zanini, A. and Fadini, U. (eds), *Lessico Postfordista. Dizionario di idee della mutazione*, Milan: Feltrinelli, 2001, pp. 278–284.

Fine, B. *et al.* (eds), *Capitalism and the Rule of Law. From Deviancy Theory to Marxism*, London: Hutchinson, 1979.

Foucault, M., *Discipline and Punish. The Birth of the Prison*, London: Penguin Books, 1977.

Foucault, M., *Discipline and Punish*, London: Penguin Books, 1991.

Foucault, M., *Dits et écrits, Tome II: 1970–1975*, Paris: Gallimard, 1994.

Foucault, M., 'Governmentality', in Burchell, G., Gordon, C. and Miller, P. (eds), *The Foucault Effect. Studies in Governmentality*, Chicago: The University of Chicago Press, 1991, pp. 87–104.

Foucault, M., *Madness and Civilization. A History of Insanity in the Age of Reason*, London: Tavistock Publications, 1967.

Foucault, M., 'Questions of Method', in Burchell, G., Gordon, C. and Miller, P. (eds), *The Foucault Effect*, Chicago: The University of Chicago Press, 1991, pp. 73–86.

Foucault, M., 'Security, Territory, and Population', in *Essential Works of Foucault 1954–1984, vol. I* (edited by Paul Rabinow), New York: The New Press, 1997, pp. 67–71.

Foucault, M., 'Sex, Power, and the Politics of Identity', in *Essential Works of Foucault 1954–1984, vol. I* (edited by Paul Rabinow), New York: The New Press, 1997, pp. 163–173.

Foucault, M., 'The Punitive Society', in *Essential Works of Foucault 1954–1984, vol. I* (edited by Paul Rabinow), New York: The New Press, 1997, pp. 23–37.

Foucault, M., *The Will to Knowledge. The History of Sexuality, vol. I*, London: Penguin Books, 1990.

Foucault, M., 'Truth and Juridical Forms', in *Essential Works of Foucault 1954–1984, vol. III*, (edited by James D. Faubion), New York: The New Press, 2000, pp. 1–89.

Francis, R.D., *Migrant Crime in Australia*, St. Lucia: University of Queensland Press, 1981.

Fumagalli, A., 'Aspetti dell'accumulazione flessibile in Italia', in Bologna, S. and Fumagalli, A. (eds), *Il lavoro autonomo di seconda generazione. Scenari del postfordismo in Italia*, Milan: Feltrinelli, 1997, pp. 147–151.

Galster, G.C. and Scaturo, L.A., 'The US Criminal Justice System: Unemployment and the Severity of Punishment', *Journal of Research in Crime and Delinquency*, 22/2 (1985): 163–189.

Garland, D., '"Governmentality" and the Problem of Crime: Foucault, Criminology, Sociology', *Theoretical Criminology*, 1/2 (1997): 173–214.

Garland, D. (ed.), *Mass Imprisonment. Social Causes and Consequences*, London: Sage, 2001.

Garland, D., *Punishment and Modern Society. A Study in Social Theory*, Oxford: Clarendon Press, 1990.

Garland, D., *Punishment and Welfare: A History of Penal Strategies*, Aldershot: Gower, 1985.

Garland, D., *The Culture of Control. Crime and Social Order in Contemporary Society*, New York: Oxford University Press, 2001.

Garland, D. and Young, P. (eds), *The Power to Punish. Contemporary Penality and Social Analysis*, London: Heinemann, 1983.

Gido, R.L. and Alleman, T. (eds), *Turnstile Justice: Issues in American Corrections*, Englewood Cliffs: Prentice Hall, 2000.

Godefroy, T. and Laffargue, B., *Changements Economiques et Repression Penale*, Paris: CESDIP, 1995.

Goode, E. and Ben-Yehuda, N., *Moral Panics: the Social Construction of Deviance*, Cambridge MA: Blackwell, 1994.

Gorz, A., *Critique of Economic Reason*, London: Verso, 1989.

Gorz, A., *Reclaiming Work. Beyond the Wage-Based Society*, Cambridge: Polity Press, 1999.

Gouldner, A., 'The Sociologist as Partisan: Sociology and the Welfare State', in *For Sociology*, Harmondsworth: Penguin, 1975, pp. 27–68.

Greenberg, D.F., 'The Cost-Benefits Analysis of Imprisonment', *Social Justice*, 17/4 (1990): 49–75.

Greenberg, D.F., 'The Dynamics of Oscillatory Punishment Processes', *The Journal of Criminal Law and Criminology*, 68 (1977): 643–651.

Greenberg, D.F., 'Penal Sanctions in Poland: A Test of Alternative Models', *Social Problems*, 28/2 (1980): 194–204.

Greenwood, P., *Selective Incapacitation*, Santa Monica: RAND Corporation, 1982.

Gutmann, A. and Thompson, D., *Democracy and Disagreement*, Cambridge: Harvard University Press, 1996.

Hadjimichalis, C. and Sadler, D. (eds), *Europe at the Margins: New Mosaics of Inequality*, New York: John Wiley & Sons, 1995.

Hale, C., 'Economy, Punishment and Imprisonment', *Contemporary Crises*, 13 (1989): 327–349.

Hardt, M. and Negri, A., *Empire*, Cambridge MA: Harvard University Press, 2000.

Harris, N., *The New Untouchables. Immigration and the New World Order*, Harmondsworth: Penguin, 1996.

Hayter, T., 'Open Borders: the Case Against Immigration Controls', *Capital & Class*, 75 (2001): 149–156.

Hempel, L. and Topfer, E., 'On the Threshold to Urban Panopticon? Analysing the Employment of CCTV in European Cities and Assessing its Social and Political Impacts', *Working Paper n. 1. Inception Report of the Centre for Technology and Society*, Berlin: Technical University, 2002.

Hobbes, T., *De Cive*, New York: Appleton Century-Crofts, 1949.

Hope, T. and Sparks, R. (eds), *Crime, Risk and Insecurity*, London: Routledge, 2000.

Howe, A., *Punish and Critique*, London: Routledge, 1994.

Hudson, B., 'Punishment, Rights and Difference: Defending Justice in the Risk-Society', in Stenson, K. and Sullivan, R. (eds), *Crime, Risk and Justice. The Politics of Crime Control in Liberal Democracies*, Devon: Willan, 2001, pp. 144–172.

Human Rights Watch/The Sentencing Project, *Losing the Vote. The Impact of Felony Disenfranchisement Laws in the United States*, Washington DC, 1998.

Huysmans, J., 'The European Union and the Securization of Migration', *Journal of Common Market Studies*, 38/5 (2000): 751–777.

Ignatieff, M., *A Just Measure of Pain. The Penitentiary in the Industrial Revolution*, London: Penguin Books, 1989.

Ignatieff, M., 'State, Civil Society and Total Institutions: A Critique of Recent Social Histories of Punishment', in Cohen, S. and Scull, A. (eds), *Social Control and the State*, Oxford: Martin Robertson, 1983, pp. 75–105.

Inverarity, J. and Grattet, R., 'Institutional Responses to Unemployment: A Comparison of US Trends, 1948–1985', *Contemporary Crises*, 13 (1989): 351–370.

Inverarity, J. and McCarthy, D., 'Punishment and Social Structure Revisited: Unemployment and Imprisonment in the United States, 1948–1984', *The Sociological Quarterly*, 29/2 (1988): 263–279.

Irwin, J., Schiraldi, V. and Ziedenberg, J., 'America's One Million Non-violent Prisoners', *Social Justice*, 27/2 (2000): 135–147.

Jacobs, D. and Helms, R.E., 'Toward a Political Model of Incarceration: A Time-series Examination of Multiple Explanations for Prison Admission Rates', *American Journal of Sociology*, 102/2 (1996): 323–357.

Jankovic, I., 'Labour Market and Imprisonment', *Crime and Social Justice*, 8 (1877): 17–31.

Jessop, B., 'Regulation Theories in Retrospect and Prospect', *Economy and Society*, 19/2 (1990): 153–216.

Jones, R., 'Digital Rule. Punishment, Control and Technology', *Punishment & Society*, 2/1 (2000): 5–22.

Kanstroom, D., 'Deportation, Social Control, and Punishment: Some Thoughts About Why Hard Laws Make Bad Cases', *Harvard Law Review*, 113 (2000): 1890–1935.

Kempf-Leonard, K. and Peterson, E., 'Expanding Realms of the New Penology. The Advent of Actuarial Justice for Juveniles', *Punishment and Society*, 2/1 (2000): 66–97.

Kemshall, H., *Reviewing Risk. A Review of Research on the Assessment and Management of Risk and Dangerousness: Implications for Policy and Practice in the Probation Service*, London: Information and Publications Group, 1996.

Killias, M., 'Criminality among Second-generation Immigrants in Western Europe: A Review of the Evidence', *Criminal Justice Review*, 14/1 (1989): 13–42.

Killias, M. and Grandjean, C., 'Chomage et taux d'incarcèration: L'example de la Suisse de 1890 à 1941', *Dèviance et Sociètè*, 10/4 (1986): 309–322.

Klein, N., *No logo*, London: Flamingo, 2000.

Kondratieff, N.D., 'The Long Waves in Economic Life', *Review of Economic Statistics*, 17 (1935): 105–115.

Kostakopoulou, T., 'Is There an Alternative to "Schengenland"?', *Political Studies*, 46 (1998): 886–902.

Kostakopoulou, T., 'The "Protective Union": Change and Continuity in Migration Law and Policy in Post-Amsterdam Europe', *Journal of Common Market Studies*, 38/3 (2000): 497–518.

Kuhn, A., 'Incarceration Rates Across the World', in Tonry, M. (ed.), *Penal Reform in Overcrowded Times*, Oxford: Oxford University Press, 2001, pp. 12–20.

Laffargue, B. and Godefroy, T., 'Economic Cycles and Punishment: Unemployment and Imprisonment. A Time-Series Study: France 1920–1985', *Contemporary Crises*, 13 (1989): 371–404.

Lahar, G. and Guiraudon, V., 'Comparative Perspectives on Border Control: Away from the Border and Outside the State', in Andreas, P. and Snyder, T. (eds), *The Wall around the West. State Borders and Immigration Controls in North America and Europe*, Lahnam: Rowman & Littlefield Publishers, 2000.

Lash, S. and Urry, J., *Economies of Signs and Space*, London: Sage, 1994.

Laufer, W.S. and Adler, F. (eds), *The Criminology of Criminal Law. Advances in Criminological Theory, Vol. 8*, New Brunswick: Transaction Publishers, 1999.

Lazzarato, M., *Lavoro Immateriale. Forme di vita e produzione di soggettività*, Verona: Ombre Corte, 1997.

Lea, J., *Crime and Modernity*, London: Sage, 2002.

Lessan, G.T., 'Macro-economic Determinants of Penal Policy: Estimating the Unemployment and Inflation Influences on Imprisonment Rate Changes in the United States, 1948–1985', *Crime, Law and Social Change*, 16 (1991): 177–198.

Lévy, R. and Zander, H., 'Introduction' to Rusche, G. and Kirchheimer, O., *Peine et structure sociale*, Paris: Les Editions du Cerf, 1994.

Lianos, M. and Douglas, M., 'Dangerization and the End of Deviance. The Institutional Environment', *The British Journal of Criminology*, 40/2 (2000): 261–278.

Loader, I., 'Policing, Securization and Democratization in Europe', *Criminal Justice*, 2/2 (2002): 125–153.

Luther Blissett Project, *Nemici dello Stato. Criminali, 'mostri' e leggi speciali nella società di controllo*, Rome: Derive Approdi, 2000.

Lynch, M., 'Waste Managers: The New Penology, Crime Fighting, and Parole Agent Identity', *Law & Society Review*, 32/4 (1998): 839–871.

Lynch, M.J., 'Quantitative Analysis and Marxist Criminology: Some Old Answers to a Dilemma in Marxist Criminology', *Crime and Social Justice*, 29 (1987): 110–127.

Lynch, M.J., 'The Extraction of Surplus Value, Crime and Punishment: A Preliminary Examination', *Contemporary Crises*, 12 (1988): 329–344.

Lyon, D., *Surveillance Society. Monitoring Everyday Life*, Buckingham: Open University Press, 2001.

Mandel, E., *Long Waves of Capitalist Development: The Marxist Interpretation*, New York: Cambridge University Press, 1980.

Mandel, M., *The Internet Depression: the Boom, the Bust, and Beyond*, New York: Basic Books, 2001.

Marshall, I.H. (ed.), *Minorities, Migrants and Crime. Diversity and Similarity across Europe and the United States*, London: Sage, 1997.

Marshall, T.H. and Bottomore, T., *Citizenship and Social Class*, London: Pluto Press, 1992.

Martinson, R.L., 'What Works? – Questions and Answers About Prison Reform', *The Public Interest*, 35 (1974): 22–54.

Marx, K., *Capital, vol. I*, Harmondsworth: Penguin, 1976.

Marx, K., *Capital. A Critique of Political Economy, vol. I*, Chicago: Charles H. Kerr & C., 1918.

Marx, K., *Grundrisse*, Harmondsworth: Penguin, 1973.

Marx, K., 'The German Ideology', in McLellan, D. (ed.), *Karl Marx: Selected Writings*, Oxford: Oxford University Press, 1977, pp. 175–208.

Marx, K., 'Preface' to 'A Contribution to the Critique of Political Economy', in Bottomore, T.B. and Rubel, M. (eds), *Karl Marx. Selected Writings in Sociology and Social Philosophy*, Harmondsworth: Penguin, 1969.

Massey, D. and Denton, N., *American Apartheid: Segregation and the Making of the Underclass*, Cambridge MA: Harvard University Press, 1993.

Mathiesen, T., 'The Viewer Society: Michel Foucault's Panopticon Revisited', *Theoretical Criminology*, 1-2 (1997): 215–234.

Matthews, R. and Francis, P. (eds), *Prisons 2000. An International Perspective of the Current State and Future of Imprisonment*, London: Macmillan, 1996.

Matthews, R. and Young, J. (eds), *Confronting Crime*, London: Sage, 1986.

Mauer, M. and Chesney-Lynd, M. (eds), *Invisible Punishments. The Collateral Consequences of Mass Imprisonment*, New York: The New Press, 2002.

McArdle, A. and Erzen, T. (eds), *Zero Tolerance. Quality of Life and the New Police Brutality in New York City*, New York: New York University Press, 2001.

McKenzie, E., *Privatopia. Homeowner Associations and the Rise of Residential Private Government*, New Haven: Yale University Press, 1994.

McKinlay, A. and Taylor, P., 'Through the Looking Glass: Foucault and the Politics of Production', in McKinlay, A. and Starkey, K. (eds), *Foucault, Management and Organisation Theory*, London: Sage, 1998, pp. 173–190.

McKinlay, A. and Starkey, K. (eds), *Foucault, Management and Organisation Theory*, London: Sage, 1998

McLean, B.D. (ed.), *The Political Economy of Crime*, Ontario: Prentice Hall, 1986.

Melossi, D., '"In a Peaceful Life". Migration and the Crime of Modernity in Europe/ Italy', *Punishment and Society*, 5/4 (2003): 371–397.

Melossi, D., 'An Introduction: Fifty Years Later, Punishment and Social Structure in Comparative Analysis', *Contemporary Crises*, 13 (1989): 311–326.

Melossi, D., 'Changing Representations of the Criminal', *The British Journal of Criminology*, 40 (2000): 296–320.

Melossi, D., 'Discussione a mo' di prefazione: carcere, postfordismo e ciclo di produzione della "canaglia"', in De Giorgi, A., *Il governo dell'eccedenza. Postfordismo e controllo della moltutudine*, Verona: ombre corte, 2002, pp. 7–24.

Melossi, D., 'Gazette of Morality and Social Whip: Punishment, Hegemony and the Case of the USA, 1970-1992', *Social & Legal Studies*, 2 (1993): 259–279.

Melossi, D., 'Georg Rusche and Otto Kirchheimer: Punishment and Social Structure', *Crime and Social Justice*, 9 (1978): 73–85.

Melossi, D., 'Georg Rusche: A Biographical Essay', *Crime and Social Justice*, 14 (1980): 51–63.

Melossi, D., 'Institutions of Social Control and Capitalist Organisation of Work', in Fine, B. *et al.* (eds), *Capitalism and the Rule of Law. From Deviancy Theory to Marxism*, London: Hutchinson, 1979, pp. 90–99.

Melossi, D. (ed.), *The Sociology of Punishment. Socio-Structural Perspectives*, Aldershot: Ashgate, 1998.

Melossi, D., 'Oltre il Panopticon. Per uno studio delle strategie di controllo sociale nel capitalismo del ventesimo secolo', *La questione criminale*, 6 (1980): 277–361.

Melossi, D., 'Omicidi, economia e tassi di incarcerazione in Italia dall'unità ad oggi', *Polis*, 12/3 (1998): 415–435.

Melossi, D., 'Overcoming the Crisis in Critical Criminology: Toward a Grounded Labelling Theory', *Criminology*, 23 (1985): 193–208.

Melossi, D., 'Political Business Cycles and Imprisonment Rates in Italy: Report on a Work in Progress', *The Review of Black Political Economy*, 16/1-2 (1987): 211–218.

Melossi, D., 'Punishment and Social Action: Changing Vocabularies of Punitive Motive Within a Political Business Cycle', *Current Perspectives in Social Theory*, 6 (1985): 169–197.

Melossi, D., 'Remarks on Social Control, State Sovereignty and Citizenship in the New Europe', in Ruggiero, V., South, N. and Taylor, I. (eds), *The New European Criminology. Crime and Social Order in Europe*, London: Routledge, 1998, pp. 52–63.

Melossi, D., 'Strategies of Social Control in Capitalism: A Comment On Recent Work', *Contemporary Crises*, 4 (1980): 381–419.

Melossi, D., *Stato, controllo sociale e devianza*, Milan: Bruno Mondadori, 2002.

Melossi, D., 'The Penal Question in Capital', in Platt, A. and Takagi, P. (eds), *Crime and Social Justice*, London: MacMillan, 1981, pp. 26–33.

Melossi, D., *The State of Social Control*, Cambridge: Polity Press, 1990.

Melossi, D. and Pavarini, M., *The Prison and the Factory. Origins of the Penitentiary System*, London: Macmillan, 1981.

Mezzadra, S., *Diritto di fuga. Migrazioni, globalizzazione, cittadinanza*, Verona: ombre corte, 2001.

Mezzadra, S. and Petrillo, A. (eds), *I confini della globalizzazione. Lavoro, culture, cittadinanza*, Rome: Manifestolibri, 2000.

Michalowski, R.J. and Carlson, S.M., 'Unemployment, Imprisonment, and Social Structures of Accumulation: Historical Contingency in the Rusche-Kirchheimer Hypothesis', *Criminology*, 37/2 (1999): 217–249.

Michalowski, R.J and Pearson, M.A., 'Punishment and Social Structure at the State Level: A Cross-Sectional Comparison of 1970 and 1980', *Journal of Research in Crime and Delinquency*, 27/1 (1990): 52–78.

Miller, J., *Search and Destroy. African American Males in the Criminal Justice System*, Cambridge: Cambridge University Press, 1996.

Miller, T., 'The Impact of Mass Incarceration on Immigration Policy', in Mauer, M. and Chesney-Lind, M. (eds) *Invisible Punishment. The Collateral Consequences of Mass Imprisonment*, New York: The New Press, 2002, p. 224.

Morris, L., 'Britain's Asylum and Immigration Regime: the Shifting Contours of Rights', *Journal of Ethnic and Migration Studies*, 28/3 (2002): 409–425.

Morris, L., *Dangerous Class. The Underclass and Social Citizenship*, London: Routledge, 1999.

Murray, C., 'The Underclass Revisited', quoted in Lea, J., *Crime and Modernity*, London: Sage, 2002.

Myers, S.L. and Sabol, W.J., 'Unemployment and Racial Differences in Imprisonment', *Review of Black Political Economy*, 16/1-2 (1987): 189–209.

Naldi, A., 'Mondi a parte: stranieri in carcere', in Anastasia, S. and Gonnella, P. (eds), *Inchiesta sulle carceri italiane*, Rome: Carocci, 2002, pp. 33–52.

Nascimbene, B. (ed.), *Expulsion and Detention of Aliens in the European Union Countries*, Milan: Giuffrè, 2001.

Negri, A., *Insurgencies. Constituent Power and the Modern State*, Minneapolis: Minnesota University Press, 1999.

Negri, A., 'Interpretation of the Class Situation Today: Methodological Aspects', in Bonefeld, W., Gunn, R. and Psychopedis, K. (eds), *Open Marxism, vol. II: Theory and Practice*, London: Pluto Press, 1992, pp. 69–105.

Negri, A., *Marx Beyond Marx: Lessons on the Grundrisse*, New York: Bergin and Garvey, 1984.

Negri, A., *Revolution Retrieved: Selected Writings on Marx, Keynes, Capitalist Crisis and New Social Subjects*, London: Red Notes, 1988.

Negri, A., *The Politics of Subversion: A Manifesto for the Twenty-First Century*, Cambridge: Polity Press, 1989.

Nelken, D. (ed.), *The Future of Criminology*, London: Sage, 1994.

Newman, O., *Defensible Space: Crime Prevention through Urban Design*, New York: Macmillan, 1972.

Norris, C. and Armstrong, G., *The Maximum Surveillance Society. The Rise of CCTV*, Oxford: Berg, 1999.

O'Connor, J., *The Fiscal Crisis of the State*, New York: St Martin's Press, 1973.

O'Malley, P., 'Criminologies of Catastrophe? Understanding Criminal Justice on the Edge of the Millennium', *The Australian and New Zealand Journal of Criminology*, 33/2 (2000): 153–167.

O'Malley, P., 'Legal Networks and Domestic Security', *Studies in Law, Politics, and Society*, 11 (1991): 170–190.

O'Malley, P., 'Risk, Crime and Prudentialism Revisited', in Stenson, K. and Sullivan, R. (eds), *Crime, Risk and Justice. The Politics of Crime Control in Liberal Democracies*, Devon: Willan, 2001, pp. 89–103.

O'Malley, P., 'Risk, Power, and Crime Prevention', *Economy and Society*, 31/3 (1992): 252–275.

O'Malley, P. and Mugford, S., 'Moral Technology: the Political Agenda of Random Drug Testing', *Social Justice*, 18/4 (1991): 122–146.

Ohmae, K., *The Borderless World: Power and Strategy in the Interlinked Economy*, New York: Harper, 1990.

Ohno, T., *Toyota Production System. Beyond Large Scale Production*, Cambridge MA: Productivity Press, 1988.

Palidda, S., *Devianza e vittimizzazione tra i migranti*, Milan: ISMU, 2001.

Palmer, J., 'Economic Analyses of the Deterrent Effect of Punishment: A Review', *Journal of Research in Crime and Delinquency*, 14/1 (1977): 4–21.

Panzieri, R., 'The Capitalist Use of Machinery: Marx Versus the Objectivists', in Slater, P. (ed.), *Outlines of a Critique of Technology*, Atlantic Highlands: Humanities Press, 1980, pp. 44–69.

Parenti, C., *Lockdown America. Police and Prisons in the Age of Crisis*, London: Verso, 1999.

Park, R. and Burgess, E., *The City*, Chicago: The University of Chicago Press, 1967.

Pashukanis, E.B., *Law and Marxism. A General Theory*, London: Ink Links, 1978.

Pasquinelli, M. (ed.), *Media Activism. Strategie e pratiche della comunicazione indipendente*, Rome: Derive Approdi, 2002.

Pasquino, P., 'Criminology: the Birth of a Special Saviour', *Ideology and Consciousness*, 7 (1980): 17–33.

Petersilia, J., 'Parole and Prisoner Reentry in the United States', in Tonry, M. and Petersilia, J. (eds), *Prisons. Crime and Justice. A Review of Research*, 26 (1999): 479–529.

Piore, M.J. and Sabel, C.F., *The Second Industrial Divide: Possibilities for Prosperity*, New York: Basic Books, 1984.

Piven, F. and Cloward, R., *The New Class War. Reagan's Attack on the Welfare State and its Consequences*, New York: Pantheon Books, 1982.

Piven, F. and Cloward, R., *Regulating the Poor. The Functions of Public Welfare*, London: Tavistock, 1972.

Platt, A. and Takagi, P. (eds), *Crime and Social Justice*, London: Macmillan, 1981.

Platt, A. and Takagi, P., 'Intellectuals for Law and Order: A Critique of the New Realists', *Crime and Social Justice*, 8 (1977): 1–16.

Quassoli, F., 'Migrants in the Italian Underground Economy', *International Journal of Urban and Regional Research*, 23/2 (1999): 212–231.

Quinney, R., *Class, State and Crime*, New York: Longman, 1977.

Rabinow, P. (ed.), *Michel Foucault. Ethics, vol. I*, London: Penguin Books, 1997.

Razac, O., *Histoire politique du barbelé. La praire, la tranché, le camp*, Paris: La fabrique-éditions, 2000.

Red Notes Collective (ed.), *Immaterial Labour, Mass Intellectuality, New Constitution, Post-Fordism and All That*, London: Red Notes, 1994.

Reich, R., *The Work of Nations. Preparing Ourselves for 21st Century Capitalism*, New York: Vintage Books, 1991.

Revelli, M., *Lavorare in FIAT. Da Valletta ad Agnelli a Romiti. Operai sindacati robot*, Turin: Garzanti, 1989.

Richmond, A., *Global Apartheid: Refugees, Racism and the New World Order*, New York: Oxford University Press, 1994.

Rifkin, J., *The Age of Access. The New Culture of Hypercapitalism where All of Life is a Paid-For Experience*, New York: Tarcher, 2000.

Rifkin, J., *The End of Work. The Decline of the Global Labour Force and the Dawn of the Post-Market Era*, New York: Tarcher, 1995.

Robinson, M.B., 'The Theoretical Development of CPTED: Twenty-five Years of Responses to C. Ray Jeffery', in Laufer, W.S. and Adler, F. (eds), *The Criminology of Criminal Law. Advances in Criminological Theory, vol. 8*, New Brunswick: Transaction Publishers, 1999, pp. 427–462.

Rose, N., 'The Death of the Social? Refiguring the Territory of Government', *Economy and Society*, 25/3 (1996): 327–356.

Rubinstein, G. and Mukamal, D., 'Welfare and Housing – Denial of Benefits to Drug Offenders', in Mauer, M. and Chesney-Lynd, M. (eds), *Invisible Punishment. The Collateral Consequences of Mass Imprisonment*, New York: The New Press, 2002, pp. 37–49.

Ruggiero, V., South, N. and Taylor, I. (eds), *The New European Criminology. Crime and Social Order in Europe*, London: Routledge, 1998.

Rusche, G., 'Labor Market and Penal Sanction: Thoughts on the Sociology of Criminal Justice', *Crime and Social Justice*, 10 (1978): 2–8.

Rusche, G., 'Prison Revolts or Social Policy: Lessons from America', *Crime and Social Justice*, 13 (1980): 41–44.

Rusche, G. and Kirchheimer, O., *Peine et Structure Sociale*, Paris: Les Editions du Cerf, 1994.

Rusche, G. and Kirchheimer, O., *Punishment and Social Structure*, New York: Russell & Russell, 1969.

Sassen, S., *Migranten, Siedler, Fluechtinge. Von der Massenauswanderung zur Festung Europa*, Frankfurt am Main: Fischer, 1996.

Sassen, S., *The Global City: New York, London, Tokyo*, Princeton: Princeton University Press, 1991.

Sassen, S., *The Mobility of Labor and Capital. A Study in International Investment and Labor Flow*, New York: Cambridge University Press, 1988.

Sayad, A., *La doppia assenza. Dalle illusioni dell'emigrato alle sofferenze dell'immigrato*, Milan: Raffaello Cortina Editore, 2002.

Schor, J., *The Overworked American. The Unexpected Decline of Leisure*, New York: Basic Books, 1992.

Schumpeter, J.A., *Business Cycle, vol. II*, New York: McGraw-Hill, 1939.

Scull, A., *Decarceration*, New Brunswick: Rutgers University Press, 1977.

Sellin, T., *Research Memorandum on Crime in the Depression*, New York: Social Science Research Council, 1937.

Sennett, R., *The Corrosion of Character. The Personal Consequences of Work in the New Capitalism*, New York and London: W.W. Northon & Co., 1998.

Shearing, C. and Stenning, P., 'From the Panopticon to Disney World: the Development of Discipline', in Doob, A. and Greenspan, E. (eds), *Perspectives in Criminal Law*, Ontario: Canada Law Book Inc., 1985, pp. 335–349.

Shearing, C. and Stenning, P., 'Private Security: Implications for Social Control', *Social Problems*, 30/5 (1983): 493–506.

Simon, J., 'Fear and Loathing in Late Modernity. Reflections on the Cultural Sources of Mass Imprisonment in the United States', in Garland, D. (ed.), *Mass Imprisonment. Social Causes and Consequences*, London: Sage, 2001, pp. 15–27.

Simon, J., 'Governing Through Crime', in Friedman, L. and Fischer, G. (eds), *The Crime Conundrum: Essays on Criminal Justice*, Boulder: Westview Press, 1997, pp. 171–189.

Simon, J., *Poor Discipline: Parole and the Social Control of the Underclass, 1890–1990*, Chicago: University of Chicago Press, 1993.

Simon, J., 'The Emergence of a Risk Society: Insurance, Law, and the State', *Socialist Review*, 95 (1987): 61–89.

Simon, J., 'The Ideological Effects of Actuarial Practices', *Law and Society Review*, 22/4 (1988): 771–800.

Slater, P. (ed.), *Outlines of a Critique of Technology*, Atlantic Highlands: Humanities Press, 1980.

Smart, B., 'On Discipline and Social Regulation: A Review of Foucault's Genealogical Analysis', in Garland, D. and Young, P. (eds), *The Power to Punish. Contemporary Penality and Social Analysis*, London: Heinemann, 1983, pp. 62–83.

Sparks, R., 'Penal Austerity: the Doctrine of Less Eligibility Reborn?', in Matthews, R. and Francis, P. (eds), *Prisons 2000. An International Perspective of the Current State and Future of Imprisonment*, London: Macmillan, 1996, pp. 74–93.

Sparks, R., 'Perspectives on Risk and Penal Politics', in Hope, T. and Sparks, R. (eds), *Crime, Risk and Insecurity*, London: Routledge, 2000, pp. 129–145.

Spinoza, B., *Theological-Political Treatise*, Indianapolis: Hackett Publishing, 2001.

Spitzer, S., 'Toward a Marxian Theory of Deviance', *Social Problems*, 22/5 (1975): 638–651.

Standing, G., *Beyond the New Paternalism. Basic Security as Equality*, London: Verso, 2002.

Stenson, K. and Sullivan, R. (eds), *Crime, Risk and Justice. The Politics of Crime Control in Liberal Democracies*, Devon: Willan, 2001.

Stern, T., 'The Effect of the Depression on Prison Commitments and Sentences', *Journal of the American Institute of Criminal Law and Criminology*, 31 (1941): 696–711.

Stolcke, V., 'Le nuove frontiere e le nuove retoriche culturali dell'esclusione in Europa', in Mezzadra, S. and Petrillo, A. (eds), *I confini della globalizzazione. Lavoro, Culture, Cittadinanza*, Rome: Manifestolibri, 2000, pp. 157–181.

Taylor, F.W., *The Principles of Scientific Management*, New York: W.W. Norton & Company, 1967.

Taylor, I., *Crime in Context. A Critical Criminology of Market Societies*, Cambridge: Polity Press, 1999.

Taylor, I., Walton, P. and Young, J., *The New Criminology*, London: Routledge & Kegan Paul, 1973.

Taylor, P., *Hackers. Crime in the Digital Sublime*, London: Routledge, 1999.

Thoburn, N., 'Autonomous Production? On Negri's "New Synthesis"', *Theory Culture & Society*, 18/5 (2001): 75–96.

Thomas, D. and Loader, B.D. (eds), *Cybercrime. Law Enforcement, Security and Surveillance in the Information Age*, London: Routledge, 2000.

Thomas, W.I. and Znaniecki, F., *The Polish Peasant in Europe and America*, Chicago: The University of Chicago Press, 1918.

Thompson, E.P., *The Making of the English Working Class*, London: Gollancz, 1963.

Thursfield, D., *Post-Fordism and Skill. Theories and Perceptions*, Aldershot: Ashgate, 2000.

Tonry, M. (ed.), *Penal Reform in Overcrowded Times*, Oxford: Oxford University Press, 2001.

Tonry, M., 'Why are US Incarceration Rates So High?', in Tonry, M. (ed.), *Penal Reform in Overcrowded Times*, Oxford: Oxford University Press, 2001, pp. 52–64.

Tonry, M. and Petersilia, J. (eds), *Prisons. Crime and Justice. A Review of Research*, 26 (1999).

Tournier, P., *Statistiques pénales annuelles du Conseil de l'Europe. Enquete 1997*, Strasbourg: Council of Europe, 1999.

Townley, B., 'Beyond Good and Evil: Depth and Division in the Management of Human Resources', in McKinlay, A. and Starkey, K. (eds), *Foucault, Management and Organisation Theory*, London: Sage, 1998, pp. 191–210.

Townley, B., 'Foucault, Power/Knowledge, and its Relevance for Human Resource Management', *Academy of Management Review*, 18/3 (1993): 518–545.

Travis, J., 'Invisible Punishment: An Instrument of Social Exclusion', in Mauer, M. and Chesney-Lynd, M. (eds), *Invisible Punishment*, New York: The New Press, 2002, pp. 15–36.

Vachudová, M.A., 'Eastern Europe as Gatekeeper: The Immigration and Asylum Policies of an Enlarging European Union', in Andreas, P. and Snyder, T. (eds), *The Wall around the West. State Borders and Immigration Controls in North America and Europe*, Lahnam: Rowman & Littlefield Publishers, 2000, pp. 153–171.

Valverde, M., 'Despotism and Ethical Liberal Governance', *Economy and Society*, 25/3 (1996): 352–372.

Van Den Haag, E., *Punishing Criminals*, New York: Basic Books, 1975.

Van Swaaningen, R., *Critical Criminology. Visions from Europe*, London: Sage, 1997.

Vaughan, B., 'Punishment and Conditional Citizenship', *Punishment & Society*, 2/1 (2000): 23–39.

Vaughan, B., 'The Punitive Consequences of Consumer Culture', *Punishment & Society*, 4/2 (2002): 195–211.

Virno, P., 'Lavoro e linguaggio', in Zanini, A. and Fadini, U. (eds), *Lessico postfordista. Dizionario di idee della mutazione*, Milan: Feltrinelli, 2001, p. 181.

Virno, P. and Hardt, M. (eds), *Radical Thought in Italy: A Potential Politics*, Minneapolis: University of Minnesota Press, 1996.

Vogel, R., 'Capitalism and Incarceration', *Monthly Review*, 34/10 (1983): 30–41.

Wacquant, L., 'Deadly Symbiosis. When Ghetto and Prison Meet and Mesh', in Garland, D. (ed.), *Mass Imprisonment. Social Causes and Consequences*, London: Sage, 2001, pp. 82–120.

Wacquant, L., *Les Prisons de la misère*, Paris: Raisons d'Agir, 1999.

Wacquant, L., 'Negative Social Capital: State Breakdown and Social Destitution in America's Urban Core', *The Netherlands Journal of the Built Environment*, 13/1 (1998): 1–36.

Wacquant, L., 'The Penalization of Poverty and the Rise of Neo-Liberalism', *European Journal on Criminal Policy and Research*, 9 (2001): 401–412.

Wacquant, L., 'The Rise of Advanced Marginality: Notes on its Nature and Implications', *Acta Sociologica*, 39 (1996): 121–139.

Waever, O., 'European Security Identities', *Journal of Common Market Studies*, 34/1 (1996): 103–132.

Waever, O., 'Identity, Integration and Security. Solving the Sovereignty Puzzle', *Journal of International Affairs*, 48/2 (1995): 389–431.

Wallace, D., 'The Political Economy of Incarceration Trends in late US Capitalism: 1971–1977', *The Insurgent Sociologist*, 11/1 (1980): 59–66.

Welch, M., 'Ironies of Social Control and the Criminalization of Immigrants', *Crime, Law & Social Change*, 39/1 (2003): 319–337.

Welch, M., *Detained. Immigration Laws and the Expanding INS Jail Complex*, Philadelphia: Temple University Press, 2002.

Welch, M., 'Detention in INS Jails: Bureaucracy, Brutality and a Booming Business', in Gido, R.L. and Alleman, T. (eds), *Turnstile Justice: Issues in American Corrections*, Englewood Cliffs: Prentice Hall, 2000, pp. 202–214.

Welch, M., 'The Immigration Crisis: Detention as an Emerging Mechanism of Social Control', *Social Justice*, 23/3 (1996): 169–184.

Welch, M., 'The Role of the Immigration and Naturalization Service in the Prison-Industrial Complex', *Social Justice*, 27/3 (2000): 73–88.

Western, B. and Beckett, K., 'Governing Social Marginality: Welfare, Incarceration, and the Transformation of State Policy', in Garland, D. (ed.), *Mass Imprisonment*, London: Sage, 2001, pp. 35–50.

Western, B. and Beckett, K., 'How Unregulated is the US Labor Market? The Penal System as a Labor Market Institution', *American Journal of Sociology*, 104/4 (1999): 1030–1060.

Williams, K.S. and Johnstone, C., 'The Politics of the Selective Gaze: Closed Circuit Television and the Policing of Public Space', *Crime, Law & Social Change*, 34 (2000): 183–210.

Wilson, J.Q., *Thinking About Crime*, New York: Basic Books, 1983.

Witheford, N.D., *Cyber-Marx. Cycles and Circuits of Struggle in High-Technology Capitalism*, Urbana: University of Illinois Press, 1999.

Wolfgang, M.E. (ed.), *Crime and Culture: Essays in Honour of Thorsten Sellin*, New York: Wiley & Sons, 1968.

Wright, S., *Storming Heaven. Class Composition and Struggle in Italian Autonomist Marxism*, London: Pluto Press, 2002.

Young, J., *The Exclusive Society*, London: Sage, 1999.

Young, J., 'To These Wet and Windy Shores. Recent Immigration Policy in the UK', *Punishment and Society*, 5/4 (2003): 449–462.

Zanini, A. and Fadini, U. (eds), *Lessico postfordista. Dizionario di idee della mutazione*, Milan: Feltrinelli, 2001.

Index